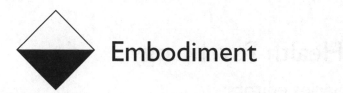

Embodiment

D1571345

Health Psychology

Series editors:
Sheila Payne and Sandra Horn

Published titles

Embodiment
Clinical, critical and
cultural perspectives on
health and illness

Malcolm MacLachlan

Open University Press

Open University Press
McGraw-Hill Education
McGraw-Hill House
Shoppenhangers Road
Maidenhead
Berkshire
England
SL6 2QL

email: enquiries@openup.co.uk
world wide web: www.openup.co.uk

and Two Penn Plaza, New York, NY 10121-2289, USA

First published 2004

A catalogue record of this book is available from the British Library

ISBN 0 335 20959 9 (pb)   0 335 20960 2 (hb)

Library of Congress Cataloging-in-Publication Data
CIP data has been applied for

Typeset by RefineCatch Ltd, Bungay, Suffolk
Printed in Great Britain by MPG Books Ltd, Bodmin, Cornwall

To
Anna, Tess, Lara
and
Eilish
with
love and thanks.

Contents

Series editors' foreword

This series of books in health psychology is designed to support post-graduate and post-qualification studies in psychology, nursing, medicine and paramedical sciences and health psychology units in the undergraduate curriculum. Health psychology has grown and continues to grow rapidly as a field of study. Concerned as it is with the application of psychological theories and models to the promotion and maintenance of health and the individual and interpersonal aspects of adaptive behaviour in illness and disability, health psychology has a wide remit and a potentially important role to play in the future.

Academic examination of the body and embodiment has been under-taken by sociologists and anthropologists for some time. This book offers a welcome alternative psychological analysis of embodiment. Moreover, attention to the body is timely as, for example, advances in health technolo-gies such as the 'new genetics' and smart prostheses raise new issues pertin-ent to notions of embodiment. On a wider scale, epidemiologists have predicted that obesity is likely to be the main public health issue for the new century in developed countries. It is predicted that in North America overconsumption of energy-dense foods, combined with lack of physical activity, is likely to reduce the life expectancy of the population; the need for action is urgent. Lifestyle determinants of health are core issues in health psychology. Consideration of the embodied self has the potential to add another dimension to our understanding of obesity, and thus to inform the design of individual and community interventions to enhance dietary changes and promote increased regular physical exercise.

In this engaging and thought-provoking book, Professor Malcolm MacLachlan explores aspects of the embodied self – the self that lives through our bodies and their disorders; the self we normally take for granted. Central to this exploration are accounts from individuals who are, perforce, living through body experiences which are often distressing. Their accounts are set alongside findings from research studies, philosophical writings, discourses on the use of language, cultural considerations – so that several perspectives and types of knowledge are brought to bear on a wide range of topics, including cosmetic surgery, pain, prostheses, eating disorders. This approach invites new insights into processes such as 'adaptation' and 'accommodation' to variations in health and bodily states, by broadening and enriching our understanding of embodiment.

Sheila Payne and Sandra Horn

Preface

In recent years there has been a plethora of philosophical and sociological considerations of 'embodiment'. However, there is still much scope and a great need to try to understand just what the term means, or could mean, in the *clinical* context. This book is therefore primarily an exploration of embodiment through a broad range of health and illness experiences. While I hope it is broad enough to encourage those who adopt a biopsychosocial model to read it, I have tried to develop something of a critical perspective in my writing. For me, such a perspective does not necessarily imply being *critical of* the myriad scientific research in neuroscience, medicine, psychology or elsewhere; instead it tries to contribute a perspective that is *critical for* understanding how these other types of knowledge relate to (and sometimes don't) people's own experience of health and illness. A third emphasis in my subtitle is the adoption of a '*cultural*' perspective, which is, I believe, essential for any truly critical understanding of human behaviour. Human behaviour is constructed according to culturally based norms and thus culture acts as a prism, scattering human concerns in different forms, and challenging absolute claims to authenticity.

In this book I have tried to emphasize the importance of *understanding*, in addition to *explaining*, people's often distressing experiences of their bodies: theorising first requires realising. I believe it is important to give voice to those who actually experience the conditions I write about, in ways that (I hope) I will be unaware of. Their personal construction – in language – of embodied experience is not simply tangential or illustrative of my arguments, but central to them. I am seeking to explain – in a different way – what they already know, in a personal way. One way I seek to achieve this is by quoting at length some of their recorded experiences. I also quote other researchers and writers at length, in order to acknowledge that my search for understanding here revisits the ideas of many who have gone before me, and as such, I see it as a dialogue, not a recitation of scientific 'case-law', but my own *re*search though other people's ideas and experiences.

My clinical training taught me that people suffered 'from' disorders, yet my clinical experience told me that often these disorders were so closely identified with the sufferer that it was more a case of them suffering 'with' the disorder, rather than from it. More recently, even this cohabitation ('me and my disorder/illness/impairment', or whatever) seems to suggest a dissociation, and I am not sure that it is justified. Certainly there may be an attempt to distance a disorder from the person who has it, and that can be beneficial. However, increasingly I now see people, in an embodied sense, as suffering 'through' their disorders. That is, disorders, particularly bodily disorders, are things that people literally 'live through'. It is this 'lived through' experience of disorder that I am particularly interested in from the perspective of embodiment.

I have tried to cover a breadth of topics in this book, but I don't make any claim for it to be comprehensive. My aim has been more to put together aspects of embodiment that aren't often seen as being such, or are not often brought together in one volume. I have for instance, omitted consideration of how the body changes through ageing or through cyclical patterns such as menstruation and ovulation. The patterns of embodiment that I do discuss here can be applied to much more than I have been able to consider. None the less, I hope that the plethora of embodiments I have considered allow justified enthusiasm for a broader understanding of the relationship between people and their bodies.

I would like to acknowledge my children, Lara, Tess and Anna, for their daily ability to open my eyes, and enliven my experience, of being-in-the-world. My wife Eilish has been more than understanding of the narrow obsession that is the writing of a book. Work colleagues at Trinity have allowed me space and time to dedicate myself to writing this book, which would not have been possible without a Berkeley Fellowship from Trinity College Dublin in 2002–3, for which I am most grateful. In alphabetical order, I would also like to acknowledge friends, colleagues and students who have stimulated my thinking on the issue of embodiment, relayed interesting articles to me or drawn my attention to areas I might otherwise have overlooked. They include: Sheila Cummins, Deirdre Desmond, Daren Drysdale, Pamela Gallagher, Olga Horgan, Alan Kent, Rik Louse, Shane O'Mara, Kieran O'Neill, Jean Quigley and Caroline Smyth. Finally, I would also like to thank Sheila Payne and Sandra Horn for commissioning this book in their excellent Health Psychology series, for the valuable feedback they provided and for their encouragement to write it. The editorial and production staff at Open University Press have had the patience of saints and I sincerely thank them for their support and charity.

 # Acknowledgements

Figure 1.3   Auckland City Art Gallery for permission to reproduce Lindauer's 1877 portrait of Te Hapuku, Te Ika O Te Moana, paramount chief of Ngati Kahungunu of Hawkes Bay, Aotearoa/New Zealand.

Figure 1.4   The Rodin Gallery, Seoul, for permission to reproduce Kim Il-Young's 1999 'Being without being' exhibited at their Bodyscapes exhibition, 2002.

Figure 5.1   BMJ publications for permission to reproduce Halligan, Zeman & Berger's (1999) Figure 2 illustrating referred sensation sites.

Figure 5.2   Alexa Wright for permission to reproduce four virtual images of phantom limbs.

Body plasticity

But O alas, so long, so far
Our bodies why do they forbear?
They're ours, though they are not we, we are
The intelligencies, they the sphere
         (John Donne, Songs and Sonnets, in *The Ecstasy*)

The world experienced (otherwise called the 'field of
consciousness') comes at all times with our body as its
center, center of vision, center of action, center of interest.
Where the body is, is 'here'; when the body acts is 'now';
what the body touches is 'this'; all other things are 'there'
and 'then' and 'that'. These words of emphasized position
imply a systematisation of things with reference to a focus
of action and interest which lies in the body ... The body
is the storm centre, the origin of coordinates, the constant
place of stress in all that experience-train. Everything
circles round it, and is felt from its point of view. The
word 'I', then, is primarily a noun of position, just like
'this' and 'here'.
        (William James 1890, cited in Thayer 1970: 154–5)

Our increasing interest in the human body is surely linked to our increasing
anxieties about *what it is*. If we assume that there remains some fundamental
truth in the basic 'plan' of life – *you are born, you live and you die* – then we
must also recognize that the means of our creation, how long and with what
sort of permutations we can live and even the finality of our death, are
becoming increasingly uncertain punctuation marks in the stories of our
lives. While for many centuries people could expect that the world they
would leave behind them was broadly similar to that which they were born
into, in the past hundred years we have had no idea of what that world we
leave behind will be like, or even if we might leave it clutching a high-tech
biological 'return ticket' – you again!

Technical transformation in medicine, especially in the reproductive area;
the epidemic of AIDS, highlighting the sexual complexities of contemporary societies; the gay and feminist movements; the changing demography of
many Western societies, especially as regards the process of ageing; the adoption of the body by consumption advertising and the consumer culture; all
of these and many other aspects of modern living effectively question the
stability of the human body (Turner 1997).

Yet I do not think that this should be seen as an age of the 'body under siege'. Instead, the loosening up in thinking about the body, at least in some quarters, offers new opportunities for some people to be *re-enabled*, often when historically they have been disabled. While recently there has been much excitement in the humanities about just how to conceptualize 'the body', much of this has not been grounded in a way that makes it relevant to people in health-related settings. I wish to apply the concept of embodiment to the increasing variety of ways in which we can understand the experience of those suffering from bodily distress and its indivisible psychological expressions.

Furthermore, in parallel to the excitement that the concept of 'brain plasticity' has recently generated in the neurosciences, I seek to develop its overlooked cousin – body plasticity. It has been overlooked because, particularly in the health sciences, we have largely failed to recognize, but certainly to take on board, the essence of *embodiment*. One reason for this is that within Anglophone Western science there has been a construction of people as 'split' between their mental life and their physical body, and their problems have been largely segregated into systems of dealing with these two domains. Outside the largely English-speaking world of 'logical positivist science' there have been parallel, but quite different, advances in how we understand such issues. In the next section of this introductory chapter we explore how the concept of 'embodiment' can constitute a middle ground between clinic and culture. Out of this consideration a more flexible idea of 'the body' arises and we consider how body images are influenced by neurological, psychological and socio-cultural factors. In the next few pages I review some relevant philosophical ideas on embodiment, and as in the old cavalry adage try and 'travel light over rough ground'.

The idea of embodiment

Let's start with a very simple definition of embodiment: *embodiment is the identification of an abstract idea with a physical entity*. The abstract idea could be the self, a nation, anger, love, God, the devil or whatever. When such ideas are identified in the flesh, we say that they are incarnate: 'the devil incarnate'; an expression of the devil, in the *flesh*. The word 'corporality', meaning *of the body*, is also used to refer to embodied ideas that are incarnate. However, for the time being, let us consider more subtle aspects of embodiment and how its conception has developed.

Being-in-the-world

The 'blame' for splitting the mind and the body is usually attributed to Plato and Descartes. Plato (fifth century BC) believed that 'truth' only existed in pure forms; that is, it wasn't embodied in physical objects. As such the physical world, and the bodies that lived in it, were at an inferior level to this higher reality. Similarly, René Descartes argued in the seventeenth century that 'pure knowledge' could only be achieved through disregard of the senses. In searching for the certainty of his own existence, Descartes came up with the Cartesian, *cognito ergo sum*: 'I think, therefore I am'. Because, Descates argued, he was aware of his own thinking, he could therefore be sure that he existed. As such, he separated mental life from physical life. The mind and the body parted. While today this may seem to have been a retrograde step, the dissociation between mental (and spiritual) life on the one hand and mere physical existence on the other hand allowed for science to proceed to work on the body – objectifying it – safe from the suspicion that God's work was being messed with. Christianity has long had a poor impression of the body, seeing it as imperfect, impure and transitory – something to be transcended (Cavallaro and Vago 1997).

Wilde (1999: 26) summarizes the implicit contemporary assumption that still prevails in many quarters thus: 'people often think that the human (self) owns the body, and that the body is separate from the self'. Whether Descartes's *cogito ergo sum* was inspired by political astuteness or whole-hearted conviction, it has endured and underpinned many of the assumptions that our understanding of human health and welfare is based on, even to the extreme of us having one sort of hospital for 'mental' problems and another sort for 'physical' problems. In striving to study ourselves scientifically – and there is nothing wrong with that – we have sought to be as objective as possible and to play down our opinions in favour of reproducible facts. This detached scientific viewpoint has been described by Nagel (1986) as 'the view from nowhere'.

While many have noted the abstractness and emptiness of the Cartesian *cogito* (Lechte 1994) it is the philosophy of Maurice Merleau-Ponty that perhaps offers the most compelling alternative in respect of the concept of embodiment. Merleau-Ponty argued against a philosophy of psychology that opposes the mental and the physical and sees them as external to each other, and therefore only associated in some sort of cause-and-effect relationship (Mathews 2002). Merleau-Ponty ties mind and body inexorably, not in seeing them as two sides of the one coin, but perhaps more in denying the possibility of the shape of the coin existing without the metal that constitutes it.

He believes that 'to be a body is to be tied to a certain [sort of] world' and that our study of that world should start from how we actually perceive it, rather than from theories of how it must be. By way of analogy, a car manufacturing plant is 'set up' to manufacture automobiles, it is configured to facilitate the most efficient assembly of these vehicles. At a stretch this production line could be modified to, say, produce motorcycles or perhaps even cranes. However, it is never going to be a suitable framework for the production of cuddly toys. The configuration of the production line means that there are certain ways in which it can relate to the world (the production of motorized vehicles) and it is limited to these. While the products of this assembly line may have different colours, engine sizes, interiors etc., their functions are also limited.

Similarly, because our experience of the world is 'grounded' in our bodies (our 'production lines'), this necessarily implies that there are certain ways in which we can – indeed must – experience the world, and there are ways in which we cannot. Merleau-Ponty's argument is that we have not taken sufficient account of the way in which our experiences are 'grounded' in our bodies. As Carey (2000: 29) puts it, 'Only a being with eyes to see and ears to hear can perceive the visible or hear the audible. Before the rational mind can dissect the world into concepts and definitions, the capabilities of the body are already engaged with the world in the activity of perception. Hence the body-subject is the basis upon which cognition and reflection take place.' This is to say that the body has knowledge that is necessarily subjective, and this is apparent in the individualistic styles of any pianist's fingers as they make music, or indeed in my own, less melodic, typing of these words.

Merleau-Ponty states that a subject that is 'in-the-world' is necessarily embodied – you have to exist in some physical form to exist at all. Benson (2001: 5–6), emphasizing the language of location, illustrates the idea of being 'in' something: 'I am in my head, two inches or so behind my eyes', 'I am in my study', 'I am in second place in the competition', 'I am in the middle of negotiations', 'I am in love', 'I am in a mess', 'I am in disgrace', 'I am working in the university', 'I am in the early stages of the disease'. Such a broad use of metaphor illustrates the pervasiveness of being contained, but also possibly of being the container.

'Existence is known through the body' (Wilde 1999: 27). Or, perhaps to put it another way, our body is our infrastructure with the world. Our experience of the world we inhabit, our subjectivity, is necessarily created from the perspective of the physical form we take. 'Our inner life as conscious persons necessarily develops out of the impersonal physiological life of a certain kind of organism: a human being', as Mathews (2002) explains. However, we are not only 'in-the-world' in our bodies – as objects – our subjectivity also influences the world we experience. Unlike a stone which is 'in-the-world', our subjectivity, our personal experiences, constitute our '*being*-in-the-world'. This *being* relates not just to other objects but also to the social and cultural world. In contrasting Descartes and Merleau-Ponty, we have moved from a dualistic claim of disembodied reason (I think, therefore I am) to one where reason is constrained by embodied form (I can only think through what I am).

This may sound anti-scientific or anti-rationalistic, but Merleau-Ponty is not saying that such approaches are wrong, simply that they are *insufficient*. Indeed, acknowledging that our 'being' is rooted to our bodies also acknowledges that our consciousness is 'mediated by bodily sense organs, brain and nervous system, and indeed, by our capacities for bodily movement' (Mathews 2002: 20). The scientific 'view from nowhere' is flawed only to the extent that those propounding it assume it to be an adequate explanation of reality. Instead, the 'view from nowhere' is an abstraction of our many 'views from somewhere' (Nagel 1986). Bringing this back to a health context Mathews states:

> Our own bodies can be viewed scientifically, as one kind of object in the world, whose causal relations to other objects can be studied in exactly the same way as any others; but more normally they are not so much perceived as experienced as expressing our way of being in the world. Similarly, the bodies of other human beings can be studied scientifically (e.g. in physiology or anatomy) as one kind of object in the world, but more normally we experience them as expressions of a person's manner of being-in-the-world; we can no more separate other human subjects from their embodiment than we can separate ourselves from our own bodies.
>
> (Mathews 2002: 59–60)

As such, the world we perceive is not only a world of objects, it is a world pregnant with meanings.

In challenging the assumption of contemporary 'Western culture', that science is the most fundamental account of the scheme of things, Merleau-Ponty believes that we can only make sense of science because we have a more fundamental – 'pre-reflective' – understanding of the world. This he nicely illustrates with his map analogy: the geographer's map, in which all features are represented by abstract symbols, only makes sense to us because we have prior experience of rivers, hills, forests etc. (Merleau-Ponty 1962).

We do not, in general, experience our own bodies or the bodies of others as objects in the way that we experience stones or cars as objects. We tend to experience others as having their own 'projects' – things they want to do – and as such are not aware of minds and bodies, but only of *human beings* (Mathews 2002). We tend to experience ourselves and others as *unified persons*. This unity is exemplified in how we express our view of the world in our bodily movements. Our experience of the world is as embodied persons and should be understood in the *first person*, rather than objectified into the third person. This idea of trying to understand behaviour 'from the inside' has important implications for illness and disability, for it implies that it is not simply a breakdown in mechanical functioning, but a disordered way of being-in-the-world, of how one relates to one's own body, or to others. As Mathews puts it, (2002: 84) 'Our bodies "express" existence just in the same way that language expresses thought.'

The mirror phase

Jacques Lacan, born in 1901 in France, has probably been the most influential psychoanalyst since Freud. While Freudian psychoanalysis predominates in North America and Britain, Lacanian psychoanalysis predominates in France, Spain, Italy and much of South America. Although Lacan died in 1981 most of his thought has yet to be formally published, much of it existing as transcripts of lectures. For this reason, and because getting to grips with that which he did formally publish is like wading through treacle with large buckets tied to your feet, I have relied heavily on secondary sources here. Lacan (1966) recounts the case of Aimee (first described by him in 1932), who had attempted to stab a well known Parisian actress. Lacan suggested that in attacking the actress, Aimee was attacking herself, because the actress represented the sort of woman that Aimee wished to be. He believed she was suffering from a 'self-punishment paranoia'. Her persecutory ideas invoked the actress as the source of threat to her. As such – Lacan argued – the 'ideal image' of the actress was the object of both her hate *and* her aspiration. In her arrest and confinement she became herself the object of punishment. This case illustrates, for Lacan, 'how the personality can be extended beyond the limits of the body and be constituted within a complex social network' (Leader 1995: 12) – the actress representing a part of Aimee herself. Such an argument is one illustration of how a person's identity can incorporate elements beyond their biological boundary: 'in a sense, Aimee's identity was literally outside herself' (Leader 1995: 13). In Lacan's analysis of this case we encounter the concept of the *image* and how it relates to embodiment.

Lacan builds on the observation that babies are born 'prematurely' in the sense that they are in no way able to look after themselves, coordinate their actions or even recognize themselves. They do not have the ability to move towards or away from things, or to pick up things. Babies have no experience of a unified body. They do, however, gain experience of other people, who appear as unified bodies, and indeed the reflection of their own self in a mirror presents a unified body – a body Gestalt. What is complex here is the paradoxical move towards acceptance of this *specular image* (seeing one's body from the 'outside', as a spectator) while still experiencing one's body from the 'inside' – *introceptively* (Weiss 1999).

Thus for the child the 'initial failure to recognise the specular image as an image of oneself must eventually give way to a recognition of the specular image as being *of* oneself, yet not identical *to* oneself' (Weiss 1999: 13). This schism between of oneself and to oneself is the source of a perpetual alienation because the specular image will never completely intersect with one's own, more fluid, body image. Merleau-Ponty, in accord with Lacan, summarizes this nicely: 'The specular image, given visually, participates globally in the existence of the body itself and leads a "phantom life" in the mirror, which "participates" in the life of the child himself' (Merleau-Ponty 1964:

133–4). It is important to realize that the images of the body from 'outside' and 'inside' are never simply superimposed over one another in a neat fit. There is no one-to-one correspondence in these two images. You will rarely see the back of your head, the bottom of your heel or the end of your spine, yet you do have an inner experience of these.

The gaze

Michel Foucault, another Frenchman, was interested in the production, regulation and representation of bodies within a context of disciplinary surveillance (Turner 1984). One aspect of this is what he refers to as 'the gaze', and Foucault (1979) uses Bentham's Panopticon to illustrate it. The Panopticon is a circular prison designed such that the cells of the prisoners are all around the outside and the wardens sit in the middle. The cells are always illuminated so that the wardens can see into them, but the central area is always in darkness. Consequently the inmates never know when they are being watched and, in effect, 'watch themselves' all the time. This sort of 'disciplinary surveillance' is not, however, restricted to prisons, Foucault argues: the 'warder' can easily be replaced by the doctor, nurse, teacher, foreman or whatever authority figures presides over whatever institution (Foucault 1990). In the case of healthcare, the scientific gaze now penetrates the skin, aiming to regulate our inner functioning. As we will see later, this 'gaze' – the sense that we are being looked at all the time – may make us feel ashamed and guilty if we fail to conform to our 'invisible observer's' expectations of the shapes and forms that our bodies 'ought' to adopt.

While Descartes and others saw the 'body as the prison of the soul', Foucault turns this around: 'the soul is the prison of the body', in the sense that the body is worked on in order that it conforms to abstract principles of propriety, these principles being the 'soul' into which our cultures socialize us. Another influential idea of Foucault, relevant to embodiment, is his suggestion that while we might think that abnormality is defined as a deviation from normality, in fact things work the other way round. We search for signs of abnormality in order to know what is normal. If we did not have abnormal, or 'improper', bodies, then we could not identify normal ones. While the definitions of abnormality may change over time and across cultures, its social function, he argues, remains the same.

An embodied brain?

The neural complexity of the human brain encourages people to think of it as a computer and this analogy has been taken up in cognitive psychology's casting of people in the role of 'information processors'. Perhaps surprisingly, much neuroscience unwittingly endorses a dualism of the mind–body type, in fact a double-dualism. Damasio (1999, 2002) states 'neuroscience has focused on functions [particularly motor functions] as if it had nothing to do with the person'. This estrangement of 'the person' from 'their' functions is one type of dualism. Another type is where neuroscience promotes a view of mental processes as residing only in the brain – *thinking is neurology* – and being distinct from bodily processes. So, for instance, neuropsychologists implicitly distinguish between neurological correlates of behaviour (including thought) and the physical body, which, at best, is treated as the site of peripheral parts of the nervous system. Thus a persons–functions dichotomy coexists alongside a brain–body dichotomy.

Nobel Prize winner Gerald Edelman challenges the mechanistic and depersonalizing view of neuroscience by arguing that the brain is not a computer: although it has structure (like a computer), it also has uniqueness (unlike a computer). Edelman (2002) says that neurons *move* (literally), and even in monozygotic twins – who have the same neuronal inheritance – they don't move in the same way. Furthermore, even neurons that perform the same function (in different individuals) have different (physical) dendritic structures. Individual differences between (individuals') brains is the rule. Brains are not pre-programmed: epigenesis occurs (Edelman 2002). In the past decade there has been great interest in the phenomenon of neural plasticity. While I was taught the 'scientific facts' that humans are hard wired, and damage to the nervous system is irreparable, the very negation of these 'facts' has become one of neuroscience's most exciting areas.

Many neuroscientists are focused on the localization of functions, reducing these functions to their neuronal and indeed molecular substrate, and in many cases this is quite approrpriate. However, Edelman upholds William James's century old idea that 'consciousness is a process', 'it's not a thing, there are no neurons for consciousness'. Consciousness is the buzz of the swarming bees. Staying at this 'broader' level of analysis, and relating the body to emotion, Damasio (2002) argues that 'The body is the theatre in which emotions play out' and he suggests that the right somatosensory cortex is a critical site for this drama, as this is where body senses are mapped on to the brain.

Of particular interest to us regarding the concept of embodiment is the situating of the brain and 'the rest of' the body in the same 'ether'. Over recent years psychoneuroimmunology (PNI) has shown the interconnectedness of what were once thought of as distinct fields: neuroscience, endocrinology and immunology. According to Pert (1997), their respective organs (brain, glands and the spleen, bone marrow and lymph nodes) are linked together in a non-hierarchical communication network mediated though electrical and chemical messages. Carey (2000: 38) notes a profound implication of this intertwining of mind and body: 'because the cells of the body, not just the brain, receive and secrete information-bearing chemicals, the whole body is an intelligence-bearing organism'.

The accumulating research from this relatively new area indicates that, for instance, the immune system can be boosted by positive experiences

(Futterman *et al.* 1994) and suppressed by negative experiences: this ranges from, for example, trivial acute stressors such as working through a difficult mathematical problem under time pressure (Delahanty *et al.* 1996) to serious chronic stressors, such as being a primary carer for a chronically sick spouse (Kiecolt-Glaser *et al.* 1991). The immune system is also influenced by many variables that probably mediate these experiences, such as levels of social support that people report having (Easterling *et al.* 1996). Thus our phenomenological experience, our *being-in-the-world*, our impression of the mirrors others hold up to us – all of these – are now underpinned by a more sophisticated understanding of our bodies.

Embodied language

Human language is surely one of the great achievements of evolution. Some have argued that its extraordinary level of sophistication indicates a specific and distinct neurocognitive ability (Chomsky 1965; Pinker 1995), a view that has disembodied language and objectified it for scientific treatment. Kelly *et al.* (2002) argue that across evolutionary time language emerged from the body, but bodily actions continue to affect language use in adults and language development in children.

Kelly *et al.*'s argument that language comprehension evolved out of body systems used in non-verbal communication in primate ancestors is supported by evidence that brain area 40 (within *Wernicke's area* and involved in language production) is also involved in facial and forearm movement in humans. In another part of the brain (*Broca's area*, involved in language comprehension) areas 44 and 45 are active both during language tasks and during simple movements of the hand and mouth. However, the claim that the link between bodily action and communication has been retained through evolution draws its strongest support from the dramatic discovery of 'mirror neurons' in non-human primates: neurons in F5 become active not only when a monkey produces a certain action, but also when it views another monkey (or indeed a human), producing the same action (Rizzolatti and Arbib 1998). If these 'mirror' neurons also exist in humans (Fadiga *et al.* 1995), it would help us to understand why other people's gesticulations, and possibly facial expressions, are so meaningful to us – because we are 'mirroring them' in our own bodies. Your smile makes me smile.

In terms of language developing within the child, Kelly *et al.*'s (2002) review of the literature concludes that there are important vocal–motor linkages throughout. For instance, rhythmically organized motor and vocal activities (e.g. rocking on all fours and babbling) coincide; while the onset of first gestures (pointing) predicts the appearance of first words. Following the in tandem development of *complementary* gestures and words (where they both convey the same information, e.g. shaking the head and saying 'no'), changes in gesture production, specifically the use of *supplementary* words and gestures (where they convey related but distinct information, e.g. pointing to a cup and saying 'mummy' meaning, it is mummy's cup), predicts the onset of two-word speech (see Goldin-Meadow and Butcher 2003).

Having examined evolutionary and developmental arguments, Kelly *et al.* (2002) also consider the 'moment-to-moment' production of language. They argue that the original lesion studies of Brocca and Wernicke that were interpreted as localizing language centres must now be reviewed in the light of evidence that language involves additional areas, including subneo-cortical areas (for instance, the cerebellum, thalamus and basal ganglia), neo-cortical areas (for instance, the temporo-parieto-occipital junction and occipital lobe) and motor areas in the cortex; even the right hemisphere, long considered as 'inferior', at least with regard to language function, seems to have an important role in language. Thus language does not seem to reside in one or two places, but seems to be an 'emergent' skill, based on interacting modalities.

Gesture and speech constitute an integrated communication system (McNeill 1992). So fundamental is this association that even congenitally blind speakers interacting with other blind speakers still use gesture (Iverson and Goldin-Meadow 1998). Kelly *et al.* (2002: 343) conclude:

> gestures appear to be linked to adult speech on multiple levels of analysis – from neural, to cognitive to social. The fact that this link is in place well into adulthood suggests that gestures are not merely a vestige of our evolutionary and developmental past, but are something that is fundamental to how fully formed humans continue to communicate in the present.

Gesture is embodied thought. *The Oxford English Dictionary* defines metaphor as 'something considered as representing or symbolising another (usually abstract) thing'. Thus gesture, in as much as it can both represent and symbolize other things, may be thought of as metaphorical. Language can obviously be metaphorical, but it can also be metaphorical in a *literal* sense. Recent research has found that semantic processing of action words activates sensory motor areas in the brain (Etard *et al.* 2000). Pulvermuller *et al.* (2001) reported that while processing action words, the areas most strongly activated in the motor cortex were those associated with the body part used to perform the action described by the words. Thus cortical activity involved in thinking about an action overlaps with that involved in performing the action. It may well be that using our hands to gesture the idea of trying to achieve balance is a very effective metaphor because it creates the experience of balance in those who perceive such a gesture (Church *et al.* 2002).

Body images

Brain plasticity

Within hours or even minutes of delivery newborn babies can imitate orofacial and head movements performed in front of them (Meltzoff 1990). This ability to identify specific bodily movements and then produce the same action with the corresponding part of their own body suggests that neonates have some sense of their own body. Such an idea would tie in well with Melzack's (1990) neuromatrix theory, which suggests that we innately inherit a sort of 'neuronal signature' of our bodies. This 'matrix', or network, is comprised of somatosensory cortex, posterior parietal lobe and insular cortex, and together they produce an implicit sense of the body.

These ideas are of course supported by the earlier work of Wilder Penfield. Penfield, a Canadian neurosurgeon working in the 1940s and 1950s, opportunistically stimulated specific regions of the brain that were exposed during operations. These patients were conscious because only local anaesthesia was used and since there are no pain receptors in the brain such stimulation is painless. He simply touched an area with an electrode and asked people what they felt. Elicited sensations ranged from images and memories to physical sensations (Penfield and Rasmussen 1950). By tracing sensations experienced down one strip of the brain Penfield 'mapped' out where different parts of the body are represented (Figure 1.1).

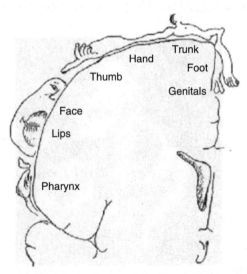

Figure 1.1 Sensory-motor areas as 'mapped-out' on one side of the brain, representing the opposite side of the body (Penfield and Rasmussen 1950)

This strip, now known as the somatosensory cortex (or sensory 'homun-culus', meaning 'little man'), reconfigures the body and allots greater space on the cortex to those body parts that are more sensitive (there is a similar pattern in the motor cortex, the strip of cerbral cortex that runs parallel to the somatosensory area, located on the other side of the central fissure of the cortex). So in both of these, the area given over to the hands, for instance, is much larger than that given over to the back or the trunk. Figure 1.2 depicts the proportional representation of the body in the brain. The good news is that most of us don't look like that! In effect, the somatosensory cortex is a map of how we *sense* the world, but not how we *make sense* out of it.

Of great importance is research indicating that how we sense the world shapes the neuronal structure of our brains. A dramatic example of this comes from the treatment of 'webbed finger syndrome' (or syndactyly), in which people are born with fingers webbed together with the result that they don't move independently of each other. Rather than the fingers having – as they usually do – their own distinct area on the somatosensory cortex, the somato-sensory representation for people with 'webbed finger syndrome' clumps all the fingers together as a 'whole hand'. For example, the distance between the sites of representation of the thumb and little finger is significantly smaller than normal. However, when fingers are surgically separated from each other so that they can move independently, within a month of this happening the somatosensory representation of the fingers has changed so that they each have their own 'patch' on the cortex and the distance between representation of the thumb and little finger has increased (Mogilner *et al.* 1993).

It would seem that a genetically inherited condition that webs the fingers together and has associated morphology in the brain is treatable not only in

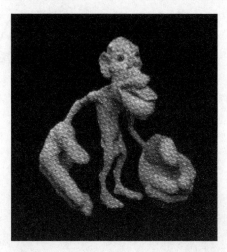

Figure 1.2   This 'homunculus' shows how the body is represented in the cortex. The biggest features, such as the hands, have the most neurons

the sense of separating the fingers, but also in the sense of changing brain structure. This is just one example of what is referred to as brain, or neural, plasticity. Robertson (1999) describes the underlying principle of neural plasticity as 'cells that fire together, wire together'. It is in this sense that he talks about 'sculpturing the brain', where people's experience of their world is *inscribed* upon their brain. Intriguingly, then, our social and cultural constructions of the world, our subjectivity, our intuitions, are neurologically 'underwritten' by the creation of Hebbian neural circuits that reverberate to our lived experience of the world. Our experience of the world is not only through *being-in-the-world* by virtue of our physical body but also through the world we construct *being-created-within-us*, by virtue of our physical body. More will be said about neural plasticity in Chapter 5, but the essential point being made here is that our neurology is dynamic, reactive and often adaptive and it reflects our subjectivity.

While the homunculi in your brain offer a representation of your body, they are very clearly not the only ones, the ones you are consciously aware of, or the ones responsible for our drive to sculpt our bodies beautiful. The fact that these neurological homunculi are so strange and foreign to us testifies to the fact that they (usually) play a limited role – if one at all – in our sense of the physical self. A range of psychological factors are involved.

Psychological images

It was not until the work of Paul Schilder that the role of non-neurological factors was incorporated into the understanding of body image. Schilder (1935) considered the broader psychological and social context in which our experience of the body occurs. He defined body image as:

> the picture of our own body which we form in our mind, that is to say the way in which the body appears to ourselves . . . we are not dealing with a mere sensation or imagination. There is a self-appearance of the body . . . although it has come through the senses, it is not a mere perception. There are mental pictures and representations involved in it, but it is not mere representation.
>
> (Schilder 1935: 11)

He was also interested in what he called the '*elasticity*' of the body image: how its properties of size and heaviness and its influence on interactions with others could fluctuate. Schilder (1935: 283) noted with disdain that 'in the voluminous books by Wundt and Tichener there is no mention of the body as an entity and as a unit'. This same situation still pertains in most psychology books, even those dealing with perception.

Schilder's term 'body image' has subsequently been used to refer to attractiveness, size, distorted body perceptions, perceptions of body boundaries and perception of internal body states. These are all legitimate aspects of bodily experience, and can perhaps be included within Grogan's (1991: 1) use of the term 'body image': 'a person's perceptions, thoughts and feelings about his or her body'. However, it may be useful to recognize a division between purely perceptual aspects of the body and evaluative aspects, while acknowledging that these may interact.

The complexity of the relationship between perceptual and evaluative images of the body is illustrated in a study by Cash (1989) which found that evaluation of individual elements of the body does not add proportionately to produce an overall impression of the body. Cash reported that for men the following were found most important (in descending order) in statistically predicting overall appearance satisfaction: weight, upper torso, face, mid torso, lower torso and muscle tone. Height was not a significant factor. For women the order was: weight, upper torso, mid torso, lower torso and face evaluation. Neither height nor muscle tone were significant factors for predicting ratings of overall appearance satisfaction in women.

While these results are interesting they are also doubtless 'culturally encapsulated'. That is, different cultural values will influence people's evaluation of their body. Even within the same societies we are now well familiar with changing attitudes regarding thinness. Grogan (1999) traces a change in the 'ideal body' of women, from the voluptuous form of the Middle Ages continuing right into the twentieth century, to the recent (1920s) idealization of slimness, propagated by the fashion industry. Until recently, to be plump was to be fashionable and erotic. This 'reproductive figure' was often portrayed with rounded hips and fullness of the stomach and breasts, in order to symbolize fertility (for example, Rembrant van Rijin's *Bathsheba*, 1654). As Grogan (1999: 12) points out, 'The ample and curvaceous woman's body was idealised as the antithesis to the taut male body portrayed by neo-classicists such as Jacques-Louis David.'

It has been argued that the pursuit of thinness arose from the fashion industries' need to mould bodies to the 'right' shape to 'show off' their garments. Thus fashion in the 1920s required women to have a boy-like flat-chested figure in order to display to greatest effect the 'Flapper' fashion of straight low-waisted dresses (Grogan 1999). In the 1930s and 1940s clothes that emphasized breasts again became fashionable – 'sweater girls'. In the 1950s it was big breasts, tiny waists and slim legs – hello Marilyn! However, the sensuality of the 36–23–36 buxom figure of the 1950s had to compete with the slimmer likes of Grace Kelly and Audrey Hepburn, who symbolized sophistication, and this thinner body became associated with 'upper classness'. By the 1960s Twiggy (all 96 pounds of her), boyish and flat-chested, had become the new role model, embraced by all social classes and seen as unconventional, free, youthful and part of the 'Jet Set' (Grogan 1999). The 'waif' models of the early 1990s, appearing painfully thin to many people, gave way to the 'heroin chic' models of the late 1990s, who not only appeared painfully thin, but, with black eye make-up, blue lips and matted hair, looked to many like heroin addicts.

There have also been changes in the idealized male body, though, at least until recently, the social pressures on male bodies have been less extreme than those on female bodies. In cultures beset with poor socio-economic conditions being thin often signifies negative attributes of malnutrition, poverty and infectious disease, while in cultures in wealthier socio-economic conditions, being thin signifies wealth, health and prosperity (Grogan 1999). In poorer contexts obesity signifies wealth because plump people are able to afford to eat to excess, while in wealthier contexts obesity may be viewed much more negatively as excessive indulgence and lack of self-control. That these 'cultural' interpretations of body image can change when socio-economic (and cultural) circumstances change was illustrated in a study by Furnham and Alibhai (1983), which compared Asian woman living in Kenya and Asian women who had emigrated to Britain from Kenya. Heavier women were more positively rated by the Kenyan as compared to the British residents. Helman (2001: 12) suggests:

> The culture in which we grow up teaches us how to perceive and interpret the many changes that occur over time in our own bodies and in the bodies of other people. We learn how to differentiate a young body from an aged one, a sick body from a healthy one, a fit body from a disabled one; how to define a fever or a pain, a feeling of clumsiness or of anxiety; how to perceive some parts of the body as public, and others as private; and how to view some bodily functions as socially acceptable and others as morally unclean.

Cultural aspects of body weight and body perception are further discussed in Chapter 4.

Cultural factors can have a strong effect on body sculpturing, even to the extent that the overlap between artificially changing the body by accentuating characteristics of beauty on the one hand and distorting the body through mutilation on the other hand becomes quite ambiguous. Polhemus (1978) has catalogued some extreme forms of body alterations that have been used (and in some cases still are). These include artificial deformation of infants' skulls, filing and carving of teeth, scarification of the chest and limbs, binding of women's feet, artificial fattening of girls, tattooing, insertion of large ornaments into the lips and earlobes and the wearing of nose and ear rings. Helman (2001) suggests that the most widespread form of bodily mutilation is male circumcision (about one-sixth of the world's population), while the most controversial is female circumcision. Although the amount of tissue that is removed during female circumcision varies across cultural groups, it can include removal of all of the external genitalia. The practice is opposed by many on the grounds of human rights, but in some cultures many women continue to advocate this 'right' for their daughters (see MacLachlan 1997).

Body cosmesis

If in some traditional societies female circumcision is seen as a way of avoiding stigmatization and becoming an eligible marriage partner (because one has adhered to the cultural rites of passage), then in the highly industrialized Western societies, cosmetic interventions can be seen as conferring eligibility in others ways. In 1999, *Newsweek* magazine ran a cover feature on 'The new age of cosmetic surgery: younger patients, more choices, greater risks'. The article by Kalp (1999) led off by recounting the 'improvements' of Holly Laganante, a 35-year-old from Chicago. She had had an eyelid lift, liposuction on her thighs, varicose vein removal and a forehead peel. And we were told that she was saving up for a forehead lift, or perhaps liposuction to fix her saggy knees. She said, 'It's been tough on me financially, but it's worth every penny . . . It's life-changing.' She is not alone. According to the American Society of Plastic and Reconstructive Surgeons, there was a 153 per cent increase between 1992 and 1999 in such operations, with more than one million in the last year. Gerald Imber, a New York plastic surgeon, recommends to his patients that they begin 'maintenance' procedures – removing fat in the neck, eliminating worry lines – somewhere between the ages of 35 and 45. He says, 'The idea of waiting until one day you need a heroic transformation is silly . . . you've wasted 20 great years of life and you've allowed things to get out of hand' (Kalp 1999: 38). California leads America in 'augs' (augmentations), where it is apparently not uncommon for 16-year-old high school girls to get breast enlargements – long before they may have finished physically maturing.

McGrath and Mukerji (2000) reported that the eight operations most commonly done on teenagers of 18 or less were (in descending order): rhinoplasty ('nose jobs'), ear surgery, reduction mammoplasty (breast reduction), surgery for asymmetric breasts, excision of gynecomastia (male breast reduction), augmentation mammoplasty (breast enlargement), chin augmentation and suction assisted lipoplasty (removal of fat under the skin). While these procedures may be necessary and appropriate in many cases, the difficulty is where to draw the line between cosmetic therapy and cosmetic recreation, and perhaps even a culturally sanctioned 'cosmetic mutilation'. McGrath and Mukerji (2000: 105) state:

> In the final analysis, *the purpose of plastic surgery is to change the patient's psyche* in a positive way. By making what the patient sees as an improvement in appearance, his or her self-perception of the body is changed, and this has an impact on the well-being and conduct of his or her life (italics added).

This raises the question as to whether plastic surgery may be the most appropriate intervention 'to change the psyche'. While the possibility of psychological disorder motivating a desire for plastic surgery certainly exists, the research evidence is equivocal on this important point (Sarwer *et al.* 1988; see Chapter 4 for more on this).

Increasingly there appears to be a mind-set of people *wearing* their body. Kalb (1999) says that many people feel under pressure to look good in order to keep their job, and cites Mary Bentley, a 43-year-old global marketing manager with IBM in Dallas: she decided to have Botox after noticing fine lines developing on her face, because 'people judge you on the way you look, dress and talk'. After the Botox she said she felt 'more competitive in the job market'. Botox is derived from botulinum toxin, which causes the potentially fatal condition of botulism. However, when injected into a muscle in minuscule amounts it paralyses the muscle (it was originally used to treat muscle spasms and Bell's palsy). When injected into the muscle behind frown lines, it prevents frown lines and removes wrinkles, for up to six months. Botox is the latest 'big thing' and is increasingly used by men as well as women (although men account for only about 10 per cent of cosmetic surgery in general).

The body as a message

The body is not simply a given physical reality, it is also shaped through cultural beliefs. In this sense we can talk of the body being a cultural construction. It is produced by the interplay between anatomy and physiology, and psychological and cultural forces. The physical attributes of the body are mute outside the context of how we refer to them. It is through language that the body acquires meaning. Indeed, the body can be seen as a text in itself on which our history is recorded: birthmarks, injuries, blemishes and wrinkles punctuating our life stories. It is this very notion of a body 'displaying a history' that treatments such as Botox seek to erase: with botox bodies can signify possibilities for the future rather than an inscription of the past.

While most people are familiar with the notion of body language – that you convey meaning through bodily movement and that sometimes this portrayal of meaning can be more truthful than verbal communication – the body infuses everyday language with many idioms, expressions and metaphors (Cavallaro and Vago 1997) (see Table 1.1). Not only can the body be a medium of language where bodily referents are used to convey abstract feelings, it can also be a canvas upon which we communicate. Just about every culture has different ways of decorating the body with these decorations symbolizing status, celebration, social roles and so on. If we think of the body as a 'peg to hang clothes on' there are infinite possibilities for the sorts of messages we can communicate about ourselves. In fact, it is just about impossible not to communicate something about yourself – even if you don't intend to or want to. Hats, heels, handbags, hair and hem heights are all understood to convey something about a woman, rightly or wrongly. You cannot switch off your image making any more than you can switch off your breathing.

Table 1.1 Bodily expressions used in English

To be an arsehole
To be limp-wristed
To be nosey
To be spineless
To be thick-skinned
To be tongue-in-check
To bend someone's ear
To bite one's tongue
To bleed someone dry
To cut one's nose to spite one's face
To elbow someone out of the way
To feel it in the bones
To get one's finger out
To get something off one's chest
To hand it to someone
To have a nose out of joint
To have guts/balls/spunk
To jump out of one's skin
To keep abreast of someone
To kick oneself
To lend a shoulder to cry on
To lend an ear
To pull a face
To put one's finger on it
To rack one's brains
To shoulder a burden
To stand out like a sore thumb
To stick one's foot in it
To swallow one's pride
To turn a blind eye
To twist someone's arm
To wrap someone around one's little finger

Source: adapted from Cavallaro and Vago (1997).

Perhaps one of the most obvious and contemporary ways to convey a message on the skin is through tattooing. Only a decade ago, in many North-Western societies a tattoo was associated with the 'working class' or with the non-commissioned servicemen 'class'; with buxom lassies adorning the wearer's skin, or renderings of daredevil daggers, or declarations of undying love. Such tattoos could also be seen as a symbol of fraternity between, for instance, prison inmates or Japanese gangsters, or as a sign of protest to symbolize alienation from mainstream society. However, now the tattooed have become the 'suits' of mainstream society, with the middle classes and celebrity-aristocracy flocking for 'tasteful' and usually discrete embellishments to convey a special little fashionable 'something' about their body, and presumably about their own self too.

The word 'tattoo' was first used by Joseph Banks and James Cook in 1769 when describing their observation of Tahitian impregnation of the skin with coloured pigments (they observed 'Tattowing' of a 12-year-old girl's buttocks). Most types of tattooing leave the skin soft, but the Maori (Aotearoa/New Zealand) way of doing it actually involved carving the skin to make a groove and then inserting the pigment into the groove (Riria and Simmons 1999). In Maori societies tattooing could be used to mark rank, status, line of descent, achievements, tribal affiliation and life history. The tattoo, or *moko*, was effectively a *personal signature*, surely something that every contemporary follower of fashion strives for. Such a 'signature' is illustrated in Figure 1.3, of a Moira chief of Ngati Kahungunu of the Hawkes Bay area of Aotearoa/New Zealand, painted in 1877. Patterns on

Figure 1.3 Portrait of Ngaiti Kahungunu, a Moira chief in the Hawkes Bay area of Aotearoa/New Zealand, painted in 1877 (reproduced by permission of the New Zealand National Gallery)

specific areas of the face (for example, above the eyes, below the chin, on the cheek) convey distinct types of information.

Contrast this traditional, highly specific and stylized method of conveying a message on the 'body canvas' with more contemporary art that seeks to convey ambiguities and anxieties concerning body identities. Recently I had the good fortune to visit the *Bodyscape* exhibition at the Rodin Gallery in Seoul, South Korea. The word 'bodyscape' has been used by American art historian Nicholas Mirzoeff to refer to scenery produced by representation of the body in visual cultures. The exhibition showed representations of the body produced by nine Korean artists. In introducing the works, Joon (2002: 12) suggests that they are ways of challenging the 'inherent limitations of the Cartesian logocentric thinking and the restrictive binary of body–mind'. While exposure of the naked body is still largely taboo in Korean society, many of the artists chose to work with the naked body, as if this is somehow more authentic. Briefly I will discuss the work of just three artists.

Kim Il-Yong takes plaster casts of body parts to produce astonishingly realistic 'life-casting' assemblages (see Figure 1.4). The female bodies he renders into plaster are presented deindividualized, without faces. His 'Being

Figure 1.4   'Being without being, 1999', by Kim Il-Yong (reproduced by permission of the Rodin Gallery, Seoul, South Korea)

without being, 1999' images are comprised of shell-like skin. The diminutive and fragile body presented challenges us to define the space inside the container and to wish for a face to put on it. A face would at once 'complete' the image and remove our awareness of its hollowness. In viewing this in three dimensions I felt an uncomfortable mix of voyeurism and nihilism.

Park Sung-Tae used very thin and fragile wire netting shaped into various body postures and suspended in mid-air. Cleverly lit, it is their reflections that take on form and substance, only hinted at in the wire mesh. For me, these striking images reflect the ambiguity between what we (biologically) are made of and the image we (psychologically) cast. These images often seem more real and life-like than their substrate. Here, however, there is both the empowering aspect of your biology – that it allows us to be more than it is – and its undermining aspect, in that whatever we do can be reduced to a simple substructure. Presumably the light that casts the shadows is the life we breath.

Finally, I also found the video works of Yun Aiyoung quite startling. The 'Abyss' series presents video images on horizontal screens immersed in the space of open-topped empty oil drums. One therefore looks down on these images, viewed though glasses that 'stabilize' the otherwise flickering footage, and this produces a distancing and 'Godlike' perspective on the video pieces. One of the pieces is of about 15 naked men and women standing in a close 'blob' of bodies, wailing and weaving in an interconnectedness that defies their own individuality and indeed their own nakedness – the individual becoming a 'dividual', a division of a many legged and armed organism. For me, the point of these and other artistic representations of the body is that they help us to question the representations that we are accustomed to. In so doing they highlight how we socially construct meanings out of our bodies. Art, no less than science, is a 'truth seeking' pursuit.

The body as a cultural icon

Why is it that certain portrayals of the body make us feel uncomfortable? Sometimes in art, sometimes in meeting people with physical disabilities, sometimes in viewing our own bodies, we are disturbed, repulsed, scared or even aggressive towards such body images. To understand this we may turn to Ernest Becker, an anthropologist who embraced the breadth of the social sciences, and dared to ask 'big' questions about the meaning of life (see, for instance, Becker 1962, 1973). Over the past 15 years a trio of experimental social psychologists have developed and demonstrated the value of Terror Management Theory (TMT) based largely upon the writings of Becker (for a review, see Solomon *et al.* 1991, 1998). The central premise of TMT is that our concerns about mortality play a pervasive and far-reaching role in our daily lives. The intelligence of human beings, coupled with their capacity for self-reflection, and the ability to think about the future, gives them the unique capacity to contemplate the inevitability of their own death.

Like Sigmund Freud and Otto Rank, Becker believed that humans would be rooted to inaction and abject terror if they were continually to contemplate their vulnerability and mortality. Thus cultural world-views evolved and these were 'humanly created beliefs about the nature of reality shared by groups of people that served (at least in part) to manage the terror engendered by the uniquely human awareness of death' (Solomon *et al.* 1998: 12). The visions of reality created by cultural world-views help terror management by answering universal cosmological questions: 'Who am I? What should I do? What will happen to me when I die?' (Solomon *et al.* 1998: 13). In effect, then, cultures give people a role to play, thus distracting them from the anxiety of worrying about what they fear most. Cultures provide recipes for immortality, either symbolically (such as amassing great fortunes that out-survive their originator) or spiritually (such as going to heaven). Abiding by cultural rules can ensure immortality, but perhaps even more important is their here and now function: 'The resulting perception that one is a *valuable* member of a *meaningful* universe constitutes *self-esteem*; and self-esteem is the primary psychological mechanism by which culture serves its death-denying function' (Solomon *et al.* 1998: 13, italics in the original).

Recently researchers have applied this analysis to the human body. Goldenberg *et al.* (2000) argue that the human body is problematic for us because it reminds us of our similarity to other animals. If we are simply animal-like then our pretensions for immortality through adherence to cultural mores make no more sense than the collective wishes of squid, lice or mice. As Becker daringly put it, we are 'gods with anuses'. I think it is this paradox that makes the body such a problem. Cultural world-views must therefore minimize the threat of the body as a reminder of our animality. This is why cultures provide norms that elevate the body from that of an animal to a cultural symbol. Such norms may specify what is worthy of disgust, what is physically attractive, what is proper hygiene, correct dress and acceptable sexual behaviour. According to TMT, then, body images, shapes and forms that do not fulfil our cultural world-view of 'good bodies' will be denigrated and rejected because they indirectly threaten our sense of being more than mere animals, finite and degradable: they suggest that 'when our bodies stop, so do we' (Cavallaro and Vago 1997). In the concluding chapter we will return to this theory. The aim of this chapter has been to 'loosen up' thinking about the body and convey how the body can be seen from a number of different perspectives and how, ultimately, it is a very plastic, in the sense of mouldable, entity.

Chapter summary

This chapter reviews the following concepts and issues:

1 The stable rigid concept of an unalterable 'given' body is increasingly being challenged by different ways of thinking about the body, the ramifications of modern healthcare and numerous aspects of modern living.
2 Embodiment may be understood as 'a physical representation of an abstract idea'. However, the body is also the site and source of the sort of abstract ideas that are developed and as such reflects a particular – embodied – perspective on the world. This perspective, most notably developed by Merleau-Ponty, challenges the mind–body split that continues to this day.
3 The difficulty of coming to terms with different experiences of self – an inner phenomenological experience and an outer 'specular image' – is seen as one of the primary challenges for people according to Lacan. This 'specular image' is also relevant to Foucault's idea of 'the gaze', where authoritative figures in society provide surveillance of the adoption of appropriate behaviour. Ultimately, people observe themselves to ensure that they adhere to social expectations.
4 While neuroscience might be expected to bridge the mind–body gap, in fact it has often increased it by using overly simplified models that take little account of people's own experiences. However, research in psycho-neuroimmunology and language acquisition indicates a great degree of interconnectedness between what have been thought of as separate mind (brain) and body systems. Much language is embodied in gesture.
5 Images of the body formed in the brain do not accord with our experience of the body. These images are, however, very adaptive to both bodily and environmental changes and reflect a high degree of brain plasticity.
6 Images of the body formed through psychosocial processes are strongly influenced by evaluative processes and cultural practices. Changing cultural norms for the body have coincided with changes in the physical form of the body. While particular bodily forms may go into or out of fashion, now surgical intervention can fashion the body to attain desired norms.
7 The body is a message, a canvas on which communications can be made. This may be through the metaphorical use of phrases relating to the body, the use of the body as a peg to parade clothes on, or intricate tattooing to indicate social position, fraternity or as a personal signature.
8 The body is also a cultural icon and artistic representations of it challenge the images that we customarily endorse. However, the iconic status of the body may also have an important role in warding off existential anxiety about our animal nature and possibly meaninglessness of life.

Discussion points

1 What assumptions does your own discipline make about the body and how open are these to the idea that the body affords the 'point of view' for your impression of the world?
2 Can a body ever reconcile its inner and outer experiences?
3 Is there such a thing as 'cosmetic mutilation', and how would you know when it happens?

Key reading

Cash, T. F. and Pruzinsky, T. (eds) (2002) *Body Images: A Handbook of Theory, Research, and Clinical Practice*. New York: Guilford Press.

Kelly, S. D., Iverson, J. M., Terranova, J., Niego, J., Hopkins, M. and Goldsmith, L. (2002) Putting language back in the body: speech and gesture in three timeframes, *Developmental Neuropsychology*, 22: 323–49.

Mathews, E. (2002) *The Philosophy of Merleau-Ponty*. Chesham: Acumen.

Sensing self

The body is a symbol. Its appearance and actions point
beyond itself to an inner world, but also beyond itself to a
total life situation. The body expresses a state of being.

(Kenny 1985: 72)

One day, for example, I can find it amusing, in my forty-
fifth year, to be cleaned up and turned over, to have my
bottom wiped and swaddled like a newborn's. I even
derive a guilty pleasure from this total lapse into infancy.
But the next day, the same procedure seems unbearably
sad, and a tear rolls down through the lather a nurse's aid
spreads over my cheeks.

(Bauby 1998: 24)

Modern North-Western conceptions of physical illness can be traced back
to Hippocrates's time and a dispute between the so-called *ontologists* and
physiologists regarding the nature of disease. The physiologists saw disease as
resulting from an imbalance within the person (in terms of different
humors) or between the person and their environment. The ontologists, on
the other hand, believed that disease was a thing, an object, which invaded
the body. It was not until the eighteenth century that the ontologists' point
of view came to predominate and can now be seen in our 'germ theory' of
disease. The microworld of biochemistry locates diseases as independent
entities; that is, independent of the person who 'has' them. This chapter is
concerned with the way in which people relate to their physical distress,
what that distress means *to them* and how this affects their experience of
embodiment. Ontologists, beware!

Embodied language

When people talk, their heart rate increases. When they talk about
themselves, it increases even more. When they talk about themselves in
situations where their personal integrity is in some way challenged, their
heart rate goes up further again – maintaining a psychological sense of self
involves active physiology. Our language, how we talk and refer to ourselves,
like a spanner, can ratchet up – 'put the squeeze on' – our hearts. However,
psychology, in particular, has treated people's conversations as though there
were only a linguistic enterprise in a social domain. Now it is becoming

clear that our talk, the conversations we engage in and the discourses we develop, are fully embodied activities. They require not just psychological work but also physical work and so we should not be surprised to learn that the work of *self-construction* has both psychological and physiological correlates. Focusing in particular on cardiovascular reactivity (CVR), Lyons and colleagues (Lyons *et al.* 2000; Lyons and Farquhar 2002) have presented a framework to explain much of the work in this area. They suggested that elevations that occur in CVR during talk, or indeed any form of communication (including sign language), are a correlate of self-construction processes: 'speakers become more engaged and show increased CVR depending on how salient their sense of self or subjectivity is during talk' (Lyons and Farquhar 2002: 2044). Physiological and psychological processes are seen not as having a causal relationship but as being correlates, in fact as being simultaneous processes.

Lyons and Farquhar also note research indicating other psychological variables that influence CVA during talk: CVR is higher when a person is in an unfamiliar context. It is lowest when with a family member, higher when with a friend and highest when with a stranger. People show lower CVR when they are in the presence of another supportive person, as compared to when they are alone or when they are in the presence of someone who is not supportive of them. It is, however, important to note that the results of the above research, and indeed the results of Lyons and colleagues' own research, is not entirely consistent with their suggested explanatory framework. This may be because not everybody reacts physiologically in the same way to 'talk' and 'self-work'. Perhaps a broader range of physiological 'correlates' (i.e. other than CVR) should be taken into account. However, for our present purposes, it can be concluded that their main point stands: 'that a sense of self occurs through social interaction and relatedness and that this process . . . [has] physiological correlates' (Lyons and Farquhar 2002: 2044). Importantly, these 'correlates' are not 'side issues' or 'physiological noise', they are part and parcel of the process of continually reconstructing and of renewing the person's sense of self though conversing with others.

Disembodied language

Talk about the self may reveal significant insights especially when considered in relation to aspects of the physical body that cause pain or distress. If modern North-Western medicine objectifies disease, do individuals do likewise? Cassell (1976) described how a woman who had a mass in her breast discussed 'my breast' and 'my nipple', but referred to the tumour in her breast as an 'it'. She didn't say to the doctor 'Make my breast well' or 'Make me better', what she did say was 'Make it go away'. As Cassell (1976: 144) notes: 'The very naturalness of the patients' words – indeed, the difficulty of even hearing the word, "it", or the word, "the", in this context, unless it is pointed out, suggests how common such speech patterns are.' Perhaps tumours that appear on the skin, with their definitive boundary, are easily spoken of as discrete objects, but Cassell argues that disease *itself* is objectified. He does note, however, that hypertension and diabetes tend not to be referred to impersonally but to be identified with the self: 'my diabetes', 'my hypertension'. Interestingly, Cassell suggests that the heart, when treated as a site of emotion, is personified ('he broke my heart'), but objectified when it is the site of dysfunction (the example he gives is 'when I had the mumps, they told me it affected the heart'). Finally, Cassell argues that some healthy aspects of the body are personified while others are not: certain organs 'hidden' from view are often referred to as objects (the lungs, kidneys, liver, ovaries), while external anatomy attracts the use of personal pronouns (my eyes, ears, skin, arms, legs). Of course these 'data' may be quite culturally specific (Cassell's sample was drawn from New York) and may also be epoch-bound (his study was conducted some 30 years ago) and so we do not know if these linguistic constructions reflect a basic human propensity or are another aspect of North-Western cultural constructions. It is, however, important to consider what function such constructions might have.

Objectifying a disease may help to distance that disease and the distress it causes from the person who is experiencing it. This can be seen as being a self-protective ploy because it disengages the self from the thing that is damaging the 'self'. Of course we are familiar with many health professions objectifying a disease. *The* tumour or *the* cancer can be attacked by *my* doctor by using chemotherapy, even when, in fact, the assault is on the whole body. This linguistic construction allows *my* doctor to be on *my* side even when she is killing me (or *parts* of me, to be more objective). It is also good for the doctor to know that she is fighting an *it* and not a *you*. Such constructions continue to reflect clinicians' and patients' (note that *patients* are objectified *people*) basic philosophical understanding of what they are about. I, for instance, prefer to talk of someone suffering *through* depression or cancer, or whatever, rather than *with* depression or cancer, or *from* depression or cancer (which I think is more objectifying – the depression or cancer is attacking the self, but not a part of the self). However, I recall a very eminent psychiatrist who lectured me during my clinical training, talking about someone who was depressed 'having a nasty dose of the illness'.

We have recently seen the mapping of the human genome, but what Cassell alludes to is a sort of 'mapping of the body and its diseases as they are portrayed in the language of a person' (Cassell 1976: 145). To paraphrase and update Cassell's conclusion, 'we know much about the function of our genes, but remarkably little about the function of our words'. If, as I have argued above, we are continually constructing ourselves in conversation, and if objectification is a form of distancing the self from the dis-ease, then what happens over time as people recover from disease? How do their linguistic self-referents change?

Distancing the body

Morse and Mitcham (1998) have described the agonizing rehabilitation of people who had experienced major burns in a series of interviews they conducted following their discharge from hospital. One person who had been electrocuted described the experience thus:

> *both hands and wrists* were burnt, which were the [electrical] entry sites. And . . . *both feet* were burnt . . . *the right side* being the worst . . . *right side* of *both hands and feet* because – my right hand was up high – so naturally it entered *the right* hand the most . . . whatever was left over came down and went into *the left* . . . *it* still sustained some damage . . . *the right hand* had to be removed . . . And the right leg was burnt quite badly, and the whole outside of *the leg* was burnt down to *the bone* – you could see *bones and sinews* in there, and at the very bottom – it also exited – not on the bottom of the foot – but . . . on the bottom of the leg, like right at the side of *the* foot was really burnt bad, too.
>
> (Morse and Mitcham 1998: 669, italics in the original)

Here the use of the definite article can clearly be seen as a distancing mechanism, effectively disembodying the person from the injury. Morse and Mitcham emphasize that this pattern did not occur uniformly across all those they interviewed, and further, that it was used to describe events only during the most painful parts of their hospitalization. In the quote above the person speaks of his hand before the burn injury as '*my* right hand was up high', but subsequently 'positions' the hand as separate from himself. As people recover, their bodily references are again through possessive pronouns: they 'take back their bodies', as Morse and Mitcham put it.

In the following instance a person is so distancing themselves from their damaged body that if they were their own doctor or nurse, we might be concerned they were excessively objectifying 'their patient': 'hopefully when we get *this* scar tissue matured, at which point then . . . depending on whether *the* skin can support itself – you also burn out the oil sites . . . you have no natural oil going into *your* skin and if you don't, it cracks'. (Morse and Mitcham 1998: 670, italics in original). Thus just as disembodying language may be used by treating clinicians, so too patients may seek to achieve the same sort of distant and detached 'interest' in the technicalities of their 'condition'. To ultimately agree to amputate 'the' leg is more manageable than is amputation of 'my leg'. This may appear in another guise as well. Recently I assessed a young women regarding her psychological preparedness to have an amputation of her left foot, which had been paining her for many years, without relief: 'the doctors know best what to do with it, whatever they think, is fine by me, I trust them completely'. Perhaps the ultimate in objectifying your illness is allowing an outsider to say what should happen to your body. While there should of course be a degree of truth in the assertion that 'doctor knows best', there is also probably a desire not to be responsible for dismembering oneself.

Morse and Mitcham explored a number of conjectures regarding the function of detached speech, and considered its use in people who had experienced different sorts of health problems. None of the spinal cord injury group they reported displayed 'disembodying language', although like the burns group they had experienced sudden, unanticipated injury that threatened their survival. Furthermore, their lengthy exposure to 'doctor talk' did not lead them to assume a more distanced rhetoric. The lack of disembodying language in this group would suggest that its function is therefore not to maintain a sense of self when an individual loses control or sensation of a body part, nor is it learned from the clinical environment.

People with myocardial infarction also showed no evidence of disembodied language, and so the threat of death which often accompanies such life threatening traumatic events does not seem to be a spur to linguistic detachment either. Finally, there was only 'scant evidence' of disembodying language in the transplant group – who had lost body parts – and this tended to refer to internal organs (liver or heart). Morse and Mitcham argue that while each of these conditions may have some aspect of pain, the pain of severe burns patients is quite simply incomparable to the much lesser degree of pain in the others. Burn patients are often quite literally 'lost for words' to describe the sort of pain they suffer:

> I remember having pain. I remember how great the pain was. I'd had four children and every one of them a hard delivery. I remember with this pain, thinking that a baby – that labour pains – didn't even hold a candle to this pain. This pain is even too great to even try to describe. It's just solid pain. I've never felt anything that comes close to it, since or before. It's the greatest pain I've ever had.
>
> (Morse and Mitcham 1998: 669)

Since disembodying language was a much stronger feature of severe burns patients than the other groups, Morse and Mitcham (1998: 676) argued that the function of disembodying language is as an attempt to retain the integrity of self during prolonged agonizing experiences: '*Disembodiment is a strategy used to remove the body part, hence to remove the pain when the agony is overwhelming*' (original italics). Schilder (1935: 104) also suggests, although without giving a mechanism, that we respond to pain by isolating it and try 'pushing it out of the body image. When the whole body is filled with pain, we try and get rid of the whole body. We take a stand outside our body and watch ourselves.'

Searching for self in chronic pain

Morse and Mircham (1998) emphasize how the language of disembodiment that accompanies episodes of severe pain reverts to an embodied language with successful rehabilitation – 'claiming back the body'. Osborn (2002) has explored what happens to concepts of self when pain endures, when, albeit less severe, pain becomes a part of life. Osborn reports on interviews he conducted in England with six people, all of whom were from white working-class backgrounds and no longer in paid employment due to their chronic pain. Using interpretive phenomenological analysis (IPA; see Smith *et al.* 1999) Osborn found that their accounts of living with pain clustered around four broad themes: living with an unwanted self, the social aspect of the self among others, a self that cannot be understood or controlled and living with a body separate from the self. Here I wish to focus particularly on the first and last of these clusters and will quote from Osborn's illuminating interviews to illustrate these themes (see also Osborn and Smith 1998).

Living with an unwanted self

Interestingly, the two segments I quote from here arise from people who asked for the interview to be stopped because they found it upsetting. It is important to note that these were the only two who asked for the interviewing to be stopped. It also conveys just how distressing and/or difficult putting pain into words can be. Helen, aged 37, had been in chronic pain for five years. Having described her pain she was asked how long it had been that way:

Since it started getting bad, I was always snappy with it but not like this, it's not who I am it's just who I am if you know what I mean, it's not really me, I get like that and I know like, you're being mean now but I can't help it. It's the pain, its me, but it is me, me doing it but not me do you understand what I'm saying, if I was to describe myself like you said, I'm a nice person, but then I'm not am I and there's other stuff, stuff I haven't told you, if you knew you'd be disgusted I just get so hateful.

Interviewer: When you talk about 'you' and then sometimes 'not you', what do you mean?

I'm not me these days, I am sometimes, I am alright, but then I get this mean bit, the hateful bit, that's not me.

Interviewer: What's that bit?

I dunno, that's the pain bit, I know your gonna say it's all me, but I can't help it even though I don't like it. It's the mean me, my mean head all sour and horrible, I can't cope with that bit, I cope with the pain better.

Interviewer: How do you cope with it?

Get out the way, [tearful] sit in my room, just get away, look do you mind if we stop now, I didn't think it would be like this, I don't want to talk any more.

(Osborn 2002: 198)

Helen seems to be struggling between contradictory aspects of her self and wondering just what her 'real self' is; it is 'nice' but 'hateful', 'It's the pain, it's me', but 'not me'. She struggles to retain a sense of worth by denying that the very thing which is hurting her so much could, in fact, be (a part of) herself. Most dramatically, she says that it is this battle for identity that is the most difficult to bear – not the actual pain itself, but the consequences of it ('my mean head all sour and horrible') for her 'self'.

Keven, aged 36, has after 13 years of chronic pain separated 'it' from himself:

> now it's me with this bit that doesn't fit, doesn't belong to me, causing all the problems, what you need to understand is that the pain is not me it's attached to me, doing it to me, but it's but it's not me, it's a part of my body that doesn't belong to me anymore, it's different.
>
> (Osborn 2002: 204).

There is a sense here of Kevin feeling that it is imperative for the interviewer to understanding ('what you need to understand') that the pain is not him, because unless he understands this (as Kevin himself does) he may get the wrong idea of who Kevin is. Later, Kevin is asked what is the hardest thing to manage in terms of how he sees himself and his pain:

> the bits that aren't me, I can't be me, the hardest part is the pain obviously, but the fact that I'm like this monster, I get mean, I do things and think things which are mean, things which I'd never tell anyone and I'll not tell you so don't ask, I get so and I can't stop myself and I hate it and I know it's wrong but I can't do much about it except to say sorry afterwards or just keep it to myself, the family understand I know but that's the hardest part now you ask. Its not me to think like that, I've had enough now . . . let's stop now.
>
> (Osborne 2002: 205)

Confronting himself, not thinking *like* himself, seems to be too much for Kevin, as if to continue the interview would be to contradict the very understanding he has made of himself – that 'it's not me'. The second phrase of this quote ('I can't be me') possibly conveys, in almost Shakespearean complexity, at once the impossibility of 'being himself' (as in 'just be yourself' and relax etc.) and at the same time the impossibility of the pain that 'comes from' and is experienced through his body, 'being me' – this can't be me, I will not let it be me.

I have noted, and it would seem to be supported in Osborn's work, another striking aspect of how people in chronic pain describe their behaviour. The pain *makes them* do things they do not wish to do, and to present an aspect of themselves (that if previously present at all) they would prefer to remain hidden. Pain is almost experienced as an authoritarian figure that compels them to act against their better judgement, for which they feel great guilt afterwards. This 'authoritarian aspect' of pain has simi-larities to Milgram's (1963) now infamous 'obedience' experiments, which subsequently, and rightly, provoked such ethical furore. Using US college students as subjects, Milgram sought to explore the extent to which people would follow inhuman orders, in this case to apply potentially fatal electric shocks to an apparently innocent victim. To his surprise they complied a great deal: even when they could hear their apparent victim screaming they continued to administer electric shocks when instructed (by the experi-menter) to do so. While I am not suggesting that chronic pain 'tells' people to 'act out' their distress on others (in thought or deed), I am suggesting that it can result in the expression of aspects of self that the person in chronic pain was previously unaware of, or perhaps which previously didn't exist. In that sense at least, these aspects may authentically be experienced as 'not me'.

Osborn's second theme, concerning the social aspect of the self, conveys how people in chronic pain are left with am impression of their inferiority to others. The third theme, that of a self that cannot be understood or controlled, highlights the sense of uncertainly that people in chronic pain live with. Not being able to anticipate their pain or their own actions in the future, they had become unreliable and unpredictable, and might indeed worsen.

A body separate from the self

Osborn found that those parts of the body which functioned 'normally and therefore silently' were given little attention, but that dysfunctional or pain-ful parts of the body were placed outside of the self, so imbibing the self with a form of dualism. Lynette, at 52 years of age, had been in chronic pain for nine years, and was asked if her pain had changed the way she sees her body:

> I suppose it's made me think about it, before I thought about what it looked like, whether I was putting on weight or what make-up to wear, but never about what was going on inside, never gave it a thought, I still don't about the bits that don't hurt, but I know I've got a back now and a bum and left leg, because it hurts and you can feel it like a solid thing like something that's gone wrong.
>
> Interviewer: A solid thing?
>
> Yeah, like a mass a bit of leather, in your back getting in the way, you know where your back is all the time, this thing you carry with you now, giving you hassle and getting in the way.
>
> (Osborn 2002: 222).

The presence of what hurts ('carrying your back around') and the absence of what doesn't ('never gave it a thought, I still don't') seem to sit so easily together in Lynette's speech. Yet both are of her body and juxtaposition that body. The hurt does not, however, seem to be of her 'self' (she carries it around) and is distanced by use of the second and third person ('a back . . . a bum and left leg', 'you carry', 'giving you hassle'). Lynette went on to describe her body in two parts: 'an old bit and the pain bit, which has gone wrong . . . it won't obey me' (Osborn 2002: 223). It seems to me that there is a profound paradox here: when you are aware of your body, it is not 'you', it is only 'you' when you are not aware of it. Taking this further we might suggest that 'you' are only embodied in what you can't sense, because only then does that body offer a clear channel for *being-in-the-world*. Just as when taking a picture we don't want to see the lens, as this detracts from the reality of the image, nor do we want to sense the body when trying to be-in-the-world.

Williams (2000, cited in Osborn 2002) also makes a clever distinction between the 'disappearance' of the body in the absence of pain and its 'dysappearance' in the presence of pain. Again Williams is emphasizing that only in the event of bodily dysfunction does its presence enter consciousness. In this circumstance there is a consciousness of 'its' being, but not necessarily a consciousness of 'it being me'. It is perhaps ironic that the dualism that the concept of embodiment seeks to erase seems to find expression in the sufferer's distinction between themselves and their body: the identification of a 'me' (*without* the body) and an 'it' in pain (*within* the body) (see also Bendelow and Williams 1995)

My quotations from Osborn's excellent interviews, and indeed his own study, are of course very selective and cannot hope to be representative of the breadth of people suffering with chronic pain. Furthermore, it is important to stress that many people suffering from a chronic illness manage their lives quite successfully, maintaining high self-esteem and being productive in their own eyes. At this stage we now broaden our consideration of how language is used in relation to embodiment.

The meaning of illness

Waitkins and Magana (1997) have discussed the role of narrative in relation to somatization. They define narrative as 'attempts at storytelling that portray the interrelationships among physical symptoms and the psychologic, social, or cultural context of these symptoms' (p. 816). They are particularly concerned with the way in which narrative integrates the cultural context with the traumatic event. The mechanism they posit for the transformation of traumatic events into somatic symptoms is one where the traumatic experience cannot be told 'as a coherent whole' (p. 818).

Waitkins and Magana (1997) suggest that, depending on the socio-cultural context, terribly distressing traumatic events are psychologically processed in different ways. For instance, in some cultural contexts the 'preferred' response may be explicit psychological breakdown and withdrawal from customary social roles, while in others psychological symptoms may not be 'preferred', while the maintenance of customary social roles is. In the latter context the distress associated with the terrible trauma narrative may be transformed into somatic symptoms (see also Chapter 3). This account chimes with Lacan's conceptualization of somatic symptoms being 'the silence in the supposed speaking subject' (Lacan 1981: 11). However, the expression of this 'silence' is channelled through cultural idioms, such that in Southeast Asian cultures that highly value the head, traumatic experiences may be expressed through headaches, while in Latino cultures, where conceptions of 'nerves' are commonplace, dizziness, numbness and weakness of extremities may predominate as symptoms (Waitkins and Magana 1997).

Mary B was referred to me because she was having difficulty mobilizing after more than three months of bed rest, following repeated falls and fractures to her femur. She had also suffered with Parkinson's disease for many years, and in addition, had been experiencing distressing hallucinations for the past couple of weeks. Mary became anxious at the thought of walking, as this incurred the possibility of falling again. Furthermore, her Parkinson's meant that when she was positioned (by a physiotherapist) sitting down between parallel bars and assisted to stand up, she experienced an intension tremor – she shook quite violently. This shaking seemed to act as confirmatory feedback to her that she was indeed 'physically not ready to walk' and also that her 'nerves' were not up to it; on several occasions she reported having a panic attack, which seemed to be associated with hyperventilation. When Mary did successfully take a few steps, she often had the experience of freezing (also a feature of Parkinson's) and of literally 'feeling stuck', which was even more anxiety provoking. She continued to experience pain associated with femur breakages and was concerned that she might experience even worse pain in the future, especially if she fell again. Mary's anxiety was of clinical severity and she also indicated symptoms of borderline depression.

Changes in the medication she was taking to treat her Parkinson's disease accounted for Mary's intermittent hallucinations. These often revolved around the theme of loss. For instance, on one occasion she believed that she had seen her entire family, including pets, all killed and that consequently she was now completely alone in the world. Mary also had difficulties concentrating and would frequently lose track of a conversation. She was distressed by forgetting things and felt quite unsure if the things she talked to people about had actually happened, or not. Frequently she claimed not to be sure if she was 'telling the truth or not' and asserted that 'I can't trust myself'. She also had grave concerns about what the future would hold for her and about her personal security in the hospital.

It appeared to me that Mary's concerns – about what was real and what wasn't, about what the future held for her, about her role and place in her family, about her safety – became embodied in her battle with mobility.

Throughout my work with her (over a period of about four months) she repeatedly used the phrase 'I don't know where I stand'. Now, on the one hand, it could be quite misleading to make too much of a phrase that might simply be a frequently used term from her personal lexicon, and as such, has no great significance. It might be that one of her 'favourite' phrases just happened to coincide with her particular type of physical difficulty, and that she might just as easily have said 'I feel disorientated', 'I can't contemplate the future' or 'I'm not sure what's happening to me'. On the other hand, her choice of words might also have conveyed something about her 'symptoms', and, indeed, her symptoms may have conveyed something about her broader life situation. Here, I think, is the crux of the difficulty with accepting the notion of embodiment within many clinical contexts: physical distress undoubtedly exists and can be shown to be underpinned by clear biological processes; so to what extent can one seriously think of organic pathology 'embodying' concerns of the self, when, in fact, the physical problem would exist without those concerns?

I believe that it is not as much a matter of the soma expressing the self here (in some sort of psychosomatic formulation) as of the self *looking for* a form of expression through the soma, *as it is*. As such, 'self-concerns', anxiety and dysphoria may paint themselves on the canvas that allows for the greatest degree of expression. Our hint that this may be happening comes from the metaphorical use of language that highlights the person's current predicament as a signifier for additional concerns. Such a process would be 'innocent' and banal were it not for the possibility that the body itself becomes a metaphor. For Mary, her anxiety about walking and 'going forward' *magnifies* the very real (organic) difficulty she has in doing just that (due to muscle wastage, gait difficulties and pain) and this in turn becomes a vehicle for her to express her concerns both physically and by routing her distress into a lexicon salient to her experiencing of the world. Thus, when Mary says 'I don't know where I stand', she means it, both literally and metaphorically.

Falling ill

I have summarized the different factors involved here in Figure 2.1, which also illustrates how the above process may mediate the embodiment of Mary's distress in her difficulties in walking. Having recounted an example of my own understanding of how aspects of the self may become embodied through physical illness, I now wish to turn to accounts ventured by others. Kidel (1988) suggests that many of us experience the onset of illness as an external blow, almost like being tripped up ('falling ill') and being 'unmasked', as illness reveals our vulnerability and dependency. Indeed, Kidel goes as far as to argue that our 'New Age' focus on perfect health is one that seeks to place us on a God-like pedestal, freed of negativity and limitations, beyond the bounds of merely being human, aged and

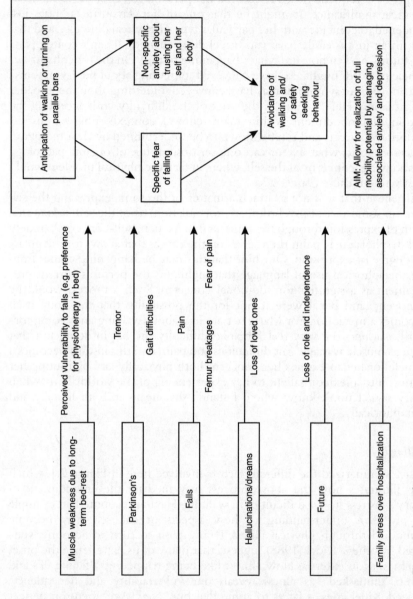

Figure 2.1   A schematic representation of Mary's difficulties and my intervention rationale

ailing. Ultimately, then, our aspiring to perfect health may be as a means to distract ourselves from our ultimate mortality and death denying wishes (see Chapters 1 and 7 on Becker and Terror Management Theory). Spiritually many religions seek to separate the immortal self from the immoral body that:

> belongs to a lower order of things; it is in some essential way inferior to mind or spirit. The 'flesh', particularly in Christian traditions, represents a source of temptation, and an instrument of the devil. It is seen as an obstacle to salvation which must be subdued: the body, as the seat of our recalcitrant 'animal' nature, is perceived as wild, unclean, autonomous, unpredictable, even dangerous.
>
> (Kidel 1988: 7)

Kidel goes on to say that given this conception of the body it is not surprising that, when we fall ill, we pass the responsibility for our body to specialists even more detached from it than ourselves. This detachment serves the needs of both doctor and patient (as previously noted), keeping 'feelings' at bay and allowing for a reassuring measuring and naming ritual. Although 'the patient' may be disempowered through this process, it is not simply a usurpation of power by the doctor, but usually also a renunciation of it by 'the patient': 'Illness makes us weak, but more often than not we multiply this by projecting the role of the healer uniquely upon the professional' (Kidel 1988: 11).

Somatic symbolism

Seeing illness as more than a mechanical malfunction for which we have no responsibility challenges us to understand what its role is in our personal life 'story', and ultimately, if it can in some way be considered as a meaningful 'role'. McCormack (1988: 37) addresses the personalized nature of a frequently objectified organ: the heart.

> And why have we forgotten what was taken for granted before the existence of the new branch of medicine called cardiology, that the heart is constantly affected by what we feel and think, the way we live, what we ask of it, that it is subordinate to the brain, that it has a language of its own and that it has for centuries carried the symbol of the centre, the spirit, the place from which love flows like the flow of blood itself, that it is the four-chambered beat and continuum of life itself.

Our hearts beat rapidly when enthused or hurt by those we love, 'bursts' with excitement, 'leaps into our mouth' when afraid, 'flutters' with pleasure, 'spills' with ecstasy, 'soars' with happiness and 'sinks' when we lose something dear to us. What may be reflected in our hearts, then, is a biological correlate of our need for human relationships (see also Chapter 3).

Perhaps one of the greatest 'advantages' of physical illness from a psychological point of view is that it 'allows' us to be emotional and excuses our expressions of need, fear, dependency and so on. To the extent that such expressions can facilitate secondary gain (benefiting because of the attention given to you and by the allowances made for you), perhaps any physical distress can be used to convey something meaningful about a person's life situation above and beyond their immediate illness. However, I have already suggested that, at least on some occasions, there may be a meaningful link between the psychological vocabulary of verbal expression and the physical vocabulary of somatic expression. None the less, it is important to caution against too simplistic or too extreme an interpretation of physical symptoms.

Guggenbuhl-Craig and Micklem (1988) warn against the desire to try to explain all diseases psychologically or symbolically. They give examples of arteriosclerosis (the narrowing of arteries) being linked to a narrow psychological outlook, or cancer of the breast being linked to a negative attitude towards femininity. The dangers of such naive and often quite offensive interpretations are apparent. Furthermore, within the psychosomatic approach there is, Guggenbuhl-Craig and Micklem (1988) argue, a conception of disease as a sort of punishment for an imbalance in their psychological functioning. Such conceptions are not just problematic because of their possible fantasy element (devoid of empirical evidence) but disturbing because of their implicit moralism: people are seen as having failed to develop properly psychologically, as insufficiently expressing their feelings, being too friendly or not friendly enough. This 'insult-to-injury' argument is terribly important to keep in mind, but because the psychosomatic conception is in some sense 'unpleasant', does not of course mean that it is wrong.

Somatic fixation

A recent term to have entered the literature is 'somatic fixation' (Biderman *et al.* 2003), which refers to the medicalization of people's problems both by 'patients' themselves and by their physicians, and other clinicians. Somatic fixation is distinguished from somatization and somatoform disorders (which are psychiatric diagnoses), although it may overlap with these. Instead, *somatic fixation* is a product of entering a system (cultural, social, institutional, medical) that has a proclivity to address somatic factors, possibly at the expense of psychological or social ones. Pre-paid health systems that operate on the basis of 'ruling out' unlikely physical causes may inculcate the assumption that a person's ailment will ultimately have a physical basis.

Biderman *et al.* (2003) give as an example that if a person in their 'late middle age' who is suffering from a headache receives a radiograph of their cervical spine, it is almost certain to find some form of pathology. Seizing on this pathology as the reason for the person's distress might be a form of somatic fixation, where the real (psychological) reason for their distress is not explored. Biderman *et al.* (2003: 1137), cautioning about somatic fixation, warn that 'Once put into motion, it leads to certain expectations of how the doctor will react to complaints and problems and can enmesh the patient in the system, preventing him or her from relating to the emotions as a potential source of bodily discomfort.' Thus, Biderman *et al.* (2003) seem to be describing a socially contrived situation (almost a *folie a deux*, in psychiatric terms) where people share a delusional belief based on somatic preoccupation.

The propensity towards 'somatic fixation' is perhaps one aspect of the medicalization of everyday life. For instance, the rate of Caesarian sections has dramatically increased in recent years, although to different extents in different countries. In the UK one-fifth of births are by Caesarian section, compared to about one in ten in Scandinavian countries (Struthers 2002). Although it may be argued that women labour better in a private familiar setting, moving about freely and keeping upright, clinical 'risk management' has them very much more publicly connected up to a monitor, and usually on a bed in an unfamiliar and often 'harsh' clinical environment. The clinical context 'tells' women that their body needs medical and midwifery expertise to deliver their baby, when often this is not the case (see also Chapter 6). One response to the harshness of medical environments and the objectification of 'patients' has been demonstrated in the, perhaps unlikely, context of neurological disorders.

Romantic science

Wasserstein (1988) suggests that the growth of the science of medicine (which seeks to generalize about patients and place them in broad disease categories) has threatened the art of medicine (which recognizes the uniqueness of 'the patient' and personalizes their experience). In reviewing the work of neurologist Oliver Sacks, Wasserstein (1988: 440) suggests that Sacks sees the disease process as having a closer relationship to the 'personal being of patients' than is usually acknowledged, and that 'an existential feeling for the patient's life situation is necessary to elucidate the mechanisms of disease'. As many of Sacks's case studies are relevant to the concept of embodiment it will be useful to review briefly some of his insights and to consider why these may be described as 'romantic science'.

The philosophy of Sacks's work picks up on the distinctions we have noted above between objectified and subjective body and self experience: he despairs of the removal of the subject from contemporary clinical case studies and the use of a cursory phrase such as 'a trisomic albino female of 21'. Sacks seeks to place the human subject at the centre, taking into account the human dimensions of suffering and affliction, but also recognizing the fighting human spirit. To do this we must 'deepen' a case history to create a narrative or tale, for only when we tell a story do we have a 'who' as well as a 'what'. Sacks is concerned with the person *in relation to* their physical disease. In the case of Dr P. (*The Man Who Mistook His Wife for a Hat*), who had severe visual agnosia (an inability to recognize familiar objects), no face, not even his wife's face, was familiar to him. Sacks describes his experience thus: 'A face, to us, is a person looking out – we see, as it were, the person through his *persona*, his face. But for Dr P. there was no *persona* in this sense – no outward *persona*, and no person within' (Sacks 1985: 12, italics in original). Dramatically Sacks sees the case of Dr P. as a warning and parable of a science excessively focused on abstract computational elements of people's distress, neglecting the judgemental, the particular, the personal aspects of experience. He goes as far as to suggest that our cognitive sciences are suffering an agnosia in that they seek the reassurance of objective fact over the meaning of subjective reality.

In *A Leg to Stand On*, Sacks recounts his personal experience of proprioceptive scotoma following a severe leg injury. Proprioceptive scotoma is best defined by Sacks's own subjective experience:

> *I knew not my leg.* It was utterly strange, not mine, unfamiliar. I gazed upon it with absolute non-recognition . . . In some sense, then, I had lost my leg . . . I was now an amputee. And yet not an ordinary amputee. For the leg, objectively, externally, was still there; it had disappeared subjectively, internally. I was therefore, so to speak, an 'internal' amputee . . . I had lost the inner image, or representation, of the leg . . . I had lost the leg as an 'internal object', as a symbolic and affective 'imago'. Thus, on the one hand, there was a severe perceptual deficit so that I had lost all feeling of the leg. On the other hand, there was a sympathetic deficit, so that I had lost much of my feeling *for* the leg.
>
> (Sacks 1984: 47–50, italics in original)

This sense of no longer 'living in' the leg is strongly conveyed by his loss of both the feeling *of* and his feeling *for* the leg. He was not embodied in the leg either through action or emotionally, and this points to two essential elements of the embodied experience. Sacks was fortunate to have correspondence with A. R. Luria, the famous Russian neuropsychologist, whom he quotes as writing: 'The body is a unity of actions, and if part of the body is split off from action, it becomes "alien" and not felt as part of the body' (cited in Sacks 1984: 115). But as Sacks (1984: 164) emphasizes:

> If a hand is 'alien', it is alien to *you*, if something is done, it is *you* who are doing it. But the 'you' or the 'I' which is everywhere implicit is formally, explicitly, denied or disallowed. Hence the peculiar double-think of . . . neuropsychology . . . It is precisely the subject, the living 'I', which is being excluded. Neuropsychology is admirable, but it excludes the psyche – it excludes the experiencing, active, living 'I'.

It would seem that even Luria felt it necessary to write two sorts of books: 'systematic' books dealing with complex neurological systems (for example, *Higher Cortical Functions in Man*, 1966) and 'neurological biographies' addressing the experiencing 'I' (for example, *The Man with a Shattered World*, 1972). In the latter work Luria goes beyond what he described as the 'veterinary' approach; or what might, in more contemporary parlance, be referred to as 'meat-with-a-beat psychology'.

One of the themes Sacks develops in his writings is the importance of the *use* of body parts and how such use is necessary in order to have a sense of 'being' in them. He also describes peripheral neuropathies that (often as a result of diabetes) had resulted in sensory and sometimes motor loss in the arms or legs. The result was that those so afflicted felt that their hands or feet were 'alien objects stuck on to arm and leg stumps' (Sacks 1984: 158). He also mentions patients with broken necks feeling that they consist of only a head and shoulders. In 1991, Sacks, after another accident, received a spinal anaesthetic and, losing all sensation of his legs, felt himself to be 'terminated' in the middle. But he emphasizes that his legs didn't feel 'missing', he felt a sort of 'seamless completeness', as though he never had had a lower half – 'a sense of wholeness ending above the legs' (Sacks 2002). Sacks's sense of being embodied would therefore seem to require some form of feedback from those parts of the body.

Luria defined a romantic science as one that would 'preserve the wealth of living reality' and contrasted this to a classical analytical science reducing 'living reality with all its richness of detail to abstract schemas' (quoted in Wasserstein 1988). In Sacks's attempt to achieve the former he, for instance, considers the role of art, music, religion and personal relationships and explores them as tools to living and rehabilitation that reach beyond rationality. Such insight is once again based in his own experience of inability to move his leg with his own volition by 'rationally' trying to through deep concentration. He contrasts this with the ease of its (effortless) movement in response to music he enjoys. While Sacks humanizes neurological and other physical disorder by allowing the reader to identify with the person's lived experience, he also often refers to such disorder as an 'it', against which the person's 'I' must struggle to integrate itself amidst perceptual, motor and other types of 'gaps'. The way in which people do this (with, for instance, defences, compensations and social relationships) is understood by Sacks to tell us something about the person. As I have also argued earlier in this chapter in the context of Parkinson's disease, so Wasserstein (1988: 444) summates: 'The symptom is not accidental to the person, *it expresses the person*; disease symptoms have unexpected significance' (italics added).

The expression of disorder/illness through particular symptoms should not be taken as a random and accidental selection of the disorder, but as the 'fall-out' of the person's struggles to combat the disorder through their own particular means. It is also in this sense that a person's symptoms, their expression of distress, may be said to embody at least an aspect of their self. It is also possible that if such symptoms became an established long-term way of being-in-the-world, then they might dominate the embodiment of self. In fact, Sacks also reports just such an instance in the case entitled 'Witty Ticcy Ray', which describes Ray, who at 24 suffered through Tourette's syndrome and was incapacitated with multiple tics (involuntary, repetitive, stereotyped movements or vocalizations) of extreme violence occurring every few seconds. Ray said that he couldn't imagine life without Tourette's, nor was he sure he wanted to: 'Suppose you could take away the tics. What would be left? I consist of tics – there'd be nothing left' (Sacks 1985: 93). Ultimately, according to Sacks, he 'dutifully' took the medication that Sacks prescribed, during the working week, only to take himself off it at the weekends, and 'let fly'.

Organic moorings

I want to end our review of Sacks's fascinating work by mentioning the case he refers to as 'The Disembodied Lady' (1985). Following abdominal pain Christina was found to have gallstones and was admitted to hospital for removal of her gallbladder. Before her surgery she dreamt of feeling very unsteady, being unable to feel things with her hands and dropping things she picked up. Later the same day, she actually developed these symptoms and, worsening, said 'I can't feel my body. I feel weird – disembodied.' On being reminded of a psychiatrist's diagnosis of 'anxiety hysteria' Sacks says this to a junior doctor: 'But have you ever seen a hysteria like this? Think phenomenologically – take what you see as a genuine phenomenon, in which her state-of-body and state-of-mind are not fictions, but a psychophysical whole. Could anything give such a picture of undermined body and mind?' (Sacks 1985: 44).

Our body sense revolves around vision, our vestibular system (balance organs) and proprioception. Proprioception is the sense of the position and movement of the body. The sense you have of where your arm is, even when you lie still with eyes closed, is the product of proprioception, and it was this sense that Christina had lost. Over time Christina's visual and vestibular systems compensated for her loss of proprioception. While initially she had been 'floppy as a ragdoll, unable even to sit up', three months later Sacks observed her sitting 'statuesquely, like a dancer in mid-pose'. Although there was no recovery from the anatomical nerve damage she had sustained she had recoverd a good deal of function. She now did everything by vision – including operating her computer – rather than by feel. Sadly, her use of vision to coordinate her body had not arrested her sense of dimembodiment, continuing to feel that her body was 'dead, not real, not hers – she cannot appropriate it to herself', or in Christina's own words, 'I feel my body is blind and deaf to itself . . . it has no sense of itself'.

Remembering Freud's assertion that 'The ego is first and foremost a body-ego', Sacks (1985: 50) states that Christina has 'lost, with her sense of proprioception, the fundamental, organic mooring of identity – at least of that corporeal identity, or body-ego, which Freud sees as the basis of self.' Christina loves open top cars that allow her to feel the wind on her body and face: 'I feel the wind on my arms and face, and then I know, faintly, I have arms and a face. It's not the real thing, but it's something – it lifts this horrible dead veil for a while' (Sacks 1985: 51). Sacks summarizes her predicament as succeeding in 'operating, but not in being', that without a sense of proprioception 'a body must remain unreal, unpossessed' (Sacks 1985: 52).

Unpossessed bodies

There are a myriad of physical conditions that restrict people's experience of different aspects or regions of their body. Perhaps one of the most dramatic of these is spinal cord injury (SPI), when a partial or complete break of the spinal cord disrupts or prevents signals from below the region of the injury from reaching the brain. While the body may live, it may be dormant of a sense of embodiment, able only to be sensed by vision, but not guided by it. In his beautifully crafted book *The Diving-Bell and the Butterfly*, Jean-Dominique Bauby, the former editor of the French fashion magazine *Elle*, describes how after a massive stroke in his brain stem (which links the spinal cord and brain) he survived with the provocatively named 'locked-in syndrome'. His 'mind' fully intact, he was paralysed from head to toe, unable to speak or to move, yet through his sole aspect of motor control – his left eyelid – he 'dictated' his book.

Bauby's metaphoric title wonderfully distils his anguish: 'something like a giant invisible diving-bell holds my whole body prisoner' (Bauby 1998: 11) and 'My cocoon becomes less oppressive, and my mind takes flight like a butterfly. There is so much to do. You can wander off in space or in time, set out for Tierra del Fuego or for King Midas's court' (p. 13). Without such escapism, 'I dissolve the landscape and there is nothing more to connect me to the world than a friendly hand stroking my numb fingers' (p. 37). Anchored to his hospital bed he feels himself fading away, 'Like the sailor who watches his home shore gradually disappear, I watch my past recede' (p. 85). He notes the paradox of the passage of time from his hospital bed: 'time, motionless here, gallops out there. In my contracted world the hours drag on but the months flash by' (p. 109).

Bauby's book is so valuable because it can speak to us from a perspective that we are mercifully spared. For me one of the most moving and significant passages in the book is where he relates a dream he has had about visiting the Paris Wax Museum:

> Entering the exhibit, I was surprised to find myself back in Room 119 [his hospital room], apparently reproduced down to the last detail. But as I got closer the photos, drawings and posters on my walls turned out to be a patchwork of ill-defined colours. Like an Impressionist painting,

it was a pattern intended to create an illusion at a certain distance. There was no one on the bed, just a hollow in the middle of the yellow sheets bathed in pallid light.

(Bauby 1998: 119–20)

On retyping these words, I feel a certain reverence due to the penetrating insight they afford us to Bauby's experience, and a certain guilt at so swiftly inserting into my own book the thoughts which he so patiently and pains- takingly conveyed with his flickering eyelid. If the uncertainly of Bauby's *being-there*, of his being-in-the-world, is conveyed through the previous quote, a more disturbing image of his certainty of being-there is conveyed as he addressed a stained-class window depicting the wife of Napeoleon III, Empress Eugenie, in the main hall of his hospital:

And then, one afternoon as I confided my woes to her likeness, an unknown face interposed itself between us. Reflected in the glass I saw the head of a man who seemed to have emerged from a vat of for- maldehyde. His mouth was twisted, his nose was damaged, his hair tousled, his gaze full of fear. One eye was sewn shut, the other goggled like the doomed eye of Cain. For a moment I stared at that dilated pupil before I realised it was only mine. Whereupon a strange euphoria came over me. Not only was I exiled, paralysed, mute, half deaf, deprived of all pleasures and reduced to a jelly-fish like existence, but I was horrible to behold.

(Bauby 1998: 32–3)

The incongruity between Bauby's butterfly-like mental eloquence and his obscene diving-bell-like physical imprisonment tempts one to see a com- plete unconditionality of the mind upon the body: indeed, it is the confron- tation between these two aspects of himself that causes him such anguish. It is as though he could get by if only he was allowed to leave the dead weight of his body behind; if he was allowed to disembody himself. The sad out- come of Bauby's predicament was his death, a death perhaps wished for at times, possibly often.

Recently Howell (2003) has reported on the experience of another 'locked-in' person, James Hall, who before a stroke in the pons varolii area of the brain was a practising Jungian psychiatrist in Dallas, Texas. Twelve years after the stroke, he can now move one finger and has described his experience, through a keyboard control, thus:

I've been thinking 24 hours a day since stroke. Afraid not to. Mind unravelled when didn't. Didn't see much at first but could soon hear everything. When you said something I would reply, no one heard. Repeating conversations to myself kept mind together. Here is what I was thinking from the time of the stroke. Silence. Blackness. Not breathing. Touch. Nothing to touch. Up or down. Nothing to feel. Where are legs, hands? Nothing to feel. No pain. Senses gone. Dead.

Hear sounds with no source can see. Not clearly. Ceiling. Slides past. Fuzzy. Can't focus. Whiteness. Is this death? No! Don't want to die. I'm somewhere between life and death.

(Howell 2003: 35)

Howell asks him if what they have discovered is really that 'the mind can do without a body'. James replies: 'Me. I'm proof. Mind has own energy. Nothing but pure consciousness' (*ibid.*) Such a sense of independence from a body must surely indicate disembodiment, at least in the sense of emotional identification, if not a physical extraction of mind. But for Hall, his *being-in-the-world*, as he describes it in the early days after his stroke, is not mediated through any normal aspect of human sensation; his eyes do not afford him a human perspective; his limbs give no sense of his being there, in *that* body. His experience is of 'being' – like Descartes, because he is *thinking*, he knows he is *existing* – but he cannot think *through* his body, as he previously did. We may wonder whether without being rooted to the world through his hearing he would have anything to think about at all, and if not, would that be death, or 'just' complete disembodiment?

Chapter summary

1 The construction of self through language is not simply a social process of conversing but also a biological process of engineering. Self-doubt quivers the heart, not in a causal sense but as a simultaneous process of being both psychologically and physically one; that is, of being embodied. In each domain we are continually renewing ourselves.

2 Language may be used to distance the experiencing 'self' from aspects of the body that cause suffering, such as pain. As the pain recedes those previously painful parts of the body (for instance, a severely burnt hand) may be 'taken back' into the body that the self identifies with. This is conveyed in a change in the language used to describe that part of the body.

3 In chronic pain, where the self may feel attacked by a part of the body over a prolonged period of time, there may be a struggle to understand which aspects of an emotionally labile and contradictory self are the 'real self', and to what extent the agency of one's actions is volitional or reactive to the pain experienced.

4 The healthy body is often outside our awareness, it is only when 'ill' in some way that we become aware of it. Paradoxically, this awareness may constitute estrangement from the body rather than a heightened sense of being embodied.

5 Physical symptoms always exist within a narrative context and may relate meaningfully to it. Symptoms may express a story of despair that cannot be put into words.

6 Even when symptoms have clear organic origins the way in which they are lived through may have a metaphorical relationship to their broader life context. Psychological distress may be painted on the canvas of the body more effectively when it is biologically challenged in some way.

7 Whatever its origin, physical illness is physical illness, and too simplistic, or too extreme, an interpretation of the meaning of the illness may diminish the integrity of the person who has the illness experience.

8 Some health care contexts necessarily predispose to finding physical problems when a somatic origin is of less significance than other factors. Some perfectly normal and healthy experiences (for instance, childbirth) have been set in a healthcare narrative that pathologizes them to such an extent that we feel specialists and special facilities are needed for them.

9 For some working in the area of brain damage, the 'who has the problem' has been replaced by the 'what is the problem'. Brain damage has been depersonalized. We can develop a more valid representation of people's experiences, by taking those experiences as being meaningful 'data'.

10 Ownership of the body requires a sense that it is there – proprioception. Without such a sense disembodiment may be experienced.

11 The ability of emotion to render motor action when focused attention cannot should encourage us to understand a person's disorder as a gestalt, as well as breaking it down to isolated neural systems.

12 In locked-in syndrome there is little to root the experiences of the person to their body and they, for all intents and purposes, may feel disembodied, even though this sense may itself be mediated through the only shred of physical being they experience and can communicate with.

13 Disembodiment may not be an all or none experience – it may be on a continuum, or indeed, it may be highly localized to certain areas. The extent to which a person who is completely disembodied – where the brain receives no sensory inputs and is thus unable to sense being-in the-world – could meaningfully exist, is problematic.

Discussion points

1 If people socially and physically construct themselves through conversation what are the biological and physical implications of objectifying pain?

2 Why are we only aware of the body when it is a problem?

3 What is 'locked-in' in 'locked-in syndrome' and what does this imply about embodiment?

Key reading

Bauby, J. D. (1998) *The Diving-Bell and the Butterfly*. London: Fourth Estate.
Morse, J. M. and Mitcham, C. (1998) The experience of agonising pain and signals of disembodiment, *Journal of Psychosomatic Research*, 44: 667–80.
Sacks, O. (1984) *A Leg to Stand On*. London: Picador.

Somatic complaints

I've been staring at this screen for half an hour now. I've got to write something and it's difficult. I don't know how to say this, how to start. My father's got Alzheimer's. No. Alzheimer's has got my dad, and it won't let go, ever . . . It's got him and it's slowly, capriciously losing him, rubbing him out so that in the end, all that will be left is the whine of dementia and a hieroglyph that looks like him.

(A. A. Gill, *The Sunday Times Magazine*
2 March 2003)

In this chapter a broad range of somatic complaints not usually grouped together are considered from the perspective of embodiment. The sorts of ailments to be discussed in this chapter may be described variously under the headings of health psychology, behavioural medicine, psychological medicine, liaison psychiatry, neuropsychiatry, disability and others. However, rarely do any of these approaches consider to what extent physical bodily distress can be understood as embodying some aspect of personal experience, or indeed, taking a broader cultural sweep, the experience of a collective group. Before considering what may be described as complaints, disorders, illnesses or diseases, it is important to note briefly how the 'normal order' of our bodily responses relates to the idea of embodiment.

Stress

Early work on the psychophysiology of stress by Cannon (1935) considered it from the evolutionary point of view of a 'fight or flight' response. When presented with a threat (a lion hurtling in your direction) the organism could respond either by fleeing the scene or by engaging with the threat – the fighting response. Cannon's insight was to realize that the basic biological reactions that facilitate responding to this drastic situation (the lion) have carried over into our contemporary environment, where in fact human relations are the predominant stressors (bosses, friends, family, lovers etc.), and the extremity of the response is often maladaptive. Thus receiving criticism may provoke not only an intellectualized reply but also a somatic reaction that harks back to a preparation for fleeing or fighting. While a discussion of the vast literature addressing the causal sequencing or simultaneous nature of the relationships between cognitive, emotional and physical responses to stress is beyond the scope of our immediate concern with embodiment, the fact of their strong association is none the less of great importance. As Cassidy (1999: 35) puts it, summarizing the relationship between biology, emotion and stress: 'Clearly, external demands *exert an influence* on the physical body through physiological mechanisms that prepare living organisms for fight or flight' (italics added).

There is a vast array of physical systems and organs that may be aroused by the psychological experience of stress mediated through (effortless) stimulation of the autonomic (i.e. self-governing or involuntary) nervous system. These reactions range from dilation of the pupils to release of glucose by the liver, dilation of the bronchi and acceleration of the heart, and to inhibition of intestinal motility and relaxation of the bladder. While each of these reactions has recognized short-term benefits in the momentary 'fight or flight' situation, it is the inability of contemporary human beings to allow a homeostatic return to a physiological 'steady state' that is problematic. Because we have evolved so rapidly, in the psychological and social sense, we now experience stressful situations that cannot easily be 'escaped' from (for instance, inter- or intra-personal stress). What is ironic is that our biology has evolved less rapidly, and physically we continue to react to our guilt, boss's criticism or lover's rejection, as if they were the literal dragons of our mythology, which we must flee or fight. Thus, in the sense that we physically respond to fear, we literally embody that fear, although that literal embodiment is the product of an atavistic and essentially *metaphorical* reaction.

Heart ache

Coronary heart disease (CHD) is a narrowing of the arteries that results in a reduced or partially blocked flow of blood and oxygen to the heart. This is often caused by a process called artherosclerosis: a build up of plaque (a hard fatty substance) on the interior walls of the coronary arteries. Chest pain (angina pectoris) may result from a reduced blood flow, while a heart attack (myocardial infarction) is a complete blockage in blood flowing to the heart, resulting in the death of some heart tissue. As the major cause of death in the North-Western world, CHD is one of the major physical health challenges of our time. Obesity, cigarette smoking and physical inactivity are all associated with hypertension. Elevated cholesterol levels are recognized as increasing the risk of CHD. We now know a good deal about just how psychological factors can influence biological factors; such as blood coagulation and blood pressure, which in turn increase the thickness or arterial walls, thus predisposing to CHD (Harenstam *et al.* 2000).

The metaphor of a broken heart to describe a person's sense of sadness may, it seems, have literal truth in it. A prospective study by Penninex *et al.* (2001) found that for both those with and those without cardiac disease at the beginning of the study, experience of depression, especially major depression (i.e. the clinical diagnosis), was significantly associated with the likelihood of dying from CHD. Another prospective study conducted by Kawachi *et al.* (1994) found that responses to five anxiety-related questions (concerning fear of people and places, sense of nervousness, feeling keyed up and jittery, getting suddenly scared for no good reason and often breaking out in a cold sweat) significantly predicted fatal coronary heart disease at 32 years' follow-up. Specifically, those who responded 'yes' to two or more of the items were over three times more likely to develop fatal coronary heart disease than were those who responded 'no' to all five.

Type A personality describes someone who displays an exaggerated sense of time urgency, great competitiveness and ambition, and aggressiveness and hostility, particularly when they encounter resistance to their goals. Much research suggests (though not unequivocally) that type A behaviour is associated with increased risk of CHD. More recently, however, research has indicated that it is the hostility component of type A behaviour that is associated with the greatest risk of future CHD. In Barefoot *et al.*'s (1983) classic study, where they followed up 255 physicians 25 years after they completed the MMPI (Minnesota Multiphasic Personality Inventory), their initial scores on the hostility scale of the MMPI significantly predicted subsequent CHD events (myocardial infarction or cardiac death).

Current emphasis is on the anger–hostility–aggression (AHA) syndrome in CHD (Richards *et al.* 2000). The pinpointing of which aspect of type A behaviour is risk inducing is of great importance, as programmes targeting other aspects of type A behaviour may be giving false reassurance to their participants. One possible explanation for the AHA–CHD link is that hostility increases cardiovascular responsivity, which in time produces physiological damage and predisposes to CHD. In essence, then, research in this area is an example of how a particular behavioural trait can be *'laid down'* in the physiological functioning of the body, with potentially catastrophic consequences. CHD may be the physical consequence of psychological frustration; at least in some instances, CHD may therefore be seen to embody – be a physical expression of – hostility. Of course, other behaviours have also been linked to CHD and to many other physical diseases, including cancer, ulcers, asthma and so on. Rather than considering possible causal mechanisms for these many associations, it is perhaps more valuable to consider the role that immunology plays in mediating the physical production of psychosocial distress.

Immunology

The experience of stress is associated with the release of a variety of hormones, especially cortisol, secreted by the adrenal cortex. Stimulation of cortisol can promote healing in the short term, but continual stimulation can be harmful because, among other effects, it inhibits the effectiveness of the immune system; that is, it creates immunosuppression. Immunosuppression is the reduced ability of the immune system to fight off pathogens, including infections. Cohen *et al.* (1998), building on previous work in the area of stress and viral infection, gave nasal drops containing 'common cold' viruses to physically healthy people who had reported high levels of stress in a personal interview. While 84 per cent of them became infected by a cold virus, only 40 per cent actually developed symptoms of the 'cold'.

The types of stressors most commonly reported in the group that developed symptoms were chronic stressors lasting over a month and often associated with conflicts with family or friends, unemployment or underemployment. Thus social difficulties can interact with viruses (also external to the body) to produce a physical illness that is, at least in part, the embodiment of a person's broader concerns. Research has demonstrated that a great range of life stresses (including being the spouse of someone with dementia, being divorced or separated, experiencing abrasive marital interactions and being bereaved) affect the immune system and can predispose to physical illness.

Specific relationships between rather abstract psychological constructs, such as where people lie on a continuum between collectivism and individualism, have also been linked to specific disorders, such as asthma. James (2001) presents data drawn from 15 countries supporting the notion that those who have a 'narrower' (i.e. more individualized) psychological identity are more likely to report asthmatic symptoms. He suggests that a differential immune function between highly individualized and highly collectivist people is the mediating mechanism that interacts with environmental factors to produce asthma. We may move even further away from proximal 'germ theory' explanations of disease by considering the relationship between economic gradients, economic inequity and physical health.

Health economics

The link between socio-economic prosperity and physical health has been obvious for many centuries in the sense that the materially better-off enjoy better health. It has been reasonable to assume that this is because of factors such as better hygiene, better access to health care, consumption of healthier food and so on. However, in the past couple of decades research on socio-economic 'gradients' has suggested that it is not simply one's absolute socio-economic position that is important for health, but also one's relative position within the hierarchy. Simply being lower in a hierarchy may be detrimental to health. This appears to be the case even *within* relatively high socio-economic groups (Adler *et al.* 1994). However, socio-economic position does not exist as a variable by itself and is inextricably linked to other factors, such as ethnicity, gender and age.

There is some controversy as to whether it is more beneficial to focus on socio-economic position as such, or the factors mediating it. However, Robert and House (2000) suggest that while the factors mediating the relationship between socio-economic position and health may have changed over time, the functional association between them has not. The considerable research evidence supporting socio-economic gradient effects on health suggests that at least some aspects of illness are not 'projections' (or consequences) simply of individual or relationship concerns, but also those of the community, state and nation. To the extent that decisions about where people 'should' be in hierarchies and how resources 'ought' to be distributed among people affect physical well-being, ill health may be seen as an embodiment of certain political systems.

One of the most interesting recent areas of research linking social and health issues has been in the related but distinct area of the health effects of socio-economic *inequity*. Considerable research indicates that the degree of income inequality within a country is strongly and linearly associated with life expectancy, even after controlling for average level of income. Wilkinson (1996) and others have demonstrated that in industrially developed countries, the larger the gap between the rich and the poor, the poorer is the health of the overall population. These effects also hold at more local levels (states, boroughs), where greater inequity is also associated with greater mortality (see Lynch and Kaplan 1997 for a review). Wilkinson (1996) has argued that those countries with the greatest social cohesion have the least income inequity, and so social cohesion may be the factor that mediates the relationship. It should not be surprising that those factors that promote 'social capital' also promote physical health, and that the lack of 'social capital' may be seen in the ultimate (dis)embodiment of mortality. Having now discussed the role that psychological, economic and social factors can play in 'real' physical illness, let us consider their role in 'false' forms of physical illness.

Somatoforms

Somatic symptoms continue to be extremely common in all cultures and are found in individuals with greatly differing levels of education and psychological-mindedness (Kirmayer and Young 1998). There is thus little evidence to support the supposition that somatic expression is somehow a more 'primitive' form of dealing with difficulties than is psychologically working through distress. Along with conversion disorder, the general DSM-IV diagnostic category of 'somatoform disorder' includes pain disorder, hypochondriasis, body dysmorphic disorder and somatization. As a discussion of all of these is beyond my scope here, and some are dealt with in other sections of this book, I will principally consider somatization and conversion disorders in the following pages. However, briefly let us note some aspects of hypochondriasis and body dysmorphic disorder.

Hypochondriasis 'describes that awareness in which the person takes undue account of the symptomatic component of his sensorium' (Sims 1988). It is a belief that one suffers from a physical illness when one does not. It may be considered as an assumption of physical disease in the *absence of its embodiment*. Sims's use of the term 'sensorium' is of interest because it posits an intermediary between a person's sensory apparatus and the person themselves. The 'symptoms' are 'symptomatic' of a belief in physical illness without organic pathology. Pain disorder, on the other hand, is a preoccupation not with illness but with a possible consequence of it – it is concerned with 'excessive' complaints of pain. While there may be some organic justification for pain, to receive a psychiatric diagnosis the complaint must seem to be out of proportion to any physical basis it may have.

Body dysmorphic disorder (BDD) refers to an imagined defect with some aspect of appearance. People are preoccupied with the idea that their appearance is in some way unattractive, deformed or flawed, when in reality any such aspect is minimal or non-existent. Preoccupation usually (but not always) focuses on some aspect of facial appearance (for example, the skin, hair or nose). Summarizing the scant research literature on body dysmorphoria, Phillips (2002) suggests that these physical preoccupations are usually associated with shame, low self-esteem, embarrassment, feelings of unworthiness and a fear of rejection. She also suggests that the majority of people suffering through this condition also experience delusions or 'ideas of reference', where one believes that other people are taking special notice of one, and that their behaviour in some way 'refers' to one's own.

In BDD some sense of inner distress therefore seems to be projected outwardly on to a supposed aspect of appearance. Perhaps akin to Bauby's Impressionist painter, the artist conveys a likeness of what is experienced, but in the case of BDD nobody else recognizes this image. BDD is often accompanied by repetitive behaviours such as excessive looking in mirrors, self-grooming and attempts to cover over the presumed 'defect' with make-up or clothes. BDD is often a chronic condition and so distressing that one study found that over half of sufferers had been admitted to a psychiatric hospital, close to 30 per cent had attempted suicide and a quarter reported being completely housebound for one week or more (Phillips and Diaz 1997). Perhaps contrary to the North-Western stereotype regarding concern with appearance, just as many men as women appear to experience clinically significant BDD.

A perhaps more extreme from of BDD is 'delusional disorder, somatic type' (or DDST), which refers to delusions whose major theme is concerned with bodily functions or sensations. In addition to delusions of extreme body odour and psychotic forms of BDD, this disorder commonly manifests as delusional infestation (the belief that one is infested with parasites in the absence of objective evidence) or hypochondriacal delusions, although it may be very difficult to distinguish between delusional and non-delusional hypochondriasis in some instances (Pruzinsky 2002). Sometimes these delusions may be of a specific symptom. I once worked with a lady who had been given a diagnosis of 'mono-delusional psychosis'. She had the singular and unshakable belief that she was pregnant, despite a complete lack of any evidence for this, including a scan that showed nothing. In fact, when I saw her she had believed this to be so for 15 months. When I pointed out to her that she must not have been pregnant, say 12 months ago, she disparagingly remarked that 'well of course I was wrong then, but I'm certainly not wrong now!' She was a pleasant, sensible, bright and articulate woman who functioned very well socially and did not seem to be otherwise distressed. She tenaciously held to her convictions despite the army of medical and psychological specialists set against her.

Somatization

If dysmorphia, and its variants, are concerned with the projection of distress *on to* the body, we now consider the 'projection' of distress *through* the body. Somatization disorder is believed to be a constellation of physical symptoms that generally group together so that some, but not all, of the symptoms that constitute the syndrome need to be present for a DSM-IV diagnosis to be made. While the syndromal nature of DSM-IV disorders is explicitly acknowledged, the requirements of a DSM-IV diagnosis of somatization disorder may seem somewhat bizarre if taken out of this context. It is worth considering the necessary symptoms in some detail. For a diagnosis to be made the following is required:

1 A history of physical complaints with onset before the age of 30, that has occurred over several years, resulting in treatment being sought, or significant impairment in social, occupational or other important areas of functioning.
2 *Each* of the following symptoms:
   (a) Four distinct pain symptoms; for instance, from extremities, chest, rectum, during menstruation or sexual intercourse, or urination.
   (b) Two gastrointestinal symptoms, other than pain, such as nausea, bloating, vomiting, diarrhoea or intolerance of several different foods.
   (c) One sexual symptom, such as erectile or ejaculatory dysfunction, or indifference to sex.
   (d) One pseudoneurological symptom; that is, a history of at least one symptom or deficient that suggests a neurological disorder.

It is also required that these symptoms are not feigned or attributable to any known medical condition. While somatization disorder as defined above may be quite rare, having a combination of physical complaints (without obvious organic cause) that don't meet all of the requirements of somatization disorder is much more common. This has led to suggestions that a new diagnosis – multisomaform disorder – which would require three chronic somatic symptoms (without organic cause), be introduced (Kroenke et al. 1997).

A study of personnel working in a mortuary during the first Gulf War (McCarroll et al. 2002) found an increase in somatization from before to after the experience. The somatic symptoms recorded included pains in the chest, nausea, faintness, difficulty breathing, feeling weak, numbness and hot and cold spells. The study compared those who had no exposure to dead bodies, those who only observed them, those who had direct exposure and those who actually handled the bodies. There was a clear linear relationship between those personnel who had greater exposure to the dead bodies and those who experienced the most somatic symptoms. This elegant, if gruesome, research design provides strong contemporary evidence for the existence of some mechanism that presents the distress associated with exposure to dead bodies in the form of somatic complaints.

Whatever the nosological complexities of the experience of somatic symptoms that have no discernible organic cause, perhaps the ultimate question of interest is what they mean, if anything. The answer to this is also somewhat complex but lies at the root of much of our culturally constructed notions about somatization. For instance, Kleinman (1980) has suggested that the way in which depression manifests itself varies across cultures. He has studied a condition known as neurasthenia, commonly reported in China, and characterized by a lack of energy and physical complaints such as a sore stomach. Kleinman has suggested that while depression and neurasthenia are different illness *experiences*, they are both products of the same underlying disease processes – depression. In other words neurasthenia is the Chinese version of the North-Western's depression.

Somatized depression

The assumption above is quite problematic and as I have previously considered it in some detail (MacLachlan 1997), I will only allude to the main issues here. Shweder (1991) suggests that such an interpretation 'privileges' a biological understanding of how depression occurs when, in fact, in addition to biomedical and psychological accounts of depression, moral, sociopolitical and interpersonal 'causal ontologies' also exist. Kleinman believes that the ultimate cause of depression and neurasthenia is the same, both involving defeat, loss, vexation and oppression by local hierarchies of power, and that such 'sociopolitical' experiences produce a biological disease process. However, the way in which this disease is expressed is influenced by the culture within which one lives. Thus, Kleinman argues that depression and neurasthenia have similar sociopolitical origins that produce a similar biological disease process, which expresses itself differently in North America and China because the different cultural conditions favour different forms of expression. However, is there any need to say that the Chinese neurasthenia is somatized depression? We might just as well say that, for instance, North American depression is emotionalized neurasthenia and that neurasthenia is the underlying disease process, not depression.

Shweder questions the value of talking about disease processes at all. For him, the concepts of 'illness' and 'disease' do not add any value to our understanding of the relationship between neurasthenia and depression; there is no need for either neurasthenia or depression to be the primary disorder. The assumed primacy of depression over somatic symptoms has been explored in Banglagore, India. Weiss *et al.* (1995) sought to explore the relationship between depressive, anxious and somatoform experiences, not only from the North-Western diagnostic perspective of the DSM classification system, but also from the perspective of individuals' own illness experience. Their study used established structured interview schedules to glean both types of information from their interviewees, who were all first time presenting psychiatric outpatients attending a clinic in Banglagore. When the same 'symptom' presentation was interpreted by the patient and by the DSM system, generally patients preferred to describe their problems in terms of somatic symptoms while the DSM system described them in terms of depression.

The experience of somatic symptoms is also common in European and North American contexts. A study of somatization in primary care settings in Spain reported that almost 10 per cent of people presenting a new episode of illness to a primary care clinic, and approximately one-third of people who presented psychological problems that were severe enough to be classified as 'psychiatric cases', fulfilled the criteria for somatization disorder (Garcia-Campayo *et al.* 1996; Lobo *et al.* 1996). Back ache, dizziness and pains in extremities were cited by over 60 per cent of somatizers (Lobo *et al.* 1996), but complaints of diarrhoea, vomiting, trouble walking and urinary retention were also encountered in 'somatizers'. The majority of these somatizing patients fulfilled the criteria for DSM-IV diagnoses of depression or anxiety.

The Spanish investigators subdivided their 'psychiatric' sample into 'somatizers' (described above) and 'psychologizers' (without somatic symptoms). Three times as many 'psychiatric' patients were rated as 'somatizers' as were rated as 'psychologizers'. The most frequent diagnosis made for 'somatizers' was generalized anxiety disorder, while for 'psychologizers' it was major depression. When it came to a DSM-IV diagnoses of dysthymia (which refers to a chronic disorder of mood, lasting at least two years, and being a less severe form of depression than major depressive disorder) there was a ratio of ten to one between 'somatizers' and 'psychologizers'. Weiss *et al.* (1995) commented thus on their results: 'These limitations of the diagnostic system identified here appear to reside more with the professional construction of categories than with the inability of patients and professionals to comprehend each other's concepts of distress and disorder.'

Functional syndromes

Such limitations have been further challenged by several researchers and recently Sharpe and Carson (2001) called for a paradigm shift in the treatment of 'unexplained' somatic symptoms, one that would 'remedicalize' treatment around the notion of a *functional* disturbance of the nervous system, and in so doing possibly remove them from the realms of mental disturbance, and thus remove their stigma. The idea of somatoform symptoms being *functional* – that is, suggesting an alteration of function rather than structure (Trimble 1982) – is common in many medical specialities: for instance, in gastroenterology, irritable bowel syndrome and non-ulcer dyspepsia; in gynaecology, premenstrual syndrome and chronic pelvic pain; in neurology, chronic fatigue syndrome; and in rheumatology, fibromyalgia (Nimnuan *et al.* 2002).

Nimnuan *et al.* (2001) set out to explore whether there was any overlap in the above mentioned disorders or whether they were in fact unique diagnostic entities. They studied 550 people who had a 'functional' diagnosis or in whom there was no detectable abnormality (three months after first being investigated). This group reported a range of 37 unexplained physical symptoms. Table 3.1 reproduces Nimnuan *et al.*'s operational definitions of each of the functional somatic syndromes that were identified as conditions (such as non-ulcer dyspepsia, non-cardiac chest pain and chronic pelvic pain have no operationally defined criteria, they constructed their own). At the level of syndromes there was considerable symptom overlap. Two clusters of symptoms, one that they labelled 'fatigue pain' and the other 'cardiorespiratory', were found to exist. These findings must question the existence of discrete functional somatic syndromes that may be identified on the basis of a 'single main presenting symptom . . . We argue that such an approach is outdated. Instead, an appreciation of the fundamental unity of those syndromes may reduce the potential for iatrogenic harm whilst encouraging continuity of care' (Nimnuan *et al.* 2001: 554).

I have argued that whatever the presenting complaint, the belief system of the person who 'owns' the complaint should be taken into account. The context of the presentation – not an abstracted diagnostic system – is often what gives the complaint meaning. In some cases of somatic symptoms the 'content' is quite recognizable, even if there is no physical evidence to attest to its existence. The research of Nimnuan *et al.* suggests that such 'meaning' can be encapsulated in two distinct groups of somatic complaints. The specialists to whom people with these symptoms are referred may often have more to

Table 3.1   Operational definitions of functional somatic symptoms

	Characteristic symptoms	Duration	Severity	Medical Investigation
Fibromyalgia	Persistent aches and pains in several parts. Non-restorative sleep. One or more of the following: felt pain all over; back pain; stiffness.	≥ 3 months	Symptoms cannot be ignored, or stops person from doing things	Negative investigation results. Final diagnosis as functional; defer diagnosis because no medical cause detectable.
Tension headache	Headache or neck pain. Pain is tight or pressing; aggravated by stress; getting worse as day progresses.	≥ 6 months	Symptoms cannot be ignored, or stops person from doing things	Negative investigation results. Final diagnosis as functional; defer diagnosis because no medical cause detectable.
Atypical facial pain	Pain in the face, jaw or mouth. Two or more of the following: teeth hurt; burning sensation in the tongue, gums or lips; pain relieved by eating or drinking.	≥ 3 months	Symptoms cannot be ignored, or stops person from doing things	Negative investigation results. Final diagnosis as functional; defer diagnosis because no medical cause detectable.
TMJ	Pain in the face, jaw or mouth. Two or more of the following: having trouble opening the mouth; pain aggravated by moving or pressing jaw; pain coming with a clicking sound.	≥ 3 months	Symptoms cannot be ignored, or stops person from doing things	Negative investigation results. Final diagnosis as functional; defer diagnosis because no medical cause detectable.

	Symptoms	Duration	Impact	Diagnosis
Non-cardiac chest pain	Chest pain. Pain, which does not usually occur after exertion; occurs at rest; usually lasts longer than 20 minutes.		Symptoms cannot be ignored, or stops person from doing things	Negative investigation results. Final diagnosis as functional; defer diagnosis because no medical cause detectable.
Non-ulcer dyspepsia	Abdominal pain above navel. Having food aggravates pain; absence of night pain	≥ 3 months	Symptoms cannot be ignored, or stops person from doing things	Negative investigation results. Final diagnosis as functional; defer diagnosis because no medical cause detectable.
Irritable bowel syndrome	Abdominal pain below the navel. Pain related to the following: having more bowel movement; having looser stool; experiencing urgency; having strain; feeling incomplete after finishing a bowel movement. Bloating; having mucus in stool. Change in bowel habit or consistency of the stools.	≥ 3 months	Symptoms cannot be ignored, or stops person from doing things	Negative investigation results. Final diagnosis as functional; defer diagnosis because no medical cause detectable.
Chronic fatigue syndrome	Having physical fatigue. Having mental fatigue.	≥ 6 months	Symptoms cannot be ignored, or stops person from doing things	Negative investigation results. Final diagnosis as functional; defer diagnosis because no medical cause detectable.
Hyperventilation syndrome	Breathing more than normal. Two or more of the following: felt dizzy or faint; heart pounding; numbness or tingling; trembling		Symptoms cannot be ignored, or stops person from doing things	Negative investigation results. Final diagnosis as functional; defer diagnosis because no medical cause detectable.

Table 3.1 – continued

	Characteristic symptoms	Duration	Severity	Negative investigation
Globus hystericus	Discomfort in the throat. Swallowing all the time; symptoms relieved by swallowing food; symptoms aggravated by saliva or dry swallowing.	≥ 3 months	Symptoms cannot be ignored, or stops person from doing things	Negative investigation results. Final diagnosis as functional; defer diagnosis because no medical cause detectable.
Multiple chemical sensitivity	Unpleasant reactions to particular substances, of which two or more can be identified. At least two different symptoms reported.		Person avoids the particular substance	
Premenstrual syndrome	Clearly defined symptom or symptoms. Symptoms disappear soon after the period.	≥ 2 cycles	Symptoms cannot be ignored, or stops person from doing things	Negative investigation results. Final diagnosis as functional; defer diagnosis because no medical cause detectable.
Chronic pelvic pain	Pelvic pain does not appear before a period.	≥ 6 months	Symptoms cannot be ignored, or stops person from doing things	Negative investigation results. Final diagnosis as functional; defer diagnosis because no medical cause detectable.

Source: modified from Nimnuan *et al.* (2001).

do with diagnostic fashions, and a person's entry points to the health system, than with their own experience of their complaint. Let us now consider one of the classical conditions of psychiatric and psychological folklore.

Hysteria

Dissociation refers to the disruption of mental processes (for instance, memory, consciousness, identity and perception) that normally occur in a seamlessly interlocking flow of ongoing experience. While Freud saw dissociation as a natural and usually unproblematic aspect of mental life, others have seen it as pathological. The classic cases of multiple personality disorder would be one example of dissociation, while dissociative fugue (sudden unplanned travel with inability to remember details of the past, identity confusion or assumption of a new identity) is another. A further example of dissociation, perhaps strangely, is what used to be referred to as hysteria, now viewed as a somatoform disorder. These are disorders that are somatic *in form only*. The assumption in these disorders, where people genuinely experience physical problems in the absence of any evidence of organic pathology, is that there is a process of *dissociation* between the mental functioning involved in self-awareness and that involved in mediating certain bodily functions or activities.

Somatoform disorders can be very dramatic, and one category of them referred to as conversion disorder includes, for example, paralysis, blindness and deafness. The idea is that mental distress is *converted into* a physical malady. These disorders resemble neurological impairments but often the experienced physical problem doesn't accord with the biology that would be required to mediate it. In this sense they lack an identifiable physical foundation, which in many cases should easily be identified by the panoply of modern biomedicine. Thus someone might report anaesthesias (loss or impairment of sensation) around the knees but not above or below the knees. However, the design of the peripheral nerves of the body makes this pattern impossible as the same nerves serve the areas above and below the knees. It is the *pseudoneurological* nature of conversion disorders that principally distinguishes them from other forms of somatoform disorder. Whether of course such a distinction is warranted is debatable.

There is great conceptual confusion regarding how the apparently dichotomized mind and body interrelate in such cases. Take as an example the following from Oltmanns and Emery's (2004) introductory *Abnormal Psychology* textbook: 'There is nothing physically wrong with the patient. The symptoms are not feigned, however, as the physical problem is very real in the mind, though not in the body, of the person with a somatoform disorder' (p. 256). Kirmayer and Santhanam (2001: 254) note the range of interpretations still left open in the case of hysteria:

These include the notion that the symptom is caused by psychological processes that may be conscious or non-conscious, wilful or outside the control of the person, due to specific plans and ideas or implicit consequences of images and metaphors, and so on. There are many more or less automatic psychological processes that could give rise to conversion symptoms, complicating the simple dichotomies of wilful/accidental, motivated/unmotivated, and conscious/unconscious.

Before we try to unpack the implication of somatoform disorders for embodiment let us first consider its broader historical and cultural context.

Hysteria must surely be one of the best justifications for feminism that there has been. Although the concept was first introduced by the Egyptians, the term derives from the Greek *hystera*, meaning uterus. The ancients ascribed a range of physical symptoms in women to a 'wandering uterus', this wandering being motivated by sexual desire arising from the need to have a baby. The uterus would move around the body and cause problems wherever it lodged – thus if it lodged in the throat, the *woman* might lose her power of speech. I emphasize *woman*, because hysteria has often been thought of as a female disorder – *hysterical woman*. Colloquially 'hysteria' connotes the often frivolous, foolish, exaggerated and irrational display of dramatic emotion (Kirmayer and Santhanam 2001).

Mass hysteria

One of the most dramatic examples of hysteria must be an 'epidemic psychological disturbance' that occurs when 'a group of people, through social contagion, collectively manifest psychological disorders within a brief period of time. Although it takes several forms such as group panic or collective delusion, its most common manifestation is an outbreak of hysteria' (Tseng and Hsu 1980: 77). In 1993 we investigated a case of 'mass hysteria' in a girls' secondary school in Malawi (MacLachlan *et al.* 1995). This began with one pupil (aged 19) reporting uncontrollable shouting, screaming and collapsing, a fear of other pupils and teachers, severe head-aches, difficulty reading and extreme sensitivity to noise. It is quite possible that at least some of this behaviour was initially associated with a bad reaction to Fansidar (an anti-malarial drug). This occurred at a time of extreme political tension in Malawi (during the toppling of President Banda). The second case occurred after a pupil had returned on the school bus – which had been stoned – after the pupils had performed dancing for the President (which was conventional – and mandatory – at his public appearances). On returning to the school one pupil (aged 16) continued to dance, started shouting loudly and developed severe pain at the back of her head. The next day another pupil (also aged 16 and from the same class as the first two pupils) started to scream and shout uncontrollably. Over the next week 10–20 pupils a day developed this behaviour, 105 in total, close to one-fifth of the school's students. Most students subsequently reported being quite unaware of their behaviour at the time, and subsequently unable to remember their bizarre behaviour.

This is by no means an isolated case and a couple of weeks later in our home town of Zomba, there was a similar, but more limited, 'outbreak' in a mixed (boys and girls) primary school. Similar cases have also been reported in the UK, USA, Japan, several African countries and elsewhere (see MacLachlan *et al.* 1995). While the 'hysterical' nature of symptoms differs it is usual that both mental and physical symptoms are 'transmitted' through a process that has been referred to as 'social contagion', but is probably a form of social learning under high anxiety. As such, it is clear that people can, in an immediate, dramatic and painful way, 'learn' how to express their emotional distress through bodily symptoms of distress. An individual's display of symptoms can act as a template for others. One can 'infect' many.

The phenomenon of koro suggests that it also works the other way around. Here the anxiety of many can produce in an individual the sensation of their sexual organs shrinking. I have described this in more detail in MacLachlan (1997) and that account draws heavily on Cheng (1994). Koro is believed to be a fatal condition and occurs mostly in southern China and Southeast Asia (Cheng 1994). Although it usually occurs in isolated cases, epidemics of koro may also occur. It is, of course, overly simplistic to assume that koro is an alternative form of a North-Western disorder, as it occurs in cultural settings that North-Western diagnostic systems have not been designed – and in my view are often unable – to encapsulate. Indeed, in terms of North-Western diagnostic criteria, koro has at one time or another been subsumed as a variant of dissociative disorder, somatoform disorder, panic disorder and even psychosis.

Although koro is most commonly associated with males through their fear of penis shrinkage, it is also found in women (although much less frequently) as a fear of retracting nipples, breasts or labia. For both sexes the fear of shrinkage is associated with the fear of imminent death, the shrinkage being only a precursor to this. Cheng (1994: 7–8) gives a vivid description of the onset of koro:

> Usually, the malady begins with a feeling on the part of the victim that his or her sex organ is shrinking. Believing that the condition is critical, the victim becomes extremely anxious, doing whatever he or she can to stop the sex organ from further retracting and crying vigorously for help. A man may be seen holding his penis, 'anchoring' it with some clamping device, or tying the penis with a piece of string. Similarly a woman may be seen grabbing her own breasts, pulling her nipples, or even having iron pins inserted through the nipples, all to prevent the retraction of the respective organs.

The process of rescuing the organs may look highly absurd to an outsider, even to a Chinese. Imagine someone shouting for help and at the same time pulling his or her genital, thus exposing it, in public. The victim's relatives and neighbours will rush to 'help out' because they too believe that the condition can be fatal . . . In fact, many so called 'patients' were diagnosed with Koro not because they themselves had initiated the complaint, but because other people around them had misinterpreted signs of discomfort to mean Koro and performed the rescue . . . For example . . . a bride was thought to have Koro on the wedding day because she appeared pale and weak. The rescue effort continued for a while until she yelled out that she was not experiencing breast shrinkage.

A full account of the way in which this disorder, when viewed from a sociocultural perspective, has both a social *function* and a meaningful *order* is beyond our scope here (see MacLachlan 1997). A vital point, however, is that koro cannot be adequately understood from the perspective of the individual's (psycho)pathology, but should be approached from the perspective of the expression of a *community's* anxiety.

Chinese folklore includes the notion of a 'fox spirit', which can seduce people, sap their 'vital energy' and thereby make them weak. The 'fox spirit' is able to shrink tissue and this provides a direct link, in folklore, to koro. A community may come to expect or experience misfortune in, for instance, its (agricultural) production or the health of its members. The 'fox spirit', it is believed, roams the world in search of victims. When things are not going well this may be taken as an indication that the 'fox spirit' has visited a community. A fortune-teller's prediction of its visitation will create considerable uncertainty and anxiety. The community becomes hyper-vigilant to detect the first arrival of the 'fox spirit'. Cheng suggests that the failure to identify any objective signs of a ghost heightens tension to such a degree that victimization becomes an inevitable outlet for the community's anxiety.

An individual's behaviour may lead others to 'realize' that the person is suffering from a koro attack. On the other hand, an individual himself may suspect a koro attack is beginning (cold sensations or insect bites in the genital area which can temporarily reduce the size of the genitalia, as can weakness or sickness, may be interpreted as the onset of an attack). Through the identification of a victim the anxiety of the whole community may be relieved. As people rush to help to rescue the victim, the failure of the victim's genitalia truly to retract is taken as evidence that the 'fox spirit' has been exorcised and moved on. The community is thus saved and tension reduced. Kirmayer and Santhanam (2001: 257) suggest that in koro, 'as with other epidemics of hysteria, social stresses create widespread feelings of vulnerability in a population or group, and combine with individual vulnerabilities to anxiety to give rise to symptoms that follow *culturally available symptom schemas*' (italics added).

These 'symptom schema', it has been argued, are not stable phenomena but, like culture itself, are continually changing ways of patterning meaning in life. Kirmayer and Santhanam (2001: 266) also stress that seeing hysteria as 'social communication, interaction and positioning can go further to explain the clinical phenomena than purely psychological or physiological explanations that ignore the social matrix of experience'. It may follow then, that as the 'social matrix' changes, so do the disorders it cultivates.

Hystories

Elsewhere I have argued that changes within a society over time can affect mental health, perhaps because of the way in which they challenge people's identities and positions within society (Smyth et al. 2003; MacLachlan and Smyth 2004; MacLachlan et al. 2004b). Thus the rate of depression, binge drinking or suicide, for instance, may increase in a specific population as it undergoes change. To the extent that society 'sculpts' the sort of disorder through which people can express their discontents, a changing society may well change the ways in which distress can 'legitimately' (i.e. while still being taken seriously – being believed) be presented. This also applies to the physical embodiment of distress. While it is widely acknowledged that 'hysterical conversions reactions' are less common now than in their heyday of the eighteenth and nineteenth centuries, when they were administered to by luminaries such as Charcot and Freud, it has also been argued that different types of somatization and conversion are now in 'style'. As Shorter (1994) puts it, there is an ever changing 'symptom pool' that constitutes the legitimate contemporary idioms of distress and this symptom pool creates 'great pressure on the unconscious mind to produce only legitimate symptoms'. Following Ferrier's description of hysteria as a 'chamelion-like condition' in 1794, Showalter (1997: 15) describes it as a 'mimetic disorder; it mimics culturally permissible expressions of disorder'.

Previous centuries have populated the 'symptom pool' with very visible neurological disorders in the form of limps, palsies and paralysis, that arose from birth defects, venereal disease, industrial accidents and so on. Although these still occur, they are much less frequent than previously, and therefore less 'available' as a recognized means of expressing inner pains (Porter 1993). Showalter (1997) argues that hysterical epidemics require at least three ingredients: physician enthusiasts and theorists to give authority to a new idea (disorder); unhappy and vulnerable patients to adopt that way of expressing their discontents; and a supportive cultural environment (perhaps of great anxiety) to facilitate its expression. This plasticity and indeed the recently enhanced mobility of hysterical epidemics is clearly indicated by Showalter (1997: 5):

Hysteria not only survives in the 1990s, it is more contagious than in the past. Infectious diseases spread by ecological change, modern technology, urbanization, jet travel, and human interaction. Infectious epidemics of hysteria spread by stories circulated through self-help books, articles in newspapers and magazines, TV talk shows and series, films, the Internet, and even literary criticism. The cultural narratives of hysteria, which I call *hystories*, multiply rapidly and uncontrollably in the era of mass media, telecommunications, and e-mail.

Showalter's list of contemporary hysterias include chronic fatigue, Gulf War syndrome, multiple personality disorder, recovered memory of sexual abuse, satanic ritual abuse and alien abduction. These 'ailments' have questionable (biological) foundations, she argues. In the seventeenth century Willis (1684) described the physician's use of the term 'hysteria' as 'the subterfuge of ignorance'. Such a statement might well be thought apt for a contemporary diagnosis of conversion disorder, somatization or any of the above. If society determines the forms that represent legitimate expression of physical distress, we must explore the boundaries of this process. Presumably there are some conditions that are beyond the realm of socially manufactured forms of physical distress. Neuropsychiatric disorders may be a case in point.

Neuropsychiatric disorders

While psychophysiological and somatoform disorders assume some functional, or at least facilitative, role for psychological processes in the production of somatic symptoms, neuropsychiatric disorders that are associated with bodily anomalies are generally understood from the perspective of brain dysfunction. In Chapters 1 and 2 we considered neurological aspects of embodiment from several perspectives, including the use of a 'romantic science' to elucidate the sufferer's experience. Here we briefly review the vast range of neurological disorders as they relate to the notion of embodiment. Cutting (1990) divided these into several groups of disorders (see Table 3.2). Under the category 'impairments of bodily identification', for instance, comes *autotopagnosia*, which is a difficulty in pointing to any part of the body. A person may not be able to indicate where their mouth or eyes are, for example. In the second category of 'bodily unawareness' is the condition known as *anosognosia*, which is usually taken to refer to someone's lack of knowledge that they are hemiplegic: they are unaware that one side of their body is not able to function. In fact, this condition is apparently quite common in those who suffer a left-side hemiplegia (and which occurs in the first week after an acute cerebrovascular accident for about half of all cases). The term *hemiasomatognosia* is used to refer to neglect of one side of the body in the absence of any weakness of the limbs. A third type of bodily

Table 3.2   Classification of neuropsychiatric disorders of self-image

---

Impaired bodily identification
Finger agnosia, autotopagnosia, right–left disorientation

Bodily unawareness
Hemiasomatognosia, anosognosia for hemiplegia, somatoparaphrenia

Anomalous bodily experiences
Any distortion of bodily experience, including:
Belonging (subjective alienation), size (micro or macrosomatognosia),
Spatial location (alloaesthesia, exosomaesthesia)

False bodily experiences
Phantom limb, autoscopy, tactile, kinaesthetic and epigastric hallucinations

Morbid emotional attitude
Anosodiaphoria, misoplegia, preoccupation

Disorders of self-image
Depersonalization, multiple personality.

Source: adapted from Cutting (1990).

unawareness is *somatoparaphrenia*: the following passage from Lishman's classic text on neuropsychiatry explains this, and some related terms:

> In more bizarre cases [of anosognosia] he [the patient] insists that the paralysed limbs do not belong to him or attributes them to some neighbouring person ('somatoparaphrenia'). He may claim that the limbs are some mechanical object, or talk to them and fondle them as though they had an existence of their own ('personification'). Feelings of anger or hatred may be expressed toward them ('misoplegia').
>
> (Lishman 1987: 61)

Such experiences dramatically suggest that aspects of the body may be quite foreign, and even hostile to, a person's sense of embodiment.

Another category used by Cutting (1990) is 'anomalous bodily experiences' and these include any distortion of bodily experience (see also Chapter 5). *Subjective alienation* describes the experience of a body part feeling strange to, or not belonging to, the person who has it. In *alloaesthesia*, stimulation to one part of the body may be experienced on another part, or even off the body altogether, such as on a chair (in the latter case this is termed *exosomaesthesia*). There are also cases where people feel that their body parts are not in proportion; for instance, a hand may have shrunk or increased in size (*microsomatognosia* and *macrosomatognosia* respectively). Another category, 'false body experiences', includes *phantom limb* sensations, where an absent body part continues to be experienced (also dealt with in detail in Chapter 5); *somatic hallucinations*, such as the body feeling wet when it isn't, or feeling that a hand is holding a toothbrush when it isn't; and *autoscopy*, seeing oneself (without a mirror being present). Cutting says that even the most vivid autoscopic hallucinations are more hazy than would be a true mirror reflection, and they may also appear as a profile or a figure at a distance rather than as a conventional reflection.

Cutting suggests that such experiences are also described as 'near death experiences' and 'out-of-body' experiences by psychic researchers. Interestingly, Cutting notes that, while what he refers to as autoscopy may be associated with brain damage, it most commonly occurs in unusual physiological and psychological conditions, especially where social isolation, sleep deprivation and fatigue are combined (e.g. lone mountaineers, shipwrecked sailors). In such instances the experiences may be that someone is 'with them' rather than it being another self.

In relation to out-of-body experiences, Blanke *et al.* (2002), using focal electrical stimulation on a person with epilepsy, found that such experiences could be induced by stimulating the brain's right angular gyrus. When this was done (with 3.5 mA) the patient they reported on said: 'I see myself lying in bed, from above, but I only see my legs and lower trunk'. She subsequently reported feelings of 'lightness' and 'floating', about two metres above the bed, close to the ceiling. A lower voltage (2.0–3.0 mA) at this same site produced feelings of 'sinking into the bed' and 'falling from a height'. When asked to watch her legs, stimulation (4.5 mA) resulted in her experiencing her legs as shortening. These visual distortions were apparently restricted to her own body only, rather than generalizing to other people or inanimate objects. The researchers concluded that:

> Out-of-body and body-transformation experiences are transitory and may disappear when a person attempts to inspect the illusory body or body part. Our findings suggest that changes in visual attention and/ or current amplitude in the angular gyrus could bring about these phenomenological modifications.
>
> (Blanke *et al.* 2002: 269)

In a further category of neuropsychiatirc disorders, 'morbid emotional attitude', Cutting (1990: 198) suggests that what might be thought of as defence mechanisms occur so frequently with damage to just one side of the brain that 'one is forced to conclude that the particular pattern of brain-damage is the prime cause'. He includes here *anosodiaphoria* (minimization of a disability in a very jocular fashion), *misoplegia* (intense hatred for a paralysed limb) and exaggerated *preoccupation* with a limb that may not even be disabled. Cutting's main point in describing these disorders is to relate them to one hemisphere or the other. He concludes that a sense that body parts don't belong, have changed in size or shape or are displaced from their usual position is usually associated with *right* hemisphere damage. A sense that body parts don't exist or are duplicated is usually associated with *left* hemisphere damage. False bodily experiences (phantom limb, somatic hallucinations and autoscopy) are not associated with laterality. Interestingly, Blanke *et al.* (2002) reported some shortening and movement effects in their stimulation study, for the person's left arm and hand only (controlled by the right hemisphere; see also Berlucchi and Aglioti 1997).

Misidentification

Some neurological disturbances may reflect a disruption of linguistic processes, while others may be associated with disruption of spatial representation. Others again may reflect disruption of the body schema itself. The body schema can reach beyond the body to include:

> non-corporeal objects that bear systematic relation to the body itself, such as cloths, ornaments and tools . . . These inclusions of inanimate objects into the body schema are generally regarded as temporary and contingent on the actual association between body and object: when the cyclist dismounts from his bike this ceases to be a part of his body schema.
>
> (Berlucchi and Aglioti 1997: 561)

Berlucchi and Aglioti cite the case of a woman who experienced a large right hemisphere stroke and who (without any indications of dementia) not only showed no awareness of her left-arm paralysis, but when made aware of it insisted that it belonged to someone else. Furthermore, the rings she wore on her left hand were also disowned, but immediately recognized if placed on her right hand. Noting William James's claim that bodily parts and personal belongings can both be experienced in self-awareness sometimes as 'mine' and sometimes as 'me', Berlucchi and Aglioti conclude that somatoparaphrenia suppresses both 'me' and 'mine' experiences.

This is vividly illustrated in an earlier report by Bisiach *et al.* (1991) in which the dialogue between an 'experimenter' (Ex) and a 73-year-old lady with somatoparaphrenic delusions (AR) is reported:

Pointing to the woman's left arm:

Ex: Whose arm is this?
AR: It's not mine.
Ex: Whose is it?
AR: It's my mother's.
Ex: How on earth does it happen to be there?
AR: I don't know, I found it in my bed.
Ex: How long has it been there?
AR: Since the first day. Feel, it's warmer than mine. The other day too, when the weather was colder, it was colder than mine.
Ex: So where is your left arm?
AR: (Makes an indefinite gesture forwards) It's under there.

Immediately following contralesional vestibular stimulation with cold water (the vestibular system is thought to be related to this type of delusion, as is unilateral spatial neglect; see Bisiach *et al.* 1991), AR instantaneously recognized the arm as her own, although only two hours later she again attributed the left arm to her mother. This case not only illustrates how 'own' body parts may be attributed to other people, but also how easily reversible somatoparaphrenic delusions may be.

Capgras delusions are characterized by a person believing that other people are not who they appear to be. For instance, Mme M, a 53-year-old housewife, developed the belief that her children and husband had been replaced by doubles. She went as far as to petition for a divorce from her husband, claiming that he was not the man she married. Many wives may get this feeling from time to time. Sadly for the woman in question, she in fact believed that he had been murdered by his double . . . Stranger still are delusions of inanimate doubles (DID), which occurs where there is a belief that certain personal possessions have been replaced by similar but inferior object.

Ellis *et al.* (1996) report two cases of DID (in the absence of Capgras syndrome) who on cognitive testing showed problems processing object information but not in identifying people. The objects that these two patients believed were substituted had a special meaning or 'valence' for them, and for such objects 'recognition involves both a sense of *identification* and a feeling of *intimate familiarity*' (Ellis *et al.* 1996: 35, italics added). While it is not clear that neurological deficits are associated with all cases of DID, and while even in the presence of neurological deficits a context of paranoia/suspicion may be necessary for them to be expressed as DID, Ellis *et al.* (1996) argue for a *functional dissociation* between neurological processes involved in recognition and the emotional valence associated with the recognized object. They suggest that it is recognition of an object in the absence of its emotional meaning that creates a sense of that object's replacement, and its inferior quality in comparison to its more warmly remembered (recognition plus valence) existence. Put another way, it is a difference between objects that embody something and objects that no longer embody that thing. As such, their proposed distinction between two visual processes that proceed from visual cortex to the limbic system, but through different roots, is of note.

The variety of mind–body relationships that spring from neurological, neuropsychiatric and neuropsychological anomalies is well beyond the scope of this brief discussion. Some disorders are hard to fit into any classification and can engulf patients and clinicians alike in their web of ontological ambiguity. Dyer (2000) reported on a Scottish surgeon who had amputated the perfectly healthy legs of two people, because they asked him to. The newly appointed chief executive in the trust for whom the surgeon worked learnt that the surgeon was planning a third such amputation and banned the operation. The trust's previous chief executive and medical director had approved the operations, and the surgeon had discussed them with both his 'defence body' and the ethics committee of the UK's General

Medical Council, as well as having the patients assessed by psychiatrists and a psychologist.

The patients in question felt 'incomplete' with two legs but that they would feel 'complete' with one leg. People with such a feeling may resort to shooting off their leg, or lying on a railway track waiting for a train to run over one outstretched leg, according to the surgeon who amputated the limbs. Interestingly, both of the people who received amputations had artificial limbs fitted, although they did not always wear them. We do not know how the artificial limbs related to these two people's sense of their body, whether the removed limbs were previously fully represented on their somatosensory cortex or what sort of psychosocial factors may have impacted on their body image. They do in a bizarre way indicate that for preferred body image, 'what you get is not necessarily what you see' as being 'you'.

Summarizing the research on neurological aspects of body awareness, Kinsbourne (2002: 25) states 'attention works by amplifying and prolonging the relevant neural activity which is then entrained in awareness'; slowing down the succession of stages involved in the body's movements causes it to falter. Thus, actively attending to one's own skilled actions brings those actions into awareness and thus interrupts their 'fluency and flow'. As Kinsbourne (2002: 27) understands it, the body image is produced by the coordination of the 'somatic senses with intention and action', which may at times be supplemented by vision. When a body part is attended to 'it comes into focus and the rest of the body provides somatosensory background'. In considering this in terms of embodiment, it seems unlikely that the attended to and 'faltering' body is not a genuine sense of embodiment and possibly more likely that the 'somatosensory background' is closer to it. Kinsbourne emphasizes that body awareness is a continual dynamic and not a matter of retrieving a stored blueprint of what the body is like. As such, it depends on an ability to deploy somatosensory attention 'on-line'. Noting that a person with a phantom limb feels ownership of it even though they cannot see it, and that a person with unilateral neglect disowns their arm even though they can see it attached to their body, Kinsbourne (2002: 29) concludes that 'somatic sensations predominate over the visual sensations when the brain represents the body. It is by somatic attention that the body, and perhaps the self, enters awareness.'

On being in-valid

Whatever the physical basis of a disorder, the way in which its effects are experienced is usually through a social context, one that continues to construct the consequences of many disorders as 'invalidity', a horrible term implying that one is *not a valid person*. Just how to refer to the situation where some people have fewer physical possibilities than others continues to be problematic. Frequently the term 'impairment' is used to refer to loss of bodily parts or functioning, while 'disability' is understood to describe the societal consequences of such an impairment, including cultural and economic disadvantage, oppression of rights, exclusion from society and so on. Thus, it is society that determines the extent to which an individual is disabled by an impairment. However, it is important to recognize that the meanings of 'impairment' are also socioculturally constructed, rather than being simply a medical classification. Related to this is a further complexity, especially with regard to the concept of embodiment: while the term 'person with a disability' has the advantage of not framing people subjectively by their disability (Lupton and Seymour 2000), it has the disadvantage of possibly overlooking that such a 'disability' is an essential part of the self, and so it may be misleading to talk of an individual self, partitioned from their body (Oliver 1990).

If one accepts that the human body mediates experiences of the self, and that impaired bodies therefore mediate different experiences of the self and the world, then there is value in recognizing someone's physical status, although not defining them by it alone. As a physical impairment is never experienced in a social vacuum, and as many people with physical impairments refers to themself as 'disabled', or as 'a person with a disability' (Lupton and Seymour 2000), I shall also use these terms. Unlike the usual 'absent' status of the 'fully able' body noted earlier (see also Leder 1990), the physically disabled person's body is ever-present, because of its difference from other – 'normal' – bodies, at least from an observer's perspective. Thus, while 'the person with a disability may not feel ill or be in pain, her or his body is coded as a dysfunctional body. It culturally exists as a transgression, a body that straddles boundaries and therefore is anomalous' (Lupton and Seymour 2000: 1852).

A colleague of mine who lives through cerebral palsy described how he hated going shopping because he could not avoid his reflection in the large glitzy shop windows. He experienced this reflection as incongruent not only with what was being 'sold', but also with his experience of himself: 'that may be *what* I am, but its not *who* I am', he protested, 'I look drunk . . . like a fool'. Contrast the lack of coordination, the involuntary movements, the grimacing and unmelodic speaking so characteristic of cerebral palsy, with the ideals of physical beauty, control and measured self-presentation. As Rousso (1982: 84) suggests, this contrast may be so stark that to some people with cerebral palsy 'their own gestures and mannerisms may be a source of self-disgust'. By representing an alternative to the culturally valued, fully enabled, body-beautiful image, the disabled may in turn be seen by the able-bodied as 'subverters' of their cherished cultural values and ideals (Murphy 1995). The *constructivist* approach to disability essentially emphasizes what the disabled body is taken to mean in sociocultural context, while the *materialist* approach is more concerned with what it can't do, socially as well as physically, in the case of access to buildings, for instance. However, it is also important to consider that an overly constructivist approach may deny what Lupton and Seymour (2000: 1853) describe as the 'phenomenological physicality of the body' (see also Lupton 2003).

How to talk about physical disability, and even how to think about it, is at the heart of a concern with embodiment. What or who is disabled, and what or who disables them? The World Health Organization (WHO) originally promoted a linear conception of disability from 'Disease/Disorder' to 'Impairment' to 'Disability' to 'Handicap'. Thus, an intrinsic biological condition would be exteriorized to create a loss or an abnormality of 'psychological, physiological or anatomical structure or function' (WHO 1980: 27) that would constitute impairment. This *impairment*, through prohibiting the execution of certain functions, would produce *disability*, and the way in which society responded to the needs of such a person would determine the extent of *handicap* they experienced. In the new conceptualization, while the first two elements remain it is now proposed that 'Activity' and 'Participation' be used and 'Disability' and 'Handicap' dropped. The implied linearity of the model has also been modified so that 'Impairment' and 'Activity' are seen to be in reciprocal relationship, as are 'Activity' and 'Participation'. The new conception also acknowledges the role of personal and environmental factors, while being wary of 'any diagram . . . [that could] be prone to misrepresentation because of the complexities of interactions in a multidimensional model' (WHO 1997: 12).

However, Turner (2001: 257) argues that even this revision overly privileges a biomedical account of impairment: 'It does not attend . . . to the subjective world view of patients as constitutive of the condition and does not recognise the role of politics and culture in shaping human suffering.' Later on Turner (2001: 258) notes: 'Because our biographical narratives are carried in our embodiment, disability has to be mediated by its meaning for the self.' Schilling (1993) argues that in modern Western society the body is held to be a representation of the self: a mirror of the soul. Featherstone (1991) has suggested that the pull of rehabilitation is towards refashioning old and impaired bodies to conform to our contemporary values of youthfulness, beauty and athleticism. Zola (1993) has also noted that people with disabilities (were in 1993, and still) are facing barriers similar to ethnic minority groups in terms of getting their perspective recognized as being of equal value as 'able-bodied' mainstream society. For some people who are disabled, it may be difficult for them to establish just what their 'own' perspective is. While conjoined ('Siamese') twins may not be a common form of disability, its implications for embodiment are important to consider.

Self-division

According to Gomel and Weninger (2003) the notion of twinship has always made people feel both curious and uneasy; perhaps because it challenges our ideas of individuality. They note that:

Siamese twins, especially, were a staple in fairs and carnival sideshows. Still today, identical twins from the world over gather annually in Twinsburg, Ohio, to seek in other twins a reassurance that they are not human oddities, while others attend the fair to gawk at them for being just that.

(Gomel and Weninger 2003: 20)

Siamese twins (a term dating back to the twins Chang and Eng, born in Thailand, or Siam, in 1811) create discomfort in many people for not only may they be difficult to distinguish physically, but psychologically too. Piaget (1958) argued that at birth a child is not capable of making the distinction between self and non-self. However, through the interaction of motor activity and perception, the child develops a sense of their physical self, and 'incorporates' (Plugge 1970) aspects of itself (such as arms and legs). Murray (2001) suggests that in the case of Siamese twins such exploration produces a sensorial experience not only of their 'own' body but also of their 'twin's' body. As such, the distinction between self and other may never be made in the same complete manner. Considering *sensation* and *function* to be two defining aspects of embodiment, Murray (2001: 119) discusses the common sentient tactile surface shared by Siamese twins, and their shared volitional movement of limbs, arguing that they have 'an experience of self through the other'.

Noting Harré's assertion that 'touch sketches out the rim of felt embodiment', Murray (2001: 23) presents evidence that Siamese twins have areas of common sensation. For instance, in the case of Chang and Eng, they both perceived touch if that touch was along the midline of where they were joined (side-by-side), but if it was more than half an inch to either side only one of them felt the touch. For other Siamese twins there also appear to be regions of common and distinct sensation.

O'Shaughnessy's conception of bodily actions emphasizes the bringing about of events by trying and in trying our volition is given ownership over the action, in a way that movement without trying cannot convey. 'When movement occurs without this intentional component, it cannot be said that an action has occurred' (Murray 2001: 120); however, see Chapter 6 where I argue that one important sense of embodiment is achieved exactly when movement occurs *without* conscious intention. As an example of shared intentional action over a common limb, Murray cites the Russian twins (aged 11 when reported on) Macha and Dacha, who each had a leg and a 'third leg' between them that was deformed and had a double foot. Each of the twins controlled the leg on her 'own' side, and each of them could move the atrophied leg in the middle.

In twins who have been surgically separated, how do they feel about themselves, if in some sense prior to their separation they have some common sense of embodiment? Katie and Eilish Holton (Galloway 1995) were born joined from the shoulder to the pelvis and sharing two legs only. At three and a half years old they were surgically separated and sadly Katie died.

While acknowledging that Eilish's distress, in particular her looking down to where Katie had been and her associated 'jerking reaction' (her mother's words), can be understood as a response to bereavement, Murray prefers to compare it to that of people who have lost a limb. However, while some may, it is suggested that most people who have had limbs amputated do not evidence bereavement-like reactions (Fisher and Hanspal 1998). Furthermore, Eilish's naming of her prosthetic limb as 'Katie' may not have been in substitution for her (as implied by Murray) but in tribute to her. None the less, the point is well made that our ambiguities in the reading of such experiences may well reflect ambiguities in the sensing of a discrete corporal self. This is nowhere better illustrated than in the delightful comment of Giuseppina Foglia, when separated from her twin, Maria Santina Foglia, in Turin in 1965: 'Is it really me? Am I really Myself', and then addressing her sister 'You're so far away' (Wallace and Wallace 1978).

Reflecting on this Murray writes:

> Consider what this really means: *is it really me?* The two sisters had now been given distinct body boundaries; for the first time Giuseppina knew her body as distinct from that of her sister. Is it – the body I now see and feel – *really me?* – mine alone, and not part of my sister. She had always seen, for the most part, her body, and also felt it – though her attached sister would affect these sensations – but now she could feel and see something quite different.
>
> (Murray 2001)

There is certainly a sense here of the shared psychological identity of Giuseppina with her sister extending beyond the mere physical conjunction between them, and of her excited existential liberty. At the time of writing, Iranian Siamese twins – joined at the head – had sadly died only a few weeks earlier, after an attempt to separate them. In the media frenzy of recriminations that followed, the individuality of the twins and their 'need' to be parted has amply conveyed the great difficulties society has with comprehending their experience. It seems clear that it was not their disability that killed them but attempts to 'correct' it. To what extent these attempts were motivated by society's discomfort with them, or their own desire for physical independence, remains an open question.

Stigma

People who are obviously 'disabled' often constitute a 'stigmatized' group. Perceptions of 'stigma' may result in disabled people being treated differently from non-disabled people: assumptions may be made regarding individuals' personality and functioning, simply on the basis of their disability; the disabled person is 'reduced in our minds from a whole and usual person to a tainted, discounted one' (Goffman 1963: 12). People without disabilities may ignore those with disabilities for fear of saying the wrong thing, or because they find encounters with disabled people anxiety provoking, and experience unease in their presence (Gething 1991). The extent to which the disabled physical body can 'frame' an interaction has been illustrated in experimental studies. Kleck *et al.* (1966) found that when a person with a simulated amputation conducted an interview with students, the students showed elevated physiological arousal as assessed by their galvanic skin response. In addition, those who expressed discomfort in the presence of a person who had an 'amputation' terminated the interview sooner than those who did not express such discomfort.

In Kleck's (1969) subsequent study, students were required to teach origami (the Japanese art of paper folding) to a confederate either with or without a simulated leg amputation. If the confederate had an amputation they were given significantly greater social distance by the students on the first trial, but not on the second trial. In fact, students in the study formed a more positive impression of the 'disabled' confederate than of the non-disabled confederate. Kleck argued that the formation of a more positive impression might have arisen because of a tendency in society to be kind to 'disadvantaged' individuals. Newell (2000: 80) suggested: 'The supposed tendency to kindness may, indeed, be little more than an aspect of establishing our dissimilarity from the disabled person.' In a sense it is almost as though the greater social distance afforded disabled bodies is an implicit statement that 'I am not embodied in (comfortable with) that body.' Kleck *et al.* quote Davis (1961) in arguing that disabled people need to develop techniques that will help them to 'move beyond fictional acceptance'. This should also be considered in terms of their own self-acceptance, so often mirroring society's 'acceptance'.

Extending our discussion beyond disability to include disfigurement, it seems that the further a disfigured body deviates from the desirable, beautiful, 'norm', the less people want to occupy space next to that body. Houston and Bull's (1994) study of seat occupancy on a train found that occupancy of the seat next to the confederate was highest when the confederate had no visible defect, next highest when they had bruising, then scarring and lowest when they had a birthmark. If this is the 'mirror' society – possibly unwittingly – holds up to those who are disabled (Taleporos and McCabe 2002), it is a reflection of discomfort that cannot easily be ignored and may often be internalized – I want to get away from my body too. How then do individuals with newly acquired disabilities develop a sense of self and identity that incorporates their altered body functioning and body image?

Reclaiming the body

Leventhal *et al.* (1999) argue, as we have noted elsewhere, that a disabling chronic illness focuses an individual's attention on their physical activities and bodily functions that were previously taken for granted. The disruption of previously automatic tasks, including walking and dressing, now becomes central to the self-concept, challenging previously held ideas about the self. The self may become embodied in what can *only just be achieved* with focused attention and effort. If such tasks were previously so menial or incidental as to be executed without conscious thought, then they will clearly not have been the seat of previous conscious embodiment. As Corbin and Strauss (1987) state, ideas of body failure 'strike at the core' of the individual. According to them, self identity is affected to the degree that these changes create a loss of valued functions and abilities. The newly disabled person must incorporate their newfound limitations into a revised self-concept.

Morse's (1997) 'responding to threats to integrity of the self' model describes several stages to this process. *Vigilance* and *disruption: enduring to survive*, the first two stages, describe the acute phase of physical illness and how these overshadow any sense of identity, disruption or change. The third stage, *enduring to live: striving to regain self*, describes how individuals are forced to recognize the physical changes and loss of function that they have experienced. In this stage they start to seek to restore as much of their physical function as possible. The fourth stage, *suffering: striving to restore self*, describes how the effects of what has happened are now being recognized, and how the person begins to struggle with grief and mourning for what has been lost. It is at this stage that individuals also start to hope and set realistic goals for themselves. Although learning to live with setbacks and difficulties, they may none the less refuse to accept their limitations and seek a more complete physical recovery than is likely to be possible. In the fifth stage, *learning to live with the altered self*, the person comes to accept his or her body and the limitations it now brings. They revalue their lives, accepting that some things will now be 'out of their reach', but learn to appreciate alternative things. In this stage their focus shifts more to the inner person rather than the outer body. In this sense they become more embodied in 'what they are', and *less* embodied in what they physically *can* do. As such they have incorporated physical changes into a new self-identity and learned to 'live with the altered self'. This last stage is similar to what Norris *et al.* (1998) refer to as 'reimaging the self'

The process of adaptation to a disability may also be influenced by prior positive bodily experiences and by being able to identify certain aspects of the current body as being positive (Taleporos and McCabe 2002). It is also interesting to note that adaptation may not be linearly related to the severity of disablement. For example, children with spina bifida who have more severe disabilities associated with the condition tend to have higher levels of self-esteem and global self-worth than those with less severe disabilities (Minchom *et al.* 1995). These authors suggested that people become more distressed about having less severe disabilities because they are closer to functioning at what they perceive to be 'normal' levels. Those with more severe disabilities are further away from functioning 'normally' and, consequently, may find it easier to accept that they cannot physically function in the same ways others do.

Body history and abuse

To end this chapter let us consider the effects, especially subsequently upon the body, of experiences of sexual abuse or rape. This section may seem to be somewhat out of place in terms of what has preceded it. I want to discuss it here because sexual abuse is often a psychologically and/or physically disfiguring and disabling experience, where the victim effectively stigmatizes their own body, and where they may develop a variety of reactions to the abuse, including somatic and somatoform conditions. As the consequences of sexual abuse for embodiment incorporate several of the themes we have already discussed in this chapter, I hope to heighten awareness that symptoms, distress and disability never occur in isolation from their psychosocial context, and personal history, including 'body history'.

The experience of physical complaints implies a sense of difficulty with living comfortably in the body. Young (1992) suggests that survivors of severe sexual abuse must come to terms with having to live with a body that has been the medium of their abuse. Often they will have a 'disrupted' view of the specific body part(s) violated during the abuse; possibly hating those parts, and possibly mutilating them through cutting or burning (Fallon and Ackard 2002). These feelings may also generalize to the entire body, or parts of it may be distorted (for example, perceived as much larger than their actual size), or intense shame and guilt felt about them. The survivor of severe sexual abuse, especially if they felt aroused at any time during the abuse, may feel that their body has betrayed them (Fallon and Ackard 2002).

We strive to maintain a coherent sense of self over time. Under usual circumstances good and bad events alike can be fitted into a personal biography that maintains personal coherence and continuity. When severely traumatic events occur they may create incoherence and discontinuity. Young (1992) suggests that the Japanese saying 'trauma stops time' accurately encapsulates this. In the case of severe sexual abuse, trauma is inscribed on, and often in, the body of the victim. In writing about this physical violation of the body Young (1992: 91) poignantly states:

> What is meant here by 'violation' is that the boundary between 'inside me' and 'outside me' is not simply physically crossed against a person's will and best interests, but 'disappeared' (to borrow a term from Latin American terror) – not simply ignored but 'made-never-to-have-existed'.

She goes on to ask two fundamental questions: How do I know what *is* me? And how do I know what *was* me? In answer to the first, she suggests that things that go on 'inside my body' (including in my head) constitute a coherent bodily experience of 'me'. Extrapolating from this to answer the second question, she suggests that anything that has gone on 'inside my body', 'last week, or last year or at any point in "my life" (that is, the life of my body) is also me or mine by virtue of my experience of bodily continuity' (Young 1992: 92). Consequently, the current sense of me or mine is continuous with its past sense. However, following severe sexual abuse 'me and mine' may be seen not as what happens inside my body, but as what goes on 'inside my head', as in 'mind': thinking, remembering, speaking etc. Furthermore, events that do go on 'inside' my body – proprioception, sensual, affective or sexual experiences, for instance – may no longer be a part of 'me'.

How does this relate to the expression of distress? Dissociation (where different facets of the self become split off from one another) may be understood as a way of 'leaving the body'. Young notes examples of abused women who learn to induce anaesthesia in parts of the body, or who attempt to remove themselves from their body by 'floating near the ceiling'. She cites a case reported by Bass and Davis (1988: 210) to illustrate its possible longer-term role in the 'post-traumatic formulation of identity':

> I do feel a good part of the time that I'm not present in my body. It's as if inside, from my neck down, it's hollow, and there's this ladder, and depending on how things are going, I'm climbing up the ladder, and this little person who is me is sitting in my head, looking out through my eyes.

While this quote suggests recognition at some level of dependence on the body, the following quote from Prince (1957: 489; cited in Young 1992) indicates even greater dissociation from the body:

> She insisted that her body did not belong to her, nor was it part of her any more than her clothes were. She simply used it but did not feel as if it belonged to her . . . she felt that she was just thought, without a body, and she seemed to have the idea that she could be independent of her body, if she wished to be, although she was not an 'astral' body. She did not believe in 'that kind of stuff'.

These quotes reflect at least some instances of difficulties of comfortably 'living in the body' for survivors of child sexual abuse.

The starving of the body through anorexia nervosa (see Chapter 4) may be the result of wishing to punish and 'diminish' the 'container' of bad experiences. Thus, extreme objectification of the 'vile' body may be experienced, as in the following extract from one of Young's own clients:

> I hate my body – it's disgusting, like some awful, dead animal. Look at it – it's white and flabby and grotesque; and the worst thing is this ugly coarse black hair growing out of it. I went to this woman gynecologist and she said I'm all scarred inside and that the yeast infections I get I'll

probably get for the rest of my life. I hate even going to the bathroom or taking a shower or looking in the mirror.

(Young 1992)

For someone suffering through anorexia as a consequence of prior severe sexual abuse, there may be an element of having to destroy their body in order to survive it. This impossibility is conceivably overcome by placing the body 'outside' of the victim, as being 'not her'.

If a mechanism to distance the self from the body does indeed exist, it would seem to be quite a different way of reacting to severe sexual abuse from the production of somatic and somatoform symptoms, which have also often been reported in this context (Fallon and Ackard 2002). However, the experience of 'present symptoms' as a sort of 'foreground' experience may also be a mechanism for distancing, or 'backgrounding', other aspects of the physical body. Young again cites one of her own clients who had suffered through somatization for three years and was previously sexually abused:

I think I've had physical symptoms all my life only I wasn't aware of it. I've struggled with the feeling that in order to keep myself alive, I have to kill my body, to save B, to save me. I don't like my body, it hurts me. I was obsessed with my body, my physical appearance. I'm still obsessed with my body but not in the same way. I'm obsessed with relieving myself of my past which I feel through my body. I feel disgusted: I feel people can see my shame in my body – it's crazy what happens with my body.

(Young 1992: 97)

Self-mutilation is possibly the most extreme form of explicitly punishing the body. A sense of being betrayed by your body during sexual abuse may create a sense in which 'it' has been an accomplice in 'your' abuse. There may be a desire to rid oneself of the body and/or to punish it. Thus what appears to be self-abuse (including mutilation and suicide) from a 'outsider's' perspective, may, paradoxically, not be experienced as 'self-abuse' from the victim's ('insider's') perspective. 'They may seem to treat the body with the same callous disregard and cruelty, the same indifference to the value and sanctity of the human body, as the aggressor' (Young 1992: 99).

Moving bodies on

Whether as a result of child sexual abuse the body comes to be punished, starved, backgrounded or dissociated from, it remains the seat of our consciousness. It is this rootedness in the body that maintains the tragic legacy of child sexual abuse, yet is also a medium for moving forward. We conclude by briefly considering some body therapy interventions in this context. These experiential treatments for traumatic events use approaches other than 'talking therapies' as a medium to 'work through' the trauma. Such approaches include dance and movement therapy, guided imagery, art and music therapies. Fallon and Arkard (2002) suggest that experiential therapies provide the means to address the shame and loss of control and to 'rewrite' the outcomes of traumatic sexual experiences. They suggest that people may use sculpting or painting to produce images of the body both after the abuse and subsequently after the body has healed. Tangible expression of this difference may then provide motivation to move forward towards the desired state. Guided imagery may be used to guide someone (who is in a relaxed state) verbally through a traumatic experience so that they come to see their body as 'strong, protected, safe and respected'.

Fallon and Arkard (2002) also note that movement, dance and the learning of self-defence techniques provides an opportunity for people to develop a different sense of their body than they previously experienced, to see it in a more positive, less vulnerable and more powerful way. The sense of an active body may transcend the preoccupations of a passive victimized body. Implicit in these experiential therapies is the idea that the body acts as a non-verbal depository of trauma, which, just as a bent nail can be seen as a 'memory' of what bent it, carries with it an imprint of trauma, especially when that trauma was done to the body. While I have argued for the necessary embodiment of everyday language within our biological substrate, it would be a mistake to assume that the only biology 'stained' by trauma is neurological. If 'the body is a symbol that reaches beyond itself', then it is also a memory that reminds itself. Experiential therapies, like any therapies, must of course be open to the scrutiny of empirical evaluation. But whatever such studies find, we know that for at least some people, experiential therapy seems a credible alternative for healing sexual abuse, both mentally and physically.

Chapter summary

1 Our physiological response to stress can be considered a literal embodiment of that stress. Yet the body's response is often both metaphorical and excessive, in that its reactivity is a carry over from an evolutionary inheritance of 'fight' or 'flight' responses to extreme acute danger. When such a response becomes chronic it depletes the body of energy and resources and creates a path for infectious and structural diseases.

2 Coronary heart disease (CHD), the leading cause of death in the North-Western world, is strongly associated with a number of risk behaviours. Anxiety and depression are also associated with subsequent CHD, as is the anger–hostility–aggression aspect of the 'type A' personality. Such effects may be mediated through stress-induced immunosuppression, as has been shown to be the case for viral infections and other diseases. Thus stress may be embodied through a variety of different somatic channels.

3 Beyond the provision of adequate material resources for healthy functioning, one's position within a societal hierarchy and the degree of
inequity in the distribution of wealth within the society have been
shown to influence physical health independently and significantly.
Thus, even rather abstract ideas (e.g. inequity and social hierarchy) may
be 'embodied', through their effects on the body, despite many people
being quite unaware of these ideas.

4 Somatoform disorder is a diagnostic category covering an array of
physical complaints without organic evidence, which other than this
have little in common.

5 Body dysmorphic disorder may be understood as a projection of distress
on to the appearance of some aspect of the body, without that distress
being embodied by any such physical appearance.

6 Somatization is a common reaction to stress and may be found in many
different cultures. Debates about whether it is primary or secondary to
depression are difficult to resolve. Many 'psychological' and 'psychiatric'
disorders present primarily as physical symptoms. Recent research questions the existence of numerous discrete functional somatic syndromes
and suggests that they may be subsumed into two broad, 'fatigue pain'
and 'cardiorespiratory', syndromes.

7 Hysteria, now referred to as conversion reaction, has been plagued by
conceptual confusion and sexist presumption. Such conversion reactions
can occur *en masse*, and while old forms of hysteria may have receded,
new forms have emerged, determined by culturally sanctioned cues and
cultivated through media preoccupation with new and unusual ailments.

8 Damage to the right and left cerebral hemispheres is often associated with
distinct anomalous bodily experiences. Regardless of actual bodily existence, the brain can mediate an experience of the body that contradicts
the evidence of its being. The brain alone can create the experience of the
'person' vacating their body; of being disembodied, either in whole, or in
part; as well as of other people and objects being 'disavowed' of their
personalized meaning, being disembodied. It is not, however, clear that
such experiences are associated only with neurological disorder.

9 A sense of the body may arise from the coordination of intention with
physical action. However, as a body part comes into conscious awareness
of it may paradoxically seem to become objectified rather than personalized. When somatic and visual sensations contradict each other, the
former often dominate.

10 Not to acknowledge a disabled person's disability may be to deny their
physicality, yet to define them by this may be to invalidate them in their
own eyes and those of society. The disabled body is 'obvious' but should
not be definitive. It embodies difference and restriction and distracts
from the person who 'occupies it'. In seeking to distinguish between the
disabled body and the able person we seek to disembody the person
from 'that body'.

11 Siamese twins who share a common part of their body may experience common sensations and be able to have control of function over the same body part. It is unclear to what extent the desire to separate such twins is derived through a wish for physical independence or psychological individuality that may be constrained when joined.

12 The mirror that society 'holds up' to people with a physical disability is often a stigmatizing experience. The disabled body questions cultural ideals of normality and beauty, and as such may be rejected, not only by society, but also by those with a disability.

13 A process of adaptation to an acquired disability, or a physical illness that permanently prohibits some aspects of bodily function, may be identified. This process of learning to 'live with an altered sense of self' is closely tied to re-evaluating the significance of the body to the self. Some degree of 'disembodiment' may therefore be therapeutic.

14 The body is a memory of past trauma. In the case of prior child sexual abuse there may be confusion between what is 'me' and what is not 'me'. The body may be 'disowned' on the one hand, or the presence of somatization may 'background' prior abuse on the other hand. The body may become seen not just as the medium of abuse but also as the instrument of abuse.

15 There are a variety of experiential therapies that seek to help people to 'learn' their body in a positive and contradictory manner to the abusive experience they may have previously had. In essence these approaches seek to make the body a welcoming place to live. Such techniques may have power beyond the reach of spoken words or ingested drugs.

Discussion points

1 Can our psychophysiological responses to stressors be considered metaphorical?
2 Why do we somatize?
3 What is disabled in disability?

Key reading

Murray, C. D. (2001) The experience of body boundaries by Siamese twins, *New Ideas in Psychology*, 19: 117–30.

Nimnuan, C., Rabe-Hesketh, S., Wessely, S. and Hotopf, M. (2001) How many functional somatic symptoms? *Journal of Psychosomatic Research*, 51: 549–57.

Young, L. (1992) Sexual abuse and the problem of embodiment, *Child Abuse and Neglect*, 16: 89–100.

Body sculpturing

Virtue? A fig! 'Tis in ourselves that we are thus, or thus.
Our bodies are our gardens, to the which our wills are
gardeners . . .

(Shakespeare, *Othello* 1.3)

The point of a sociology of embodiment is to go beyond
a Cartesian medical framework in which mind–body
dualism is replaced; there is little advantage in substituting
a psychology–biology dualism for the traditional mind–body
dualism.

(Turner 2001)

'We' have now mapped the human genome, celebrated the fiftieth anniversary of the discovery of DNA and cloned that now famous ewe, Dolly. Genetic enhancement of our lives could become an almost mundane aspect of our being, were it not for us swinging between utopian speculation about achieving our full potential, and dire predictions of a biological totalitarianism that would keep us all perfectly humming the same tune. We are both the producers and consumers of a social order that prescribes to rid ourselves of what is proscribed: short people can be given synthetic growth hormones, inattentive school kids can be given Ritalin, introverted folk can get Seroxat; because shortness, poor academic performance and shyness are stigmatized. Those who market these treatments aim them at parents who are afraid of having stigmatized children.

Elliot (2003) reminds us of the tale of *The Wizard of Oz*, and the salience of our ideas about self-improvement. As you may recall, the Scarecrow (who wants brains), the Tin Woodman (who wants a heart) and the Cowardly Lion (who wants courage) all travel along the Yellow Brick Road to meet the Wizard, only to find that they are, in fact, already intelligent, compassionate and courageous, respectively. The problem of these seekers lies not in what they are, but in who they think they are. Self-doubt is the source of their angst and thus what the Wizard provides them with is not a brain, heart or courage, but self-esteem. The Wizard's real trick, however, is not only to sell the Lion a vision of himself at odds with what he fears himself to be, but also to convince the Lion that this is how he really is; it is his *true self*. Elliot notes that whether it be cosmetic surgery, Prozac or a sex change, 'No transformation is so dramatic that it cannot be described as a means to achieve the "true self"' (Elliot 2003: 14). In this chapter we consider the relationship between the self and ideas about how the body appears, how it can be shaped by personal, cultural and market forces and the contemporary roads that people may travel, sometimes seeking new bodies, at other times seemingly trying to rid themselves of their 'old' bodies.

In this chapter, as if by sculpturing a form, I move towards and away from several themes, returning to some of them many times. We begin, however, with a very brief history of how the body has been related to personality.

Physiognomy

> Always and everywhere, the normal blond has positive, dynamic, driv-
> ing . . . and variety-loving characteristics; while the normal brunette
> has negative, static, conservative . . . characteristics.
> (Blackford and Newcomb 1915: 141)

Perhaps one reason why we are attracted to the idea that how someone looks relates to what they are like as a person is that physical characteristics are among our most easily measured features. I had to dig into LaPiere and Farnsworth's third edition of their *Social Psychology* (1949), first published in 1936, to unearth some of the more 'quaint' and quite unhelpful stereo-typing that has occurred concerning the relationship between physical chara-cteristics and personality. It was Aristotle's treatise on 'physiognomy' that first described how character could be judged from physical features. Lavater's *Essays on Physiognomy*, published in 1878, detailed 100 physiog-nomical rules by which to judge people. For example, Rule 77 states 'a broad, brown wart on the chin is never found in truly wise, calmly noble persons'.

Such 'insights' were preceded in 1876 by the famous French criminolo-gist Cesare Lombroso's own physiognomical rules. It is worth quoting LaPiere and Farnsworth's (1949: 212) appropriately sarcastic recounting of these:

> Lombroso, however, presented the ingenious and intriguing theory that
> all mankind was divisible into the criminal type and the non-criminal
> type and that, since nature had fortunately stamped the criminal per-
> sonality with a criminal physiogamy, all that was necessary to prevent
> further crime was to round up the people who looked like criminals.
> After long study, Lombroso provided criminologists with a set of
> pictures showing the types of physiognomy indicative of personalities
> typical of people who would commit specific types of crimes.

Phrenology

It is important to remember that physiognomists considered themselves to be men of science, involved in the serious and systematic pursuit of import-ant problems. Another aspect of 'scientific' thinking of the time was that of phrenology, where the exterior configuration of the skull was believed to reflect personality characteristics. Initially Gall and Spurzheim in the early nineteenth century had identified 27 regional faculties such as 'secret-iveness', 'parental love' and 'spirituality'. However, this had subsequently to be increased to 35 faculties. The idea was that the more a person used particular faculties the larger that area of the brain grew and this produced distortions in the shape of the skull. A huge industry spawned; a science with royal patronage and wall charts, journals and specialists sprung up. Queen Victoria had her own children's heads measured and analysed (Stirling 2002).

Such was the fervour for phrenology that it was felt that things could be learnt even from the remains of great men who were now deceased. For instance, Jonathan Swift was exhumed from his resting place in St Patrick's Cathedral, Dublin, and men of science busily spent a week feeling the bumps on his skull so as to ascertain the faculties he must have used most in his various writings. Incidentally, alongside the phrenological model of Swift's skull that is now displayed in the cathedral in which he was once dean, there are two death masks made of Swift. Perhaps these are attempts, along with his adjacent marble bust, to retain not just a physical likeness but also perhaps some sense of physical presence?

Somatotypes

Still quoted in some textbooks, although usually as historical titillation, are Sheldon's system of 'somatotypes', in which body build is classified into the three basic components of endomorphic (or fatty), mesomorphic (or mus-cular) and ectomorphic (or linear), with each being measured along a seven-point scale (Sheldon *et al.* 1940). Thus, in Sheldon's system an individual's somatotype was represented by three numbers reflecting their position on each of these components. LaPiere and Farnsworth (1949) illustrate the system with reference to Jesus Christ and Superman. Christ's portrayal by early religious painters as thin, lightly muscled and delicately boned would earn him a 2-3-5 rating on Sheldon's scales: low in the endomorphic com-ponent, relatively low in the mesomorphic component and slightly above average on the ectomorphoc component. Superman (at least the rather 'modest' Superman of the 1940s comics) they suggested would be a 2-7-6: thin, exceptionally developed musculature and relatively small boned. I reckon our steroid-supplemented real life 'supermen' of today (more of that later) would bump the 1940s comic version down a few notches, as many of them exceed what would have been judged credible back then.

While a 'neutral' Sheldon system, as a means of categorizing bodies, might have had its uses to anatomists and physical anthropologists, its greatest deficit was that it wasn't neutral. Body types and personality type were seen to be associated. Specifically, endomorphy (being fat) was associated with viscerotonia (being jovial); mesomorphy (being muscular) with somatonia (being enterprising); and ectomorphy (being 'fragile') with cerebrotonia (being intellectual). Thus, one's rating on Sheldon's somatic components, it was claimed, described not just physical characteristics but also where one lay on different dimensions of personality: by looking at someone you could judge what sort of person they were.

I have somewhat laboured this notion of physical and psychological association for several reasons. First, it goes to the heart of the notion of embodiment; to the extent that we have some influence over the type of body we have, one can see how it can be argued that physical features may therefore 'embody' aspects of the psychological self. Second, it is perfectly clear that for many of us, although we may have some influence over our body, the degree of this influence is constrained by biological inheritance and environmental factors. Third, even back in the 1940s people were rubbishing the very notion of some of the stereotypes that still pervade: the 'jovial fat guy', the 'entrepreneurial athletic guy' and the 'introverted tall guy'.

I think that we may now have come full circle: despite the lack of credible evidence of somatic–personality links, in our modern consumer culture, people, or more precisely their images, are commodities that we 'consume'. 'You are what you eat' and 'what you see is what you get' are strange bedfellows of embodiment; representing both a health-foody emphasis on purity, naturalness and goodness on the one hand, and an 'I'm not too deepish' focus on (usually) cosmetic beauty on the other hand. Let us look at the young, and how they are acquiring bodies that 'we' never had (sorry, you may be one of them), and how they are striving to acquire bodies that nobody has.

Tweenagers

The idea of 'adolescence', as a period of storm and stress, always was a social construction. While some societies have an adolescent period, others quite simply don't. In some societies, for instance, people move from childhood through to adulthood directly, often facilitated by some sort of initiation ritual. In other societies 'adolescence' is a rather long and drawn out process of moving slowly and sometimes with conflict from dependence into independence. If the boundaries between adolescence and adulthood may be blurred, those between childhood and adolescence have been seen as less blurry, at least until very recently. A couple of years ago, Kidscape, a child protection charity, championed a campaign opposing the selling of G-strings, targeted at preteen girls, which were embossed with a cherry and the words 'Eat Me'. The Channel 4 documentary Skinny Kids reported on the availability of padded bras for seven-year-olds, and children of nine shaving their legs and wearing full make-up. The cropped tops and high heels that even little girls of four and five seem to adore are also adored by paedophiles according to Kidscape. There is thus a moral issue here of what message we wish to endorse concerning what our children are interested in – what our children are for.

Driscoll (2003) reports that the latest figures available (for the year 2000) indicate that eight 11-year-old girls gave birth in England and Wales, while in the previous two years none of that age did. Driscoll argues that the identification of 'tweenagers' (10–13-year-olds) as a market segment, with an estimated combined spending power of £1 billion in the UK alone, along with the increasing individualization of society and the need for children to 'assert themselves and find an identity early on', have at least partly driven this sexualization of our children. Glitzy and fleshy fashion magazines such as *Elle* and *Cosmopolitan* are now publishing special editions for teenagers, and *Teen Vogue* has been launched in the USA. Our female children are being made into small women, premature teenagers; little girls are no longer 'cool'. So just what is it that they are being encouraged to emulate, body-wise?

Svelte as a gazelle

There has been a good deal of research on how the female body has changed in shape, particularly over the past few decades. In the now classic study, Garner *et al.* (1980) got access to the self-reported measurements of *Playboy* centrefolds across the years 1959 to 1978. They also got measurements for Miss America contestants in the same period, and compared these to the population norms. The mean weight for 'playmates' (expressed as a percentage of the mean weight for all women of the same age and height) showed a statistically significant decline from 91 per cent in 1959 to 83.5 per cent in 1978. While the average height and waist sizes actually increased, bust and hip sizes decreased, suggesting a decrease in the curvaceousness of the 'preferred' female body. However, over the same period, the average weight of Miss America contestants reduced by 0.13 kg per year, and for pageant winners the average decrease was 0.17 kg. Furthermore, during this same period the population mean for women under 30 had actually increased by an average of 0.14 kg per year. In a more recent study Voracek and Fisher (2002) looked at the trends in *Playboy* centrefold models' body measurements from the magazine's inception in December 1953 to December 2001. They concluded that significant change had taken place over time:

> The typical body mass index of *Playboy* centrefolds has further descended below corresponding population levels, whereas their typical waist:hip ratio now approaches population levels. In sum, centrefold models' shapely body characteristics have given way to more androgynous ones. These temporal trends are at odds with claims that

centrefolds' body shapes are still more 'hourglasses' than 'stick insects' and that the maximally sexually attractive female waist:hip ratio is stable.

(Voracek and Fisher 2002: 1448)

Of course it may be argued that *Playboy* centerfolds, Miss Americas or *Vogue* models (see the study by Barber 1998) represent only idealized feminine images from the perspective of men or fashion magazine editors, rather than a more pervasive change in the 'average woman'. If women had a hard time emulating the vital statistics of *Playboy* centrefolds, Miss Americas or *Vogue* models (although I recognise that many smart women chose not to), these were, in retrospect, quite easy targets in comparison to the contemporary 'airbrushed' icons who grasp our gaze.

My own little erotic myopia includes the one-time earthy and delight-fully voluptuous Kate Winslet, whom fortunately I did not feel compelled to emulate, but just appreciate. Woods (2003) has a go at Kate: 'svelte as a gazelle splashed across GQ magazine. She looks drop-dead, pick-off-the-shelf flawless and gorgeous. Swell breasts and wasp waist perch on legs like stilts, while a perfect complexion glows on her chiselled cheeks (top and bottom).' Continuing in his humorous and compelling piece, Woods describes the process of Kate's photographic digital manipulation, alluding to her recent blockbuster: 'Like the iceberg that sank the Titanic, a fair chunk of her remains submerged.' But sure, what harm if Kate wants to tweak her bits and pieces, especially if they don't represent the 'real' her.

There is, however, real harm to be done here, because what is being sold is the earthy, happy, girl-next-door, at one with herself, 'Kate Winslet' image, squeezed into the digital wish-world of somatic freaks. I use this cruel word 'freak' because it is a cruel trick to play on us and conforms, in at least one sense, to the *Oxford Reference Dictionary* definition of a freak as an 'abnormally developed individual or thing'. The problem is, we don't quite know whether our 'GQ Kate Winslet' is indeed an individual, or a thing. The crucial point here is that the person that we are presented with by GQ is not the embodiment of the personhood of Kate Winslet, as we think we know her (prior image).

I am sure that Kate Winslet would not be too bothered by the (unlikely) prospect of losing a single fan – me. The more important concern is that Kate, and those like her, are as much a 'victim' of the PR machine as are the rest of us. Indeed, Woods reports the editor of GQ, Dylan Jones, as saying that 'Almost no picture that appears in GQ – or any other magazine or newspaper – has not been digitally altered in some way.' And Woods says that when Michael Jackson was reunited with the Jackson Five on stage, the film was doctored to make him look blacker, and therefore to 'fit in' with the image being sold. The former editor of *Cosmopolitan*, Marcelle D'Argy Smith, commenting on the digital airbrushing in fashion magazines, says 'the truth is nobody has any idea what anybody really looks like'. She argues that ordinary people believe that they should be like non-existent gorgeous people, and that we are living in a 'lunatic world'.

To her credit, Winslet subsequently commented on her *GQ* cover image: 'I don't look like that and, more importantly, I don't desire to look like that. It isn't real . . . I want to be clear that I haven't suddenly lost 30 lb. It is important to say that magazines do this; they make perfection' (Woods 2003). Thank God for those unofficial opportunistic trashy photographs that portray our icons in ways that we can hardly recognize them; in fact, they look rather like us. The popular portrayal of celebrity soma is an area deserving of much more serious study and research, not least because it at least partly contributes to our continuing desire to recast our bodies in new likenesses.

Regenesis

For those of us who wouldn't mind a bit of airbrushing ourselves, the Internet offers a panoply of soma-changing and regenerating possibilities. Once upon a time, against my better judgement and under the guise of 'book research', I actually opened an e-mail with the following in its subject line: 'HUMAN GROWTH HORMONE – Decrease Body Fat/Increase Muscle/Sexual Vigour/Anti-Aging!' That exclamation mark is well placed. On a 30-day trial no-risk money-back guarantee basis, *Regenesis* is sold as being 'clinically documented by medical doctors, and there are many testimonials attesting to the success of this product'. The actual effects are quite appropriately described as 'TRULY INCREDIBLE'. These include:

IMMEDIATELY –
  ♦ Decrease Body Fat – Increase Lean Muscle Mass
  ♦ Slow Down the Aging Process Gradually
  ♦ Feel Young Again with Renewed Energy
  ♦ Improve Sexual Vigour

TAKING A LITTLE LONGER TO –
  ♦ Erase Lines and Wrinkles
  ♦ Restore Hair Loss and Color
  ♦ Continuing Process to Decrease Body Fat – Increase Muscle

LONG TERM – Add Years To Your Life And Life to Your Years

And all this in an oral spray: 'TRULY INCREDIBLE', indeed! Now I am not qualified, and I am not sure who would be, to attest to the validity of these claims, but for my publisher's legal piece of mind, my point is not to contest any of these claims, but to indicate that they are a reflection of the desires of our times, coupled with the realization that with biotechnological innovations apace, they might just be achievable. Our desires – indeed fantasies – we are increasingly being told are not at all unreasonable: in fact, we deserve them; 'real me-isms' again; because 'I'm worth it', no doubt. Thus, on the one hand we have digitally manipulated bodies that we can't possibly hope to be like, while on the other hand we have a simple (and relatively inexpensive) oral spray that promises us the possibility of inhabiting just such bodies. No wonder we are uncertain about our bodies. But what has happened to the eugenic-cosmetic dream of celeb-somas when the inhabitants of the largest constituency of this dreamland are fatter than ever? In a time when thinness is increasingly valued, why are we getting fatter?

Fat land

Greg Critser's *Fat Land* (2003) presents some frightening statistics: 61 per cent of US citizens are overweight, such that they will experience health-related problems associated with their weight; while 20 per cent meet the criteria for morbid obesity, qualifying for gastroplasty, a radical surgical technique that limits the amount of food being digested. The percentage under 19 who are overweight or obese has doubled in the past 30 years. Critser ponders on Ivan Illich's assertion that 'every man is his own author'; if each of us is responsible for what has been made of us, what does this say about citizens of the USA? Critser charts the increase in the girth of his nation's average body through a number of interlocking social, economic and psychological forces.

He explains that when retailers attempted to get their clientele to buy more when at the movies, for instance, they hit a plateau. They could not get people to buy two burgers, or two packets of chips, or two Cokes each. People didn't want to look gluttons, it seemed. Then a marketing 'genius' struck on the idea not of selling more, but of selling bigger. So a serving of McDonald's 'French fries' rose from 200 calories in 1960 to 320 calories in the late 1970s to the whopping 610 calories of today. People had come to see big as the norm, and getting bigger was smartly priced to be proportionately cheaper than staying smaller. Being bigger was not just about more intake, it was also about power – wimps don't eat Big Macs. The increasing culture of permissiveness in consumption, and what might be called 'individualized authenticity', banished notions of gluttony and shame.

The argument about what harm overeating does has raged for years and has political, commercial and many other interests feeding into it. What does seem clear, however, is that obesity has some obvious health consequences, diabetes possibly being one of the most widely recognized. With possible consequences of blindness, limb amputation and immobility, diabetes is now being taken very seriously. Indeed, pharmaceutical giant Eli Lilly's new insulin production facility (the biggest single-drug production facility in the world) was built in response to its increasing sales, with 24 per cent growth a year (Critser 2003).

Obesity is not, however, socially, culturally or economically inert. Its greatest effects, at least in the USA, are felt among 'the poor, the underserved, and the underrepresented' (Critser 2003: 109). For instance, 33 per cent of black people, 26 per cent of Hispanic people and 19 per cent of white people with an annual household income of less than $10,000 are obese in the USA. For those same groups in the $50,000 plus bracket, the respective figures are 23 per cent (blacks), 22 per cent (Hispanics) and 16 per cent (whites). In trying to partition the causative factors Critser (2003: 110–11) summates that 'The point is not that culture or race does not matter. They do. The point is that class almost always comes first in the equation: class confounded by culture, income inhibited by race or gender, buying power impinged on by ethnicity or immigration status.'

The contemporary clash of culture and metabolism, the seeds of which were planted by European conquerors hundreds of years ago, has been described by Bogin and Loucky (1997). They argue that cultural exploitation of the Guatemalan Maya with their resultant poverty produced an environmentally adaptive metabolic proclivity to retain fat in their context of scarcity. However, when they migrate into a culture of abundance, such as the USA, this proclivity predisposes them to obesity. It is not thus a 'regular' immutable genetic inheritance that causes the high rates of obesity in the Guatemalan Maya who migrate to the USA, but an adaptive metabolism inherited from generations of poverty that just can't 'turn off' that fast a survival mechanism that has worked over many generations. It is in this sense, Bogin and Louckey argue, that metabolically the original traumas of conquest are today played out on the streets of Los Angeles.

As weight and body composition are a reflection of daily consumption, while height reflects health and nutritional history, increases in body weight precede increases in height when people from impoverished regions migrate to regions of abundance (Bogin and Louckey 1997). Such an argument clearly questions comfortable implicit assumptions about health being affected by physical factors or social or cultural factors; about health problems either being nature or nurture. Metabolic changes that adaptively arise due to cultural and economic exploitation, but subsequently disadvantage their 'carriers', surely represent the embodiment of a history of inequity. This is no abstract pondering of an academic nature. Consider, for example, the rates of obesity among Mexican American children: for 5- to 11-year olds they are 27.4 per cent for girls and 23 per cent for boys. The rate peaks in the fourth grade for girls at 32.4 per cent and in the fifth grade for boys at a staggering 43.4 per cent (see Suminski et al. 1999).

Critser (2003: 132) quotes a neurologist, Dr Scott Loren-Selco who works in Los Angeles, as explaining to him that the immigrant population especially 'get' the TV advertising, that the USA is the 'place about "more"'. Where they can get more. It's "Look at me! I'm just a poor kid from

Xapotecas and even I can get more". They can afford supersized burgers and fries – and so they get them'. Critser concludes that 'the price of abundance is restraint' (p. 175). So how do ideas of restraint translate to ideas about our bodies?

Ideals and actuals

Fallon and Rozin (1985) had undergraduate students (in the USA) evaluate nine figure drawings of female body builds and nine of male body builds, scaled so that they ranged from being very thin to very large. The students were asked to identify the same-sex figure that most closely corresponded to their own current shape, their ideal shape and the shape they believed would be considered most attractive to the opposite sex. They also rated the opposite-sex figure that they themselves considered most attractive – other attractive. There were no significant differences between self-reported *current, attractive* and *ideal* figures for males, but for females their current figure was significantly heavier than what they rated as the most attractive figure, which was in turn heavier than their own ideal figure. This ties in with the idea, at least for female US college students, of striving for an ideal that is excessive in the sense of being 'beyond' attractive.

Following various other comparisons between the above variables, Fallon and Rozin (1985) suggested that women's ideal figure was influenced by factors other than a desire to attract heterosexual partners, and argued that weight loss may be used as a means of establishing control over their lives, or that women believe that others, including other women, view thinness as a positive characteristic in females, possibly connecting it with higher social class. However, it is important to point out that while various studies have used the methodology of comparing current, attractive and ideal ratings of figures, they do not all produce the same findings. For instance, Cohen and Adler (1992) found that female college students rated their current figure as significantly heavier than their own ideal figure; however, they estimated their peer ideal figure to be significantly thinner than their own ideal figure. Thus in this study women felt that other women wanted to be significantly thinner than they themselves wanted to be. In agreement with previous studies, the figure women thought was most attractive to men was significantly thinner than men preferred.

The suggestion that men are less troubled by their body image than are women has, however, been challenged on the grounds that most studies have been concerned with body shape, while muscular definition is of greater concern to men. That cultural preferences for male muscular definition have changed was supported by Pope *et al.*'s (1999) study of the muscularity of popular action toys, which showed increasing muscularity over a 30-year period, and their contemporary observation that today many such toys are of a more muscular build than most human bodybuilders. Dittmar and colleagues' (2000) investigation of ideal characteristics among English adolescents first identified a range of ideal male and female characteristics through qualitative methods. In the second part of their study adolescents were asked to indicate the extent to which they agreed with the personality and body descriptors of the ideal man and woman.

While personality characteristics were seen as more important overall, greater importance was attached to bodily characteristics when describing the ideal of the opposite sex, especially by boys. The ideal male was described as athletic, trim, with a thin waist, a muscular upper body and short hair. The ideal female was deemed to be pretty, skinny but still voluptuous (quite an achievement) and had long hair. These preferences are clearly multidimensional, rather than simply being dictated by body shape. Finally, Dittmar and colleagues (2000) also looked at the relationship between body mass index (BMI, weight in kilograms divided by the square of height in metres) and the extent of the above preferences. Interestingly, they concluded that adolescents of greater body mass tended to distance themselves from conventional notions of attractiveness.

While adolescents' strong rating of personality characteristics as being important in judging attractiveness is in some ways encouraging, in other ways a psychological versus physical dichotomy does not accord with research findings. In fact, it seems that the two are intimately and intricately linked. In a summary of the sociocultural perspective on physical attractiveness, Jackson (2002) concludes first that beauty is not only in the eye of the beholder; in fact, there is considerable agreement not only within US culture about what constitutes attractiveness, but also cross-culturally, especially regarding facial attractiveness. Second, physically attractive people are viewed as possessing a variety of other non-physical positive characteristics, such as academic, interpersonal and occupational competence, and this stereotyping holds 'regardless of culture'. Third, not only do people appear to be judged on the basis of their physical attractiveness, but others behave differently and more positively towards them.

Jackson's (2002: 16–17) final conclusion is that 'attractive people are "better" in ways consistent with their preferential treatment by others', by which is meant that attractive adults actually do experience more occupational success, have better social skills, higher self-esteem, better health, are more self-confident and so on. This indeed seems to add privilege to praise (as opposed to 'insult to injury'), although it is important to note that these effect sizes (i.e. how much difference attractiveness really makes), although statistically significant, are rather small in scale. None the less, is it any wonder that people want to be attractive when there seems to be so much to be gained? Overall, it seems very clear that 'The more discrepant one's self-evaluation is from the cultural ideal, the greater the dissatisfaction with appearance' (Jackson 2002: 20). Let us now consider one extreme and tragic form of such dissatisfaction.

Eating disorders

The diagnostic criteria for anorexia nervosa have changed from when it first entered medical parlance in the 1870s, although the fear of weight gain has continually been seen as its primary motivational factor (Habermans 1996). Currently the DSM-IV (Diagnostic and Statistical Manual of the American Psychological Association, fourth edition – which is very similar to the World Health Organization's International Classification of Disease, tenth edition, ICD-10) identifies four key symptoms: (a) refusal to maintain normal body weight (less than 85 per cent of that expected for height); (b) intense fear of weight gain, even though underweight; (c) disturbance in the way in which one's body weight or shape is experienced, self-evaluation being overly influenced by body weight or shape, or refusal to recognize the significance of low body weight; and (d) amenorrhea in postmenarcheal females, specifically the absence of at least three consecutive menstrual cycles. Two subtypes of anorexia nervosa are identified: a *binge-eating/purging type*, where the person regularly eats in binges and may use various methods of purging, such as self-induced vomiting, misuse of laxatives, diuretics or enemas; and a *restricting type*, where the person has not regularly engaged in binging/purging. However, as with so many attempts at classification of people's distress, the validity of these subtypes has been called into question by a recent longitudinal study that showed significant cross-over between people in these groups and no difference in impulsivity, assumed to be a factor in the binging/purging subtype (Eddy *et al.* 2002).

Clinical classification of anorexia nervosa, however, hardly captures the desperate anguish of those caught up in the tragedy of self-starvation: obsessive preoccupations with food, struggles to control hunger, the 'shutting out' of loved ones, the mood disturbances and the 'diminishing' of that person, not only physically, but also through a slipping away of the person that others feel they can identify with. Self-starving also has a profound effect on blood pressure and body temperature, and these changes in the body's environment can result in changes in the bones, teeth, hair and skin, as well as impaired renal and cardiovascular functioning. Indeed, some people with anorexia die from multiple organ failure. To spend time with those who suffer *through* anorexia nervosa is to witness a frightening trajectory where the progressive embodiment of a desperate belief undermines the person's possibilities for life.

From the perspective of embodiment, perhaps the most intriguing primary symptom of this syndrome is the presence of body weight or shape disturbance. Distorted body size perception has long been considered a core aspect of anorexia nervosa. The person's actual physical appearance and their own experienced appearance are discrepant. Even though people with anorexia may intellectually appreciate that they are dreadfully underweight, they still perceptually see themselves as being bigger than they actually are. For those not familiar with this phenomenon a similar experience is perhaps the experience people have when viewing their own image in a distorting mirror, except then you are very much aware it *is* a distortion.

Research on this issue has indicated that some people who do not have an eating disorder still experience distorted body perception. Cash and Deagles's (1997) meta-analysis of over twenty years of research on body image disturbance found that on average people with an eating disorder distort their size to a greater extent than 73 per cent of the non-eating disordered comparison groups used in the research studies. Garner's (2002) recent summary of research on aspects of size distortion suggested that for those who are anorexic, overestimation of total body size seems to be greater than overestimation of the size of particular body parts (such as face, chest or hips). He suggests that this may be because whole-body estimation involves more direct exposure to one's self-image, rather than the more 'indirect' estimation of width of a particular body part. Most importantly, Garner concludes that while people with anorexia and those in 'control' groups may differ in the accuracy of their estimation of their own body size, they do not differ in estimating the size of objects in general, and thus the distortion is motivated around the self, rather than a general perceptual distortion.

While this is interesting, it is a mistake to make too much of body size overestimation in eating disorders, as it appears to be an unstable effect (being influenced by mood, viewing thin images of other women or per- ceived overeating). While not all of those who have anorexia nervosa experience body size overestimation, its occurrence is often associated with the presence of other symptoms of greater severity – for instance, depression and eating problems – which are associated with poorer outcomes (Garner 2002). Oltmanns and Emery (2004: 341) cite an anonymous student's attempt to explain how a person with an eating disorder sees a distorted image of herself:

> It's almost like she sees herself as bloated – of course she sees herself, she recognizes herself, but as bigger than usual. Also, the skinnier she gets, the more she notices fat deposits around the waist, under the arms, etc., because the more fat is lost, the more attention is drawn to the little bit of fat that still exists . . . Also, it's the point of reference in the background that may sometimes be distorted. She looks at the bath- room mirror and thinks, 'Did I take up that much space against this wall yesterday?'

This description clearly indicates processes of thinking and focusing that may be found to a lesser extent among many 'non-eating disordered' members of Western societies.

There have of course been many different explanations put forward to account for anorexia nervosa, and it is well beyond our scope to discuss them here. However, some are relevant to the concept of embodiment. Williamson *et al.* (2001) characterize the cognitive approach as emphasizing the interplay between environmental pressure for thinness because of its cultural association with social acceptance and prosperity, the social modelling of dieting through media outlets, the existence of cognitive biases for body-related information and the principle of reinforcement. Thus fear of gaining weight, it is suggested, motivates restricted food intake, excessive exercise and/or purgative behaviours, and thereby releases the individual from the anxiety accompanying weight gain. This negatively reinforcing cycle – i.e. escaping from a feared situation – becomes very difficult to break. Furthermore, evidence of weight loss can be positively reinforcing because it may be associated with feelings of achievement and self-control through the ability to deny strong biological urges to eat.

From a more psychodynamic perspective it has been suggested that anorexia may be seen as a phobic avoidance of adult weight and body shape, and sexuality (Crisp 1997). The anorexic is able to avoid these fears (and often the onset of menstruation). Related to this is a systems theory perspective that sees anorexic symptomatology as symbolically representing the individuals' fear of negotiating and failure to negotiate, the separation/individuation aspects of family life. Thus the anorexic symptoms represent an attempt to establish power, autonomy and independence while not having to engage with the challenges (including body changes) of adolescence (Casper 1982).

Up to this point, masculinity has been conspicuously absent from my description of anorexia nervosa, and with good reason. It is a predominantly female preoccupation, although when it does occur in men (about one in ten cases) it is often more difficult to treat, perhaps because it does not reflect compliance to Western male cultural values, but a rejection of them (Anderson 2002). Indeed, Western male cultural values might be thought of as quite the opposite of the anorexic figure and this realization has led to the coining of a new term.

Reverse anorexia nervosa

'Reverse anorexia nervosa' is concerned with an excessive focus on fat-free muscularity and may involve the abuse of anabolic steroids (Anderson 2002). These ideas have been popularized in Pope et al.'s (2000) book The Adonis Complex. Pope et al. note that the 'GI Joe' action 'doll' of the 1960s was significantly less muscular than his 1990s successor. The 1960s model, if he stood 5 feet 10 inches tall, would have had a 44 inch chest and 12 inch biceps. The 1990s model, standing at the same height, would have a 55 inch chest and 27 inch biceps. This enlargement of the body was also found for other boys' toys, and often represents dimensions physically unobtainable. Barbie, it would seem, has at last found a man worthy of her own dysmorphia.

Male bodies are now much more to the fore in advertising than previously. For instance, Olivardia (2002) notes that while the proportion of undressed women in women's magazines (such as *Cosmopolitan*) has remained fairly constant over the past three to four decades, the proportion of undressed men shot up from about 3 per cent in the 1950s to 35 per cent in the 1990s. Male mannequins now possess larger genital bulges and more defined muscular build than previously, and – mimicking the changes in female cultural sexual iconic imagery – over the past 25 years the average *Playgirl* centrefold has lost 12 pounds of fat and gained approximately 27 pounds of muscle (Leit *et al.* 2001).

Corson and Andersen (2002: 194) suggest that 'males want to be heavier but see themselves as lighter, and females want to be lighter but see themselves as 10–15 pounds heavier than they really are'. Whatever the direction of body image distortion, they suggest that it is motivated by similar factors: preoccupation with physical appearance, popularity and attractiveness. While females may want to lose weight, males want to lose body fat while maintaining lean muscle mass. It has been argued that the relative empowerment of women in most Western societies has had a consequential disorientating effect on men and that because of their threatened masculinity, they are seeking increasingly to define themselves through what distinguishes them most from woman – their bodies (Olivardia 2002).

I am not suggesting that the difficulties of masculinity arise simply from the relative empowerment of women, but more that the changing nature of gender roles, 'the dying phallus' as Clare (2001) refers to it, can have broad implications. Elsewhere, we have argued that changing cultural contexts, particularly the changing role of young men in many rapidly 'modernizing' countries, are associated with an alarming increase in young male suicide (Smyth *et al.* 2003). This is proving a terribly difficult problem for educators to approach. Recently the Irish government sought effectively to withdraw its 'Exploring Masculinities' programme aimed at 15–16-year-olds, amidst complaints that it was making boys soft and sissy, and might even incline them towards homosexuality!

One reaction to the obscuring of masculinity, as suggested by Olivardia above, is to accentuate it, in terms of musculature. Anabolic steroids (which generally are synthetic forms of testosterone) are now being consumed in a greater variety of forms by more men – and boys – than ever before. While woman may prefer men to have a slightly more muscular than average body physique, an increasing number of men are seeking to outstrip by far this heterosexual 'ideal' in favour of a much more extreme (presumed) muscular male 'ideal'. The physical side effects of steroid use include acne, breast enlargement, liver cancer, arteriosclerosis, mood disturbance and severe aggressiveness (Olivardia 2002). The fact that a study, now 16 years old, found that even then 6 per cent of high school boys reported using steroids before turning 18 (Buckley *et al.* 1988), often not for athletic purposes but purely to sculpture their bodies towards what they conceived of as aesthetic ideals, must surely be of great concern to us.

Cultural change and eating disorders

I have argued that popular culture has had a strong impact on how both men and women view their bodies. Gordon (2000: 1) claims that 'eating disorders are unique among psychiatric disorders in the degree to which social and cultural factors influence their epidemiology, development and perhaps their aetiology'. This is perhaps too conservative a claim in its suggestion of uniqueness, and in only suggesting the possibility of social and cultural factors being implicated in the cause of eating disorders (MacLachlan, in press). However, Gordon's point is to emphasize the rapid acceleration in reports of anorexia from the 1960s through to late 1980s, and also the appearance of the previously unknown condition of bulimia in the late 1970s, and its rise to a position of greater prominence than anorexia in only a few years by the mid 1980s. This 'modern epidemic' of eating disorders, it is suggested, reflects a number of societal forces in the West, such as: the rise of the consumer economy, with its concomitant emphasis on achieving individual satisfaction, often at the expense of more collective goals; increasing fragmentation of the family and intergenerational conflict; and changes in traditional gender roles (Gordon 2000; see also Keel and Klump 2003).

It remains unclear whether the media simply reflect or actually produce the trends in wider culture that seem to impact on our value judgements about our own and other people's bodies. Whatever the cause–effect relationship, it is clear that not all people are affected equally by a culture's somatic iconography. It is likely that those least sure of themselves and their identity – whose self-esteem is more anchored in being accepted by complying with cultural standards, and who experience personal difficulties for situational, constitutional or personality reasons – are most inclined to embark on eating behaviours that lead eventually to disorders of eating. For many women in the latter part of the twentieth century, the possibilities and expectations for high performance and personal achievement often contradicted traditional demands for dependency and submissiveness, resulting in self doubt that, for some, has been channelled into the cult of the physical, and of the less curvaceous (and traditionally feminine) woman's body. Gordon (2000: 3) suggests: 'the contradictions and transitions in female identity represent the most profound basis of eating disorders throughout history and across cultures'. If this is true, how do different 'cultural vocabularies' express such conflict through the symptoms of eating disorders?

While once considered a culture-bound disorder, anorexia nervosa is now recognized in many non–Western countries, perhaps because they have recently undergone rapid industrialization and experienced facets of globalization. Gordon (2002) notes that almost all the countries that had reported instances of eating disorders prior to 1990 were European or North American (with the exception of Japan and Chile), while countries reporting eating disorders since 1990 include Hong Kong, mainland China, South Korea, Singapore, South Africa, Nigeria, Mexico and Argentina. It is instructive to consider cases of anorexia nervosa in Hong Kong because these differed from the typical North-Western cases in several important ways: most were from lower socio-economic levels (as opposed to the middle classes); patients often interpreted their inability to eat as gastric problems (as in bloating) rather than a fear of getting fatter; and the majority of these people did not experience body image distortions, or express body image concerns. The research that Gordon cites was primarily conducted by Sing Lee, but his later research did show a developing concern with body image, even though plumpness is understood to be a sign of health in traditional Chinese culture. This might suggest the interplay of modernist and consumerist forces with more traditionalist values.

In 1999 Lee and Lee reported a study explicitly designed to explore these relationships. They compared eating attitudes among secondary school pupils in Hong Kong (highly Westernized), Shenzhen (an increasingly Westernized city in mainland China) and the Chinese province of Hunan (relatively untouched by Westernization media and fashion trends). Despite students in Hunan having the highest body mass index (BMI) they showed the lowest desire to lose weight. Gordon (2002: 11) suggests that one theme uniting the 'new' countries where eating disorders have been reported is that 'they are either highly developed economies (such as Hong Kong or Singapore) or they are witnessing rapid market changes and their associated impact on the status of women'.

Veiling the body

The symbolic meaning of anorexia nervosa has been much debated and a recent and unusual perspective on it that resonates with the notion of embodiment has been provided by Nasser (1999), who has linked it to the increasing popularity among some Muslim women, particularly in the Arab world, of wearing a veil. Nasser argues that one must look beyond the notion of reactivation of tradition, an Islamic revival or Western stereotypes of veil wearing. She sees the voluntary adoption of the veil by educated working women as a kind of 'veiled resistance' (see also Nasser 2001) to the experience of conflicting gender roles. Nasser notes a similarity between anorexia and veiling in terms of them both being means of reproducing the self through hiding or evading, or of negating the body. In each case the body 'appears to disappear'.

Arguing for a common dialectic between the visible and the invisible, Nasser (1999: 176) notes: 'The ever-diminishing body is clearly disappearing while remaining firmly visible and ironically more noticeable, imparting a clear message through its apparent invisibility.' Both veiling and anorexia may be seen as attempts to establish boundaries around the self through what is perceived as a morally elevated position which encompasses purity and superiority: 'Each woman pursues her externally different but psychologically analogous and culturally approved objective with fanatical and compulsive devotion' (*ibid*.), intertwining self-control with self-discipline, with self-denial, with self-validation. The theme of making something more apparent by obscuring it somehow resonates with the idea of only noticing ability through disability. To embody an idea may be to deny that which ostensibly represents it, and in so doing focus more critically on the idea itself, herself or himself.

Cosmetic surgery

Curtaining off the body may be one way to alter its appearance; cosmetic surgery is another. According to the American Society of Plastic Surgeons over 1.3 million North Americans underwent cosmetic surgery in 2000, and this figure represents a 225 per cent increase on the year 1992. In order of decreasing popularity these included liposuction to remove fat, breast augmentation, blepharoplasty (or eyelid surgery), Botox injections (see Chapter 1) and 'facelifts'. It is often implied that those seeking cosmetic surgery are driven by feelings of personal inadequacy that represent basic neurotic insecurities. In a comprehensive review of the literature Sarwer *et al*. (1998) found that interview-based research on individuals who sought cosmetic surgery indicated some evidence of 'psychopathology', while research conducted using standardized psychometric measures did not. With no obvious reason for these different findings, the 'neurotic-vanity' debate looks set to run. However, what probably can be agreed upon is that cosmetic surgery is a psychological intervention, or, at least, a surgical procedure with psychological consequences.

So what are those consequences? Once again, according to Sarwer (2002), the research is equivocal. Post-operatively some studies indicate slight 'improvement' psychologically, while others report no such changes. However, at the very least it seems reasonable to assume (if somewhat circular) that people motivated to have cosmetic surgery have a higher level of body image dissatisfaction than those who do not consider it. Sarwer and colleagues (2002) found that while people who undergo cosmetic surgery report less dissatisfaction post-operatively with the body part altered by the surgery, they do not report any greater overall body satisfaction as a result of a specific procedure. It would therefore seem that while specific body parts may be a focus of (and embody?) a sense of dissatisfaction, alteration and 'improvement' of that body part still leaves a more diffuse embodiment of dissatisfaction.

Sexual response and dysfunction

Sexuality allows for communication and gratification through the medium of the body. Surely there is no more obvious example of the physical expression of an abstract idea than when a man gets an erection in response to remembering an erotic experience, or indeed anticipating the possibility of one. While women also have plenty of erectile tissue to their credit, it is undeniable that the male's is designed to be more demonstrable. In the space of a few seconds a sexual possibility can be embodied through a series of physical changes that pay scant respect to any notion of mind–body disjunction.

The classic work by Masters and Johnson (1966, 1970) provided a systematic and scientific understanding of the physiology of sexuality, delineating different phases of what they called the sexual response cycle: excitement, plateau, orgasm and resolution. From the point of view of considering how physical changes may embody 'states of mind' let us just consider the excitement phase. Cognitive, sensory, motor or emotional stimulation that produces erotic feelings triggers the excitement phase, where there is a general increase in muscle tension throughout the body and engorgement of blood vessels, particularly those in the genital region. Women experience vaginal lubrication (within 5–15 seconds), thickening of the vaginal walls, flattening and elevation of the labia majora, expansion of the vaginal barrel and elevation of the cervix and uterus. Men experience penile erection (within 3–8 seconds), thickening, flattening and elevation of the scrotum and an elevation and increase in the size of the testicles.

While Masters and Johnson's sexual response cycle may be criticized for its overly physiological focus, its omission of a sexual desire phase and its focus on orgasm as the culmination of sexual arousal (Malatesta and Adams 2001), it remains a fairly accurate, if partial, account of 'normal' sexuality. However, if the engorgement of the penis and its subsequent erection can be seen as a very literal and rapid embodiment of erotic desire, then erectile dysfunction (or impotence as it used to be called) can be similarly seen as an embodiment of anxieties about sexuality. While such men may report feeling sexually aroused, sufficient blood is not pumped to the penis either to create or to maintain an erection sufficient to allow penetrative sex and/or orgasm to be achieved. Although many men may now and again (due to stress, tiredness, alcohol consumption, marijuana use or other factors) experience erectile problems, for some it is a recurrent and long-term problem, for which treatment may be sought.

In many cases, vascular, neurological or hormonal impairments, along with the 'side effects' of prescribed medication, can account for erectile dysfunction. However, nothing seems to create a problem more than a cure. Kaye and Jick (2003) reported that after the introduction of Viagra (seldenafil) to the UK in 1998, the rate of erectile dysfunction doubled over the next two years. Of course many of those seeking Viagra may simply not have come forth prior to its release. It seems likely that for some people who experience erectile dysfunction for psychosocial reasons, the prying of a psychologist into their sex life is more aversive than the disorder itself, and this may have kept them from seeking help. Equally there are probably now many psychosexual problems being held at bay by medication, without their underlying causes being addressed. In sexuality, the subjective and objective relationship to the body may collide in emotion and contradiction.

Bending gender

The importance of biological sex and social gender are becoming increasingly recognized with regard to health. Many genetic, hormonal and metabolic factors shape distinctive male and female patterns of morbidity and mortality (Doyal 2001). While sex-specific diseases such as cancers of the cervix and prostate are very obvious examples, the incidence, symptoms and prognosis of other diseases differ between the sexes. For instance, men seem to have a much greater propensity to develop heart disease early in life. Continuing gender inequalities in income and wealth place women at greater risk of 'disorders of oppression' such as depression and anxiety, disorders for which there is no evidence that women are at greater constitutional risk (Bushfield 2000). While Doyal calls for greater sensitivity to sex and gender in terms of current health research, service delivery and social policy, her concern is with what might pejoratively be called 'normal' sex and gender. Even greater challenges confront us with regard to sex and gender that fall outside our bipolarized norms.

Gender identity disorder, if 'disorder' is what it is, refers to dissatisfaction in one's sense of being either male or female. For most people their gender identity reflects their physical anatomy: those with a penis learn that they are boys and those with a vagina learn that they are girls, and this sense is established from very early on (at about two years of age). Sex roles (masculine and feminine behaviours) are influenced by cultural norms and in many Westernized countries they have changed and indeed merged to a certain extent in recent decades. But sex roles and gender identity are different. Having a certain gender identity may imply the adoption of certain sex roles in particular cultural settings, but the degree of influence that social factors have in gender identity remains controversial, and for some, problematic.

Money (1975) reported the case of a 7-month-old identical twin whose penis was accidentally destroyed during circumcision. Because there was no satisfactory way of replacing his penis, Money recommended that the boy be castrated, an artificial vagina created and the child raised as a girl. In addition to this, at puberty, oestrogen was administered so as to feminize the boy. This 'nurturing' was thus pitted against nature's male genes and prenatal hormones. In 1975 Money reported that at the age of 12 the child was a 'normal female'. This work is often taken as providing strong support for the social-learning theory of gender identity. However, a follow-up by Diamond and Sigmundson (1997), neither of whom were involved in the initial treatment decisions, reported that as a child she tended to act in masculine ways and rebelled against the oestrogen regime she was put on, because she didn't want to develop breasts and refused to wear a bra. At age 14 she decided to live as a male, subsequently requesting a mastectomy (surgical removal of the breasts), phaloplasty (surgical creation of a penis) and androgen treatment. He subsequently married at the age of 25. He is now completely heterosexual, able to ejaculate and experience orgasm, but his early castration destroyed his ability to reproduce.

On the face of it, this long-term follow-up documenting the distress and anguish of a person biologically born male, but forced into a female identity only subsequently to reclaim his manhood, seems to support the primacy of biology over social learning when it comes to gender identity. However, Phillips (2001a) cites another similar case where again a Canadian baby boy suffered the same type of injury and at the age of 7 months was 'surgically remodelled' into a girl. Although Tomboyish as a child, she is now a young woman, who is bisexual but firmly convinced she is a woman.

The term 'transgendered' refers to 'anyone who doesn't conform to the most rigid definitions of male and female, from the teenage boy rebelliously wearing eyeliner and nail polish to the most committed candidate for sex change surgery' (Phillips 2001a: 33). There is also a spectrum of 'intersexed' conditions where up to 1 in 500 people are born with sex chromosomes that don't correspond to their anatomy. It can be argued that transsexualism (where, for instance, a man feels that he is really a woman and therefore has the wrong body for the gender he identifies with) is a type of intersexualism, where the organ at odds with the chromosomes is in fact the brain. Transsexuals, who want to escape a body that does not embody their gendered experience, draw into question both social learning theories (they have been reared in accordance with their biological sex) and hormonal theories (they have the same hormonal complement as other members of their biological sex). However, perhaps the real problem is with the thinking of the sexually conventional rather than the experience of the intersexed. The comfortable dichotomy of male/female (male or female, male versus female) may be more of a social comfort than a biological or phenomenological reality. We make freaks out of what we are scared of, are unfamiliar with or find incomprehensible. Furthermore, while officialdom may be adamant that a child be either male or female on their birth certificate, for some people the reality is that this is a nonsensical distinction.

Phillips (2001b) reports that 1 in every 200 babies in Western countries (more than the number born each year with Down's syndrome) have surgical interventions because their bodies fail to conform to our categories of male and female. The Intersex Society of North America (ISNA) is campaigning against the 'normalization' of babies born with intersex conditions or ambiguous genitalia, because they question the benefit of such interventions and some members give testimony to the associated sexual and emotional difficulties that follow. Just as previously 'treatment' was suggested for homosexuality, which was illegal (and still is in some jurisdictions) and given as a psychiatric diagnosis, it may now be argued that, at least in some cases, surgery for intersexed children is being performed to alleviate the anxieties of parents and society at large, rather than those who are intersexed themselves.

People can be born intersexed as a result of a number of different 'conditions'. These include: congenital adrenal hyperplasia (CAH), where prenatal exposure to androgen hormones masculinizes an XX foetus and may produce ambiguous genitalia; androgen insensitivity syndrome, where the foetus has testes along with an X and a Y chromosome, but its cells don't respond to testosterone, with the result that the baby appears completely female; Klinefelter syndrome, where boys with an extra X chromosome who have masculine genitals develop only limited secondary sexual characteristics at puberty, and may also grow breasts. Some of these, or other conditions that are associated with intersexuality, may of course produce physical problems such as incontinence or persitent urinary tract infections that deserve to be treated in their own right.

What is more controversial is whether a deviation from a clean-cut sexual dichotomy is in-and-of-itself something that should be surgically altered. To the extent that such individuals experience social discomfort because of their sexuality, intervention may be appropriate, but to the extent that such individuals themselves embody social anxiety about gender identity, then more explicit societal recognition and discussion of sexual variation may be the more appropriate intervention. 'Intersexed' should be an identity worth living.

Paraphilias

Paraphilia literally means love (philia) beyond the usual (para). The psychiatric classification system DSM-IV includes under this category sexual masochism, sexual sadism, exhibitionism, voyeurism, frotteurism (sexual arousal through rubbing up against other people), paedophilia fetishism and transvestic fetishism. Beyond objectification of the body as a source of erotic stimulation, most of these conditions are beyond the scope of our immediate concern with embodiment. However, transvestic fetishism is worthy of further consideration in this context. A transvestite enjoys dressing in the clothes of the 'other' gender – cross-dressing. The 'diagnosis' of transvestic fetishism is applied only to heterosexual men. Their behaviour may involve just wearing a single item of women's clothing, such as knickers, underneath male clothing, but usually the person will completely dress as a woman, often including using make-up and jewellery. The person may then masturbate while cross-dressed.

Docter (1988) identified five key characteristics of this behaviour: (a) a heterosexual orientation; (b) sexual arousal to cross-dressing; (c) the cross-dressing is periodic; (d) there is no desire for surgical or hormonal gender reassignment; and (e) gender identity is masculine except when cross-dressed. Transvestic fetishism should therefore not be confused with gay men who wish to dress as 'drag queens' but who do not find the cross-dressing in itself sexually arousing. It is not clear exactly what aspects of cross-dressing are arousing in transvestic fetishism. It may be that the image of the self in women's clothing (either literally in a mirror or figuratively in the 'mind's eye') is arousing because it presents an alternative embodiment of the self: a self that can 'turn on' the self.

Spitzer (2003) has recently published a study on 'homosexual reorientation'. Now, of course, homosexuality has nothing to do with paraphilias, but the reason I mention it in concluding this chapter is that the paper has been met with a hail of criticism. This has probably been somewhat lessened, however, by the fact that it was the same Robert Spitzer who contributed so much to getting homosexuality removed from the DSM classification system as a psychiatric disorder, decades before. Spitzer's paper reports that following 'reparative therapy' the majority of his voluntary participants (143 men and 57 women) changed from predominantly or exclusively homosexual activity to predominantly or exclusively heterosexual activity in the year following therapy. Some have felt that this study was unethical because it implies that a homosexual orientation is something that is suitable for therapy. Others have felt that therapy ought not to be pitted against a natural biological drive. For others again, it merely indicates that even our most basic biological and bodily functions can be shaped by social and psychological means, and that in any case sexual orientation (like gender identity) simply lies along a continuum, along which we may travel.

Chapter summary

1 There is a danger of focusing on 'self-improvement' through changing physical aspects of the body, when in fact self-esteem should be the primary focus.
2 Physiognomy, phrenology and somatotypes were among the early attempts to link physical structure to personality attributes. Although such links have been discredited, modern consumer culture emphasizes the link, perhaps more than ever.
3 Increasingly girls' bodies are being sexualized and encouraged to resemble women's bodies. What sort of body is deemed to be attractive is influenced by cultural and temporal trends. However, the 'ideal' bodies being marketed today, especially through celeb-somas, are often digitized, air-brushed images that, in reality, do not exist.
4 At the same time we are bombarded with a plethora of beauty enhancing, life prolonging, youth making advertisements for products that claim to be able to achieve what we have hitherto been led to believe it not possible.

5 Strangely, at a time when somatic perfection and technological sophistication are so strongly emphasized, the average body is probably further from these ideals than ever before. Obesity is a serious health problem for millions of people in affluent countries, and its effects are greatest among those who are socially and/or economically most marginalized.

6 Attractive – shapely – people benefit not only in terms of immediate health but also by being favoured across a whole raft of social and cultural rewards. For some women their *ideal* body figure preference is thinner than that which they believe is necessarily *sexually attractive*, and their *current* figure is heavier than either of these. Likewise, some men seem to be aspiring to bodies with a higher degree of musculature than they believe is sexually attractive.

7 It is possible that celeb-somas are projecting new cultural norms for bodily form, deviation from which makes people feel dissatisfaction. People may be emulating these bodily forms, even though they do not deem them to be the most attractive.

8 Anorexia nervosa is one example where a preoccupation with the body is taken to an extreme. While there are many different theoretical orientations to explaining and treating this problem, most recognize that distorted experience of the body as an important factor. 'Reverse' anorexia is perhaps also an extreme reaction to the changing roles of men in society and to the increasing uncertainty about masculinity.

9 Eating disorders, particularly anorexia, may be an attempt, like veiling, to make something more apparent (feelings about the body and self) by obscuring it. By diminishing the body, more attention is given to it.

10 Cosmetic surgery may improve satisfaction with the aspect operated on (although not in all cases), but despite this it may still fail to enhance overall body esteem.

11 Sexuality offers clear evidence of how thoughts change physiology and anatomy. The balance between excitement and relaxation in sexual intercourse is delicate and failing to achieve this often produces difficulties. Some forms of treatment objectify the body and establish a schism between the embodied person and the wish for embodiment.

12 The relationship between gender identity and biological sex remains ambiguous. The identification of biological sex is not, however, a binary choice: there are multiple intermediates and additions, and the 'intersexed' are increasingly arguing for their biological (and psychological) authenticity.

13 Paraphilias remind us that sexual satisfaction is not a one-fits-all commodity. Transvestic fetishism presents the intriguing experience of some people being 'turned on' by themselves in the garb of the 'opposite' sex. Sexuality will continue to be one of the most hotly debated aspects of embodiment because of the moral and biological arguments that encircle it.

Discussion points

1 If there is little evidence of a link between somatic form and personality, why is it such a compelling idea?
2 To what extent are cultural forces responsible for making us fat or thin?
3 How mutable are gender and sexuality?

Key reading

Bogin, B. and Loucky, J. (1997) Plasticity, political economy, and physical growth status of Guatemala Maya children living in the United States, *American Journal of Physical Anthropology*, 102: 17–32.
Diamond, M. and Sigmundson, H. K. (1997) Sex reassignment at birth: long-term review and clinical implications, *Archives of Paediatric and Adolescent Medicine*, 151: 298–304.
Gordon, R. A. (2000) *Eating Disorders: Anatomy of a Social Epidemic*, 2nd edn. Oxford: Blackwell.

CHAPTER 5

Illusory body experiences

I'm tired of this, I'm tired of that,
Tired of everything in fact,
Tired of eating such a chore,
Tired of drinking through a straw,
Tired of having no hands at all,
Frustration drives me up the wall,
Can't hug a child nor pat a dog,
Just sit here helpless like a log,
Can't shed a tear unless someone knows,
Cos I can't dry it up and I can't blow my nose,
Can't scratch an itch or rub my head,
And I can't turn over in my bed.
But this does not mean I'm always blue –
What matters the loss of a limb or two?
(An elderly person (name not reported),
cited in Day 1998: 101)

We respond viscerally to the spectre of amputation: it
challenges our own sense of bodily integrity, and conjures
up nightmares of our own dismemberment. We feel an
instinctive sympathetic identification with the amputee by
virtue of our own embodied being, but our identification
frightens us; thus we are drawn toward and repelled by
amputees simultaneously, both feeling and afraid to feel
that we are (or could be) 'just like them'.
(French 1994: 73–4)

'Tis but thy name that is my enemy.
Thou art thyself, though not a Montague.
What's Montague? It is not hand, nor foot
Nor arm, nor face, nor any other part
Belonging to a man. O, be some other name!
What's in a name?
(Juliet, reflecting on her lover being of a family that is her
family's enemy, in Shakespeare's *Romeo and Juliet* 2.2)

While other chapters in this book seek to cover a plethora of 'conditions'
and experiences related to the concept of embodiment, this chapter focuses
much more narrowly on illusory body experiences. These are experiences
of the body that do not appear to coincide with its reality. Probably the best

known of these are phantom limbs. Phantom sensations occur when there is an 'attribution of a sensation to an absent body part' (MacLachlan *et al.* 2003). Most of this chapter is given over to phantom experiences and associated aspects of the rehabilitation of people with these experiences, especially with reference to the use of prostheses. Some of the major thinkers on embodiment, including Merleau-Ponty, have recognized the importance of phantom phenomenon for understanding embodiment, and it is for this reason that we consider them in some depth.

A phantom limb is likely to be experienced after an amputation: the person continues to experience the presence of a limb when all the evidence is to the contrary and they can clearly 'see' for themselves that there is no limb there. They experience a *being-in-the-world*, even when there is nothing there to *be in.* The often accompanying phantom limb pain (PLP) can for some people be excruciatingly painful, last decades and be very disruptive to daily functioning. The understanding and treatment of such pain is also therefore a clinical imperative.

Phantom experiences very greatly. Some, or all, of an absent body part may be experienced and this experience may be painful or pleasurable, or simply of the missing part's presence. Phantoms have been reported after the removal of limbs, breasts, colon and rectum and even teeth. However, they have also been reported without the removal of body parts: in people with spinal cord injury, stroke, lesions of the parietal lobe of the brain, in people born without limbs (congenital limb absence), in some people who have had an anaesthetic 'block' and in people who have suffered avulsion of brachial plexus (when nerves from an arm are ripped from the spinal cord, most commonly in a motor vehicle accident) (see Horgan and MacLachlan 2004 for a review). Below we consider historical, psychological and neurological perspectives of phantom phenomena and illustrate some of the fascinating aspects of this very real and very intriguing problem. We also outline how such phantom phenomena may be turned to the person's advantage.

Deities, fictions and phantoms: a brief history

There is anthropological evidence that people survived amputations as long as 45,000 years ago. Cave paintings in Spain and France, about 36,000 years old, show the imprint of a mutilated hand. Similar paintings in New Mexico suggest that self-mutilation was used to appease the gods as part of religious ceremonies (perhaps a forerunner of circumcision?) In some cultures amputation was feared more than death, as the amputation was believed to affect the person in the afterlife too. Ablated limbs were therefore buried, but then disinterred and reburied when the person with the amputation died, so that they might be whole for the afterlife. Some gods were also amputees: the Peruvian jaguar god Aia Paec was an above elbow amputee; Tezcatlitoca, the Aztec god of creation and vengeance, was a right foot amputee; and the Irish Celtic god New Hah was a left arm amputee with a four-digit silver prosthesis.[1]

While there is much evidence of prostheses being worn in ancient times (by the Egyptians, Greeks and Romans) and during the 'Enlightenment', one of the earliest available accounts of phantom phenomena comes from Ambroise Pare, who in 1552 wrote:

> Verily it is a thing strange and prodigious, which will scarce be credited unless by such who have seen with their own eyes and heard with their own ears, the patients, who have many months after the cutting away of the leg, grievously complained that they yet felt exceedingly great pain of that leg so cut off.
>
> (Cited in Sherman 1997: 72)

Herman (1998) asks why certain phenomena are reported in the medical literature but not others. For instance, he asks, if Galen could report in detail on gout and migraine, then why not on phantom limb pain? Indeed, Pare's description of PLP, although recorded in his momumental ten-volume work, lay dormant for over 300 years. Riddoch (1941) states that Lord Nelson took the phantom fingers he experienced – after having had his arm amputated due to injuries incurred in an unsuccessful attack on Tenerife in 1797 – as direct proof of the existence of the soul. In literature, Captain Ahab, in Melville's *Moby Dick* (1851), has the following exchange with the ship's carpenter who is making him a new 'prosthetic' leg:

> Le ye, carpenter, I dare say thou callest thyself a right good workman-like workman, eh? Well, then, will it speak thoroughly well for thy work, if, when I come to mount this leg thy makest, I shall nevertheless feel another leg in the same identical place with it; that is, carpenter, my old lost leg; the flesh and blood one, I mean. Canst thou not drive that old Adam away?
>
> Truly, sir, I begin to understand somewhat now. Yes, I have heard something curious on that score, sir; how that a dismasted man never entirely loses the feeling of his old spar, but it will still be pricking him at times. May I humbly ask if it really be so, sir?
>
> (Melville 1851: 435)

Herman marvels at how, despite personal and popular awareness of phantom limbs, textbooks of neurology at the time make no reference to the subject. In 1866, an anonymous short story in *Atlantic Monthly* ('The Case of George Dedlow') describes how a young man, who during the American Civil War has both legs severely injured and awakes to ask an orderly to massage his left calf to relieve a cramping pain, then learns that both his legs have been amputated. Subsequently Dedlow attends a séance and summons up his amputated legs. He walks a few steps on them, but then they shorten until he is again walking on 'his stumps'. During the American Civil War amputation was very common, as it was used (in the absence of antibiotics) to prevent gangrene setting in. Five years after 'The Case of George Dedlow' was published, Silas Weir Mitchell (who as it turns out was its author) published his first accounts of PLP in a scientific journal. It is widely presumed that he published the Dedlow case in *Atlantic Monthly* to gauge reaction to the 'risky' (as in 'wacky', not scientifically respectable) suggestion of the existence of the phantom limb phenomenon. This is an illuminating illustration of how the scientific community may not be open to empiricism, unless it is nested in the comfort of well woven established theories. At that time, phantom phenomena simply weren't explicable.

The meaning of limb loss

There is much in the experience of amputation and phantom phenomena that remains elusive to explanation, and there is also much that has to be confronted and navigated through on a personal level by those with limb loss. Before considering the large-scale or 'high-tech' studies that have been conducted in this area, it will be illuminating to consider how the individual, their prosthesis (if they have one fitted) and their pain form a dynamic, integrated, yet differentiated, identity in various different ways at different times. We consider below a man who will be referred to as Colin, who was referred to me for assessment. As it happened, he had also been participating in a study conducted by a colleague who was working with me as a research assistant (Olga Horgan), and so these longitudinal data (five previous assessments) were used to augment my own assessment (certain details have been changed to protect anonymity).

Colin, a 25-year-old block layer's mate, had got his right leg caught in a steel rope, resulting in a crushing injury below the knee, so that this portion of his leg had to be amputated. While he did not appear to be suffering from post-traumatic stress disorder (PTSD), his continued rumination concerning the accident and leg loss reflected his distress and difficulty in coming to terms with these events. He was clearly emotionally affected by the accident and limb loss and even two years after the accident was experiencing clinical levels of anxiety and a borderline depressive state.

The following, highly selected, quotations reflect something of the difficulties he encountered over the two years that we tracked his progress. Five months after his accident, during his first interview with Olga Horgan, Colin described his impressions of his stump and of his phantom pain. Although diminished, this pain persisted despite his continuously being on a fairly hefty dose of pain-killing medication since the accident (Neurontin, 900 milligrams per day, at the time of interview):

my stump, as stumps go, is a very ugly stump.

Q: Why do you think so?

Basically, with most stumps you'll just see a scar. Mine has skin grafts, so it's all home-made. That's the bottom of my old foot there, that's the heel. They actually took it off my old foot, and they sewed it on. And that skin's grafted off this leg here . . .

Q: Do you like to look at it yourself or do you prefer not to look at it?

Sometimes I'm transfixed, nearly. You know, I'll be just staring at it. I can't believe it, like.

Q: You can't believe it's yours?

Yea, yea.

Q: You still don't feel it's part of your body?

Ah, I know it is, but I don't believe it, you know. It's kind of a weird way to phrase it, but in some ways I don't believe that I don't have the leg. You know, I still get shocked if I look down, and it'll take me aback for a second, you know.

Here Colin is expressing his difficulty in coming to terms not just with the emotional aspect of his leg loss but also with the 'mechanical' aspect of how 'bits' of him can be moved about, to make up the stump. There is not only a sense of disbelief at what is *not* there 'when I look down', but also a sense of disorientation regarding what is there – on his stump. Thus the integrity, the 'natural' orderliness, of his body parts has has been disturbed, and possibly along with that his view of himself.

Colin then describes his phantom pain:

Oh, when I first had phantom pain, it was months ago. I was, I think, shortly after the amputation. You know, because when I had the leg and it was still there, there was a lot of pain in the leg and the foot. And, so maybe that's instilled in my head for a little while.

Q: So does the pain that you're experiencing in it now resemble the pain that you had before you lost the foot?

Sometimes, sometimes. I'll get pain in my phantom ankle, I'm not sure that's the correct term. Em, and I had a problem spot on my ankle.

Q: Was that after the accident you had the problem spot?

Yeah. I forgot what it was, it was like a sore basically. But, like right now I have it. It kind of feels like my toes, almost like they're asleep.

Q: And do you feel them right at the stump or is your leg . . .

Right now, its at the stump . . . At the stump, yeah. Kind of toes, feel the toes . . . If I'm wearing the leg [i.e. the prosthesis] they'll go down to the foot. Where the, my new foot is. They'll end up going down there . . .

Q: Can you draw on the diagram where you feel the phantom pain?

That's really about it, toes and ankle. There's also just regular pain, and I won't be able to hit a spot *per se*, but I'll just feel like there's pain.

Q: All over the area?

. . . With that, it'll tend to be just the stump. Because if I'm wearing the limb, a lot of times I won't feel, I won't feel it sometimes. But basically, If I'm wearing the limb or not, it'll just be like a jabbing pain, like I'm being stuck with a big hot poker or something like that.

Colin refers at the beginning of this quotation to 'the leg' and 'the foot', and not 'my leg' or 'my foot', when describing himself before the amputation. It may be that just as they have been physically taken away, he now attempts to place them outside of himself, and in doing so objectifies them. However, he also experiences the prosthetic leg as object – 'the leg' – and the phantom toes, as object ('they' as opposed to my toes), will go down to 'the foot' of the prosthesis (object). But then, reflecting his ambivalence towards the prosthesis, he says, 'where the, my new foot is'. Clearly there is confusion and possibly conflict over how to identify with what has been lost and what has replaced it. While he refers to 'the leg' (meaning the prosthesis), he at the same time accepts ownership of 'my new foot'.

He doesn't know what to call the pain in his phantom ankle. Or even if there is such a thing. He also refers to what may be described as 'pain memory', the idea that pain prior to an amputation is somehow 'instilled in my head' after the painful limb is removed. There are other pains as well, more diffuse, but these may not be felt when wearing the prosthesis. Regardless – and unsure if it is phantom or stump pain – there is still that treacherous pain, 'like I'm being stuck with a big hot poker'.

Four months later, again talking about phantom pain, he says:

There's . . . actual times when I, when it's hard to tell which one is phantom which one is real, yeah. And this stabbing pain could actually be a phantom pain as well, like . . . 'cos it's hard to tell . . . the stabbing pain I'd almost think to be phantom pain, because eh, as far as I know there's nothing wrong with the leg, like, you know, it wasn't like I em, I smacked it against something, 'cos if I do, it'll hurt like, you know, but that just, it wouldn't be, unless I banged it against something, you know.

Here Colin distinguishes between 'phantom' and 'real' pain, seeming to suggest that only if there is something physically 'wrong' with the leg (like it being banged) *should* it hurt. In the second interview (eight months after his accident) Colin was asked whether his feelings towards his prosthesis had changed since he left the hospital as an inpatient:

I have grown accustomed to wearing it and em, maybe I've eh, I don't know, the word 'relationship' isn't really appropriate . . . cos I still think of it as like a tool, kind of thing. But em, you know, it's, it's become part of my day, and having to deal with it every day, yea you just get used to I and, but it's still, it's not really, I don't, don't talk to it or nothing, ha! Or make it coffee!

There is an awkwardness here in the way Colin tries to convey to us alternative impressions of the prosthesis as a 'tool' in one sense, and also something much more personal, that you might talk to. He tries to navigate a mid-line ('you know, it's become part of my day') but almost blows it with 'yea you just get used to I': 'I' and 'it' are interchanged, possibly just in a random slip of speech, or possibly not. He humorously reassures us that he knows it is not a person and doesn't talk to it, or make it coffee! Colin's skilful use of rhetoric and humour is an excellent defence, not just against how he anticipates others will react, but also against his own reactions. The very conversation he is having positions him in a bizarrely 'meta' perspective where he is observing himself, commenting on 'himself'.

When asked about the loss of his leg later in the same interview he says:

I'm still at the point where I feel like a little child having a tantrum, you know, wanting my leg back . . . it brings me down quite often thinking about it . . . it's almost like there's still hope that my leg'll come back. You know, which I know is complete rubbish, like, but it's still kind of there, you know. And I would say in, in time it'll just realize or just see it isn't going to grow back like, you know, you know plant little leg seeds or something . . . its almost, almost like I had this weird idea that if I give up hope of having my leg back, you know, kind of thing, even though I know I'll never have it back, you know, ah, it's almost like I don't want to lose it yet. You know, it em, I never had a . . . I don't know if this has anything to do with anything really, but when I first, em, had, like had it taken off, I was told that they hold on to it for months, you know, and em, you tell them what to do with it, or that eh, just eh burn it up with the rest of the rubbish, which is what they do like, or if they, to burn it and let you have the ashes, or let you actually take it and bury it or whatever like. And em, so at first, I was like you know, 'maybe I'll have the ashes, 'cos I don't want the leg itself', like. 'I'll have the ashes and sprinkle them somewhere', like, you know, just to, after watching these talk shows, you know, the term 'closure', and all this business, like you know. But as it turns out, immediately after the operation, they, they, they em, they burned it with all the rubbish

Q: When did you find out it was gone?

It was em, like a month later, something like that. I thought that em . . . but em, I really wanted it, you know and then, it was almost like em, it wouldn't be near as bad, but its almost like if you lose a friend, kind of thing, and you do, and you know, its almost like, if, if a friend, if a friend of yours or a family member works on a boat, and the boat goes down, and they never find the body, you know, and you don't, you can't really go to a funeral, like, you can't eh, you can't say goodbye kind of thing. You know, I never had a chance to say goodbye, like, so it's almost like 'it's still out there', ha, ha, 'it's hopping its way towards me'. Which is kind of a scary notion, Stephen King kind of thing. But em, yeah, uugh. I, I kind of hated that aspect. I didn't have a chance to do something with it really – whatever.

When Colin says 'it's still kind of there, you know', what we don't know is whether he is referring to the *wishing* that he still had his leg, or to the phantom experience of it being there. He feels like a child having a tantrum and punishes himself for it – 'complete rubbish'. Yet he cannot resist the childlike notion that somehow the leg will grow back, like 'Jack and the Beanstalk', if only he could 'plant little leg seeds'. Again in a child-like magical thinking way, he says that he is not ready to give up hoping it might return, because if he does, he really will have lost it.

Colin then comes out with a phrase every therapist lives for: 'I don't know if this has anything to do with anything really, *but* . . .' He goes on to describe that he had heard that the patient has some say in what happens to their limb; for example, it could be buried or they could – and he uses a very gentle word – 'sprinkle' the ashes. But, almost as a second wrenching of the limb from his being, he hesitates to say that immediately after the operation, in fact, 'they, they, they em, they burned it with all the rubbish'. This is sad punishment, resonating with the, 'complete rubbish', self-punishment of his child-like tantrum.

In the third paragraph, he is out with it: 'I really wanted it'. He compares the experience as being like losing a friend at sea and not having their body to mourn. Even more emphatically, 'I never had a chance to say goodbye'. This incompleteness, this unfinished business, is gruesomely evoked with 'it's still out there, ha, ha, it's hopping its way towards me. Which is kind of a scary notion'. Once again humour – Stephen King – comes to the rescue, of one and all. However, this is not quite sufficient: 'But em, yeah, uugh'.

In the fourth interview (15 months after his accident) Colin was asked if he would agree with some people who describe losing a leg as being like experiencing a bereavement.

> Yeah. I lost a friend of mine. You know, and eh, like a friend that you'd call every day, and talk to every day, you know, rain or shine, and eh, then just one day, they're not there any more. And you still want to call them, and you have to call them, but they're not there. So, you have to talk to a machine instead, kind of, you know. This being the, this being the machine, like [pointing to prosthesis].

Fifteen months after the injury Colin seems to have settled on a complex metaphor linked to the idea of bereavement, but which goes beyond it. He clearly states that 'I lost a friend of mine', on whom he was completely reliant. Colin feels compelled to try to make contact but only gets the mechanical (answering) machine; a semblance of his friend, but not his essence. These few quotations, taken from Olga Horgan's many hours of interviews with this one man, illustrate to some degree the process of navigating a passage between what is 'him' and what is not, what it is reasonable to have emotions about, what wishes are realistic and what he is left with at this stage, two years after his leg loss. Clearly this is no ending. We can hope that his anxious and depressive feelings reduce over time, possibly along with a process of further redefinition of what happened, what is happening now and what will happen in the future. Perhaps in the future, as some others have reported, he may come to feel that he has gained a 'friend'; that the answer phone talks back. A more comprehensive longitudinal analysis of Colin's and many other people's experiences across time, considered from a grounded theory perspective, can be found in Horgan and MacLachlan (submitted).

Characteristics of phantom limb pain (PLP)

People contemplating an amputation to relieve peripheral vascular disorder are sometimes told that although PLP does often occur, it gradually goes away. Such advice may be based on an influential study that reported diminishing PLP over its two-year follow-up (Jensen and Rasmussen, 1994), yet others have reported PLP persisting, at least for some people, over several decades (Sherman and Sherman 1983). Further, clinical folklore often has it that amputations incurred through traumatic injury (for instance, a car accident) are more likely to result in PLP than are 'elective' procedures, where people 'opt' for an amputation to relieve problems associated with a chronic disease (for instance, peripheral vascular disease). However the evidence for this has been inconclusive (Friedmann 1978; Dijkstra *et al.* 2002).

In a recent study of almost a thousand people who had amputations an average of half a century ago (mean of 43.7 years, median of 56 years) we found an incidence of PLP ranging from 94 per cent for amputations due to diabetes down to 70 per cent for amputations due to active combat-related injuries. Across the group as a whole significantly fewer people with 'traumatic' amputations reported PLP than those who had amputations as a result of 'elective' procedures (Desmond and MacLachlan submitted). However, while PLP may persist for many decades it varies considerably in terms of its frequency, duration, intensity and the amount of interference with normal lifestyle it produces. For a small minority it does, however, continue to diminish their quality of life seriously for many decades. The actual pain experienced in PLP has been variously described as stabbing, shooting, burning, tingling, pins-and-needles, itching, throbbing and cramping. Sometimes pain is associated with the amputated part feeling cold or contorted; perhaps assuming an unnatural position (for instance, a hand bent backwards) and sometimes with the feeling of the leg 'jumping' (see Sherman 1997; Horgan and MacLachlan 2004; Desmond and Maclachlan 2004).

Paradoxes of pain

Phantoms are now scientifically 'very respectable' phenomena to have and surf the zeitgeist of neuroscience with alacrity: they are seen as the very manifestation of neural plasticity, at once explainable and mysterious. We will therefore review this perspective on phantom phenomena and then in later sections of the chapter 'pan out' to consider phantoms in broader psychological and rehabilitative context, and review some other examples of illusory body experiences. The contrast between Mitchell's reluctance to go public on phantoms in the nineteenth century and the twenty-first century's race to publish the latest high-resolution images of neural remapping – apparently resulting from amputation – could hardly be greater.

One of the most fundamental neurological distinctions when it comes to pain, any sort of pain, is whether it is 'felt' centrally (in the brain) or peripherally (at the site where it is located). If you bang your finger with a hammer the sensation in your finger stimulates nerves (C-fibres) that travel up your arm to the spinal cord. At the spinal cord sensation is directed upward and onward (through the anterolateral system) by nerves passing through the medulla and midbrain regions, through the thalamic nuclei and ultimately to cortical projections. But where is the pain actually felt? Is it in your finger, or in your brain? The answer to this rather basic question continues to be a puzzle, with some bodily pain having no detectable peripheral injury or pathology and therefore assumed to be more centrally mediated, while other peripheral pains continue to be felt, despite the use of powerful nerve blocks to prevent the transmission of impulses up the spinal cord. Of course, it is very likely that the one mechanism may not underlie all pain experience. Although the consensus is that pain is felt centrally, we must be careful, from the perspective of embodiment, not simply to replace mind–body distinctions with central–peripheral distinctions.

Neurologically, there are three very interesting paradoxes concerning pain (Pinel 2003). First, despite it being so unpleasant, we actually need to be able to experience pain in order to avoid situations that might do us damage. Melzack and Wall (1982) described a woman who was unable to feel any pain whatsoever. As a child she bit off the tip of her tongue when chewing food and suffered third degree burns after kneeling on a radiator to look out a window. Strong electric shock, very hot water and prolonged ice baths produced no sensation of pain or changes in blood pressure, heart rate or respiration rate. She required several orthopaedic operations to relieve pathological changes in her knees, hip and spine that her surgeon attributed to a lack of feedback from these areas. She failed to shift her weight when standing, to turn in her sleep or to avoid certain postures that would be painful after a short time for most people. Sadly, she died at the age of 29 from infections, skin and bone trauma.

A second paradox concerning pain is that although we now know that our sensations are represented in the cortex, pain itself has no obvious cortical representation. For instance, removal of SI and SII (primary and secondary somatosensory cortex) does not appear to be associated with changes in pain threshold, and patients who have had one complete hemisphere removed (hemispherectomized) can still feel pain on both sides of their body. Although both analgesia and hyperalgesia may be produced by central stimulation, it seems unlikely that pain is mediated in the same way as touch, sight or sound (Pinel 2003).

A third paradox of pain is that despite being such an utterly compelling – physical – sensory experience, it can none-the-less be effectively suppressed by emotional and cognitive factors. Such factors can effectively situate pain in contexts that appear to override a simple physical transmission of sensation. Episodic analgesia is said to exist when injury occurs in the absence of the pain normally expected to be associated with it. In such instances, it is not that the people don't feel pain, as in the case described above, but that for a fixed period of time after the injury they are 'pain free', although pain is subsequently experienced.

The example of Indian hook-swinging rituals is now well known. 'Celebrants' have hooks, from which they are suspended, inserted into the small of their back under the skin and muscles. They are then wheeled, swinging supported only by these hooks, through neighbouring villages in order to bless the children and surrounding fields. This ritual is intended to represent the power of the gods (Kosambi 1967: 105) and indeed there is no evidence that the celebrant is in any pain. There are also numerous reports of soldiers receiving severe injuries in battle and reporting no sensation of pain until sometimes hours later.

Melzack and Wall's (1965) gate-control theory suggested that there are descending pathways (from higher to lower levels of a sensory hierarchy, with the highest levels in the brain) that when stimulated can activate a neural mechanism, effectively 'closing the gate' to ascending painful stimuli. The implication is that contextual, cognitive and emotional processing of injury are factors capable of closing the gate to pain through some form of descending analgesic circuitry.

If the state of knowledge regarding pain is incomplete and indeed often insufficient to help many sufferers, this is unfortunately even truer of phantom pain itself (Halbert *et al.* 2002). There is evidence of the involvement of peripheral factors in PLP: for instance, it is associated with stump pain, with percussion of the stump or with stimulation of neuromas (the lumpy, hypersensitive cut ends of nerves). However, it also occurs in the absence of stump pathology and without nerve damage in the case of people born without a limb (see Horgan and MacLachlan 2004; Desmond and MacLachlan 2004, for reviews). Melzack's (1995) 'neuromatrix' theory attempts to account for such findings. It suggests that we have a genetically 'hard-wired' network of neurons from which is created our sense of body awareness, or body schema. Each individual's 'neurosignature' represents their unique experience of their body, generated from habitual patterns of sensing that occur between the thalamus, cortex and limbic system. While this theory may be more of a description of those regions that appear to be involved in phantom sensations than an explanation of how the sensations arise, its notion of a 'neurosignature' that one is born with, may account for why people born with limb loss can still experience phantom pain. Yet if brain cells can demonstrate plasticity, and we can learn that we don't have a leg, why is this not incorporated into a 'modified neurosignature'?

Phantoms in the brain?

Referred sensations are sensations attributed to one part of the body but experienced in a different part of the body. If someone has an arm amputated, parts of that arm may be experienced through stimulating (touching) either the stump area, or bizarrely, the face. Intriguingly, both the stump and face may have mapped on to them the 'plan' of the missing limb as a result of neural plasticity. Thus touching the face on certain 'trigger points' may produce the experience of fingers being touched (see Figure 5.1) and touching the stump may produce similar experiences. The explanation for sensations being referred to the face is that once the limb is amputated the area of the somatosensory cortex normally innervated by the hand has no 'inputs' and effectively becomes vacant. The areas on the somatosensory strip

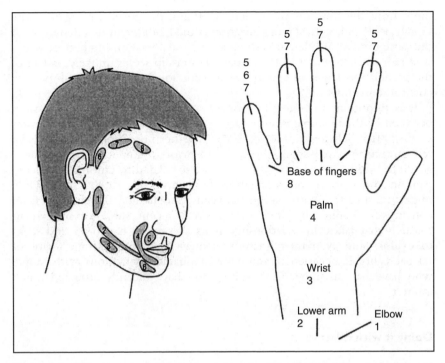

Figure 5.1   The areas depicted on the right side of the face in this patient elicited the precisely localized referred sensations in the phantom hand, shown in supine position (reproduced by permission from Halligan *et al*. 1999)

that border this vacant area (the face) then infringe upon it and provide it with alternative inputs. So while the neural 'image' of the amputated limb remains on the somatosensory strip, it is actually stimulated by inputs from elsewhere. While this remapping occurs rather quickly, it appears to be a transitory phenomenon, diminishing over time. However, of greatest interest here is that the reorganization in both motor and somatosensory cortex following amputation is associated with PLP (see Horgan and MacLachlan 2004).

Flor *et al*. (1995), using neuromagnetic imaging techniques, found a strong relationship ($r = 0.93$) between the extent of cortical reorganization and the extent of phantom limb pain experienced. Birbaumer *et al*. (1997) hypothesized that if pain was reduced by anaesthesia this would lead to a reduction in cortical reorganization. When the stump was anaesthetized, three of the six people with amputations who experienced pain reduction also showed a reduction in cortical reorganization. However, the reasons for this are unclear. First, stump anaesthesia may have reduced input that could have affected the cortical reorganization. Second, the anaesthesia may have eliminated the PLP, which then affected the cortical reorganization. Third, input from the stump may maintain PLP and the cortical reorganization. Finally, PLP and cortical reorganization could be different manifestations of the same process. While establishing a functional relationship between cortical reorganization and PLP, a causal relationship seems unlikely, as half of the participants failed to experience a reduction in phantom limb pain or cortical reorganisation.

It is important to note that not all studies have found a relationship between PLP and somatosensory reorganization (see, for instance, Grusser *et al.* 2001b; Schwenkreis *et al.* 2001). Furthermore, significant levels of reorganization have actually been found prior to amputation (Grusser *et al.* 2001a) and cortical reorganization is also related to chronic and acute pain in the absence of amputation (Knecht *et al.* 1998). Thus while research points to an association between plasticity and PLP, it is far from conclusive. Despite this there has been a recent surge of interest in research that takes this relationship as its theoretical backdrop, and seeks to explore and even treat phantom experiences with various forms of virtual reality. Experimental inductions of 'phantom sensations' with people who have had an upper limb amputation have recently attracted much interest.

Doing it with mirrors

Ramachandran and Rogers-Ramachandran (1996) used a 'mirror box illusion' to treat phantom limb pain. In this procedure, people with an upper limb amputation placed their intact arm into a box with a mirror down the mid-line, so that when viewed from slightly off-centre, the reflection of their arm gave the impression of having two intact arms. There were significant individual differences in the extent to which participants were susceptible to the illusion that the reflected arm was their 'phantom arm'. Of the ten patients the procedure was carried out on, six reported feeling their phantom move when they saw the reflection of their right arm move. For one person, repeated exposure to the mirror box procedure resulted in the experience of the phantom arm telescoping into the stump (as though it was disappearing into the stump leaving only the hand attached to the stump). For four of the five people who experienced painful spasms, the sight of the reflected hand opening up relieved the spasms. For three people, when the right arm was touched, they also felt these sensations on their phantom arm.

It must be noted that not all the people experienced exclusively positive effects. Although PN was relieved of the clenching of her phantom limb, the burning pain she experienced was not affected. RL's spasms were eliminated but his tingling paraesthesias were not. BD could not move his phantom limb with or without the mirror box. Nor did he feel the transferral of sensations from his real arm to his phantom limb, despite the use of the mirror box. Thus, although this technique had quite dramatic therapeutic value for some people, it was only moderately effective, or completely ineffective, for others (See also Brodie, Whyte and Walker 2003).

A second induction of illusory body experience, the Extending Nose Procedure, also described by Ramachandran, produces the illusion of one's nose extending. This sensation is induced by having a volunteer sit in front of a blindfolded participant (both individuals face in the same direction), while the experimenter taps the nose of the participant and manipulates his or her hand to tap the volunteer's nose simultaneously and in synchrony. Although the experience of one's nose extending is not suggested to have any therapeutic value, it is, like the mirror box, thought to relate to neurological mechanisms underlying proprioceptive and somatosensory feedback. This is also true of a third type of induced illusory body experience, the Rubber Hand Procedure, described by Botvinick and Cohen (1998). In this procedure, the illusion that a prosthetic hand is one's own is induced by experiencing the stroking of a prosthetic hand while feeling the synchronized stroking of one's own obscured hand – placed behind a screen, to the side of the prosthetic hand.

Plastic Bodies

An important question arising from these demonstrations is whether the individual differences in susceptibility to these illusory body experiences are associated with other variables. In particular, it seems that each of the induction procedures not only constitute a highly suggestible situation, but also that one's sense of 'body plasticity' (see Chapter 1) might be an equally, if not a more, relevant variable than possible individual differences in neural plasticity. Furthermore, the extent to which one is preoccupied by somatic experiences might also be relevant to the induction of these illusions, such that people highly focused on their bodily experience may be less likely to accept alternative accounts of them. To see if such factors were indeed associated with the occurrence of these 'virtual' embodiments, we implemented the three experimental protocols detailed above with fully able-bodied participants (MacLachlan *et al.* 2003).

We found no association between the extent to which participants had illusory body experiences across the three induction procedures, but scores indicating greater 'body plasticity' were associated with the occurrence of all three illusions. Body plasticity was measured using the Trinity Assessment of Body Plasticity (TABP: Desmond *et al.* 2001), a 20-item questionnaire designed to assess how 'rigidly', or 'fluidly' individuals identify with their somatic body. Low scores reflect the belief that the self is identified with a discrete physical body that should not be altered or interfered with in any way. High scores reflect the contrary belief that self-identity is not restricted to the physical body but that it may include places or objects, that it can be modified and that it does not 'limit' the individual.

It could be that different induction procedures influence different aspects of illusory body experience, and therefore scores on the procedures need not be related. Perhaps it is also the case that people are likely to have illusory body experiences to different extents depending on the mode of presentation and the body part involved. Supporting this is the suggestion that culture and familial rearing influence our awareness of different body parts, and our propensity to feel 'phantoms' in them (Frazier and Kolb 1970; see MacLachlan *et al.* 2003, for a more comprehensive discussion of these findings).

Augmenting reality

In Ramachandran's work it was argued that the therapeutic effects of the mirror box resulted from the presentation of feedback that was consistent with people's actual phantom experiences, and that the removal of the usual contradiction between proprioceptive and somatosensory feedback was therefore in some way beneficial. If this analysis is accurate then a more compelling version of the mirror box illusion may have greater therapeutic benefits. As has already been noted, there is great variability in the experienced authenticity of the mirror box illusion, and in its therapeutic value. One reason for this may be that the mirror necessarily reflects the image of the 'good' intact limb. However, computer-generated 'composite' images of experienced phantoms often differ greatly from that of the limb before amputation, and from the corresponding intact limb (Wright 1996; see Figure 5.2). For instance, in comparison to the original limb, the phantom limb may be shorter, or longer, be continuous or have 'gaps' in it, and have some parts of it thinner or thicker (Wright 1996).

Augmented reality technology could be developed to produce authentic 'phantom limbs' by giving pre-eminence to the person's description of their own phantom experience, and encoding this into the parameters used to generate the virtual phantom image. The production of a virtual limb that corresponds to the experienced phantom in terms of shape, size etc. would allow for greater integration of people's subjective (verbal) description of their experience with a customized visual representation. Figure 5.2 represents how four people who have had amputations have their own idiosyncratic experience of a phantom. Using computer-generated 'composite' images Alexa Wright (1998) has given their phenomenological experience visual representation. It should be clear from these images that the use of virtual and augmented reality could provide a more tangible and accurate way of representing the anomalous phantom perception. Indeed, we have reported a case study describing the successful (but brief) alleviation of phantom pain using a computer-generated virtual mirror (computer screen) image that allowed for asynchronous movement of the intact hand (which wore a data glove) and the 'reflected' image of the phantom hand

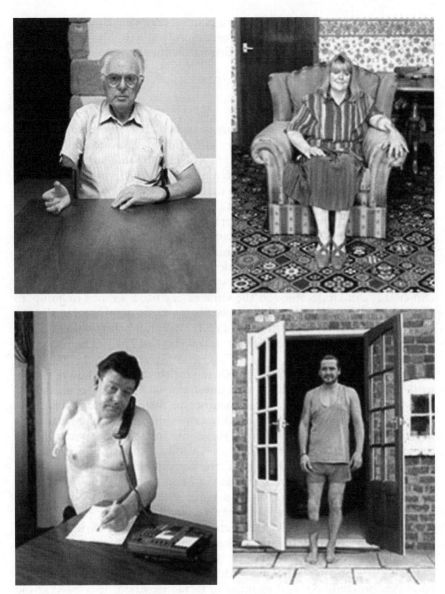

Figure 5.2   Visual representations of phenomenological experiences of phantom limbs (reproduced by permission of Alexa Wright: www.medphys.ucl.ac.uk/ mgi/alexa/alexawright.html))

(MacLachlan *et al.* 2004a). We hope that ultimately a more authentic 'virtual limb' would also provide a more stringent test of Ramachandran's hypothesis that visual feedback (which with virtual reality could coincide with proprioception) may reduce phantom pain by removing the contradiction between these two sources of information and possibly stimulating a reversion of any cortical remapping that had occurred.

What is me?

Based on the Rubber Hand Procedure described above, it would seem that in the event of conflict between information provided through the differing modalities of vision, touch and proprioception, information derived through vision and touch overrules that provided by proprioception. Those who referred the tactile sensations to the rubber hand during the induction procedure also reported that they had a sense of the rubber hand being 'their own'. Admittedly this is hard to accept in the abstract. In my own experience, as I watched the rubber hand being stroked and felt the stroking on the same fingers of my obscured hand, initially I was fully aware that my hand was obscured and it was the prosthetic hand that I could see being stroked. However, less than a minute after this strange procedure started, and without consciously thinking it through, the sense of 'my hand' seemed to 'jump' to the prosthetic hand that I could see. Even being aware of this process did not revert my experience to what it was before the 'jump': the prosthetic hand seemed like 'my hand', although I was aware also that I had a hand obscured behind a screen.

   What you see and what you sense being touched may be the key factors in helping to identify 'what is me'. Interestingly, Graziano et al. (1994), working with monkeys, identified neurons in their premotor cortex that responded to stimulation on the hand, but the same neurons also had receptive fields extending outwards from the tactile field into the space around the hand. In other words, when these cross-modal neurons were activated by visual stimuli delivered near the hand, the corresponding visual representation of the hand was also activated in the brain. We now know that these neurons respond to both tactile and visual stimulation, with their visual receptive fields (those areas that stimulate them) extending outward from their tactile receptive fields (Farne et al. 2000). There is thus very close integration of visual and tactile information in the brain: what you feel is (usually) what you see.

   In an intriguing experiment, Rorden et al. (1999) found that the rubber hand illusion could be used to improve tactile sensations in a 64-year-old man who had severe left spatial neglect and impaired tactile awareness due to intercranial pressure from a large right hemisphere fronto-temporal arachnoid cyst: he only reported being able to feel taps on his left hand when he could actually see the hand being tapped. Prior to surgery, which successfully restored the man's normal sensations, Rorden et al. (1999) obscured the man's hands under a table. They attached a solenoid (a mechanical device that delivers taps) to his left index finger, which had impaired tactile sensitivity. In addition, a pair of rubber hands were placed above the table with a small light attached to the index finger of the left hand. This light flashed regardless of whether a tap was delivered or not, its function being to attract the man's attention. This complex procedure revealed that the patient was able to correctly identify 51 out of 100 taps, significantly more than when the light was attached to the (misaligned) experimenter's finger rather than the rubber finger that had been aligned in a natural position (32 of 100 taps correctly identified). Rorden *et al.* concluded that visual and tactile stimulation interacts more when applied to the same limb. Subsequently, Farne *et al.* (2000) showed that people with right-brain damage, again with left tactile extinction (loss of feeling), can form visual representations of peripersonal space (the space immediately adjacent to a limb) of a rubber hand as if it were their own hand. Their results suggest that people can unwittingly treat a prosthetic body part as if it were a part of their own body as long as it is aligned in a life-like orientation to their body. At a more technical level these results imply that visual–tactile sensory integration occurs in the 'peripersonal' space of an artificial limb, as if it were a personal belonging.

In general, the above experiments support the idea that when visual and proprioceptive information about the body is contradictory, the visual sense predominates. In these experiments people tend to 'feel' what they see. However, in the case of phantom limb sensations it is the other way around: they feel what they don't see. Perhaps for them proprioception is dominant (at least in the absence of salient visual information). As reported, for instance, by Colin (earlier in this chapter), if phantom toes are experienced at the stump end and a prosthetic limb is then put on the stump, the phantom toes may 'go down' to where the prosthetic toes are. Thus when presented with a suitable visual stimulus, phantom sensations may again be dominated by vision.

Schooling the phantom

There is considerable anecdotal evidence that the experience of phantom limbs can be used to, for instance, help people to learn to walk again (Sacks 2002). Sacks suggests that 'one needs a phantom to fit into a prosthesis, like a soul into a body, if one is to adapt fully to the prosthesis'. He also quotes remarks by Kramer commenting on the phantom limb thus: 'Its value to the amputee is enormous. I'm quite certain that no amputee with an artificial lower limb can walk on it satisfactorily until the body-image, in other words the phantom, is incorporated into it' (Sacks 1985: 64).

Not only do some people feel their phantom 'go into' their prosthesis when they put the prosthesis on, but a man interviewed in one of our own studies reported actually being able to get relief from an itch in his phantom ankle by scratching his prosthetic foot. While virtual and augmented reality technology (as described above) may have some potential to alleviate phantom pain, non-painful phantom limb sensations may continue to be experienced. Using such technology, these sensations could be 'schooled' to mimic the movement of the prosthetic limb, helping to coordinate body movement and enhancing the patients' capacity to identify with their prosthesis.

Reaching with electricity

It may be that identification with – embodiment of – a prosthesis is more likely the more 'life-like' its functioning is. In 1982, Campbell had his left arm amputated at the shoulder after discovering he had a rare form of cancer. He quickly returned to work and had a myoprosthetic arm fitted – one controlled by muscle power. Campbell has worn this arm for over 20 years now and he feels a certain emotional attachment to it. However, in other respects he became frustrated by its limitations. Over the past ten years he has therefore participated in the development of the world's first myoelectric prosthetic arm – powered by electricity and capable of much greater movement. The current model not only allows for electronically mediated movement of the whole arm; it has got a rotating wrist and elbow and allows the wearer to reach upward; it also allows for individual finger digit movements (see Gow *et al.* 2001). The mechanical part of the arm is covered with a silicon cosmesis, making the arm look very realistic.

Although the myoelectric prosthesis looks good and can behave in a more authentic fashion, Campbell does not feel it is a part of him in the same way that his original prosthesis was. There are probably several reasons for this, including greater familiarity with his original prosthesis, a greater sense of 'safety' having mastered the original prosthesis and, quite simply, because it does less, there is less to go wrong with it. In addition, Campbell explained that 'the thinking required to make it [the myoelectric prosthesis] work is very different, you have to flick a lot of different areas of your shoulder to make it work, so you're conscious of making it work all the time'.

Campbell believes that if he had had the opportunity to wear the myoelectric prosthesis from the start, it would feel as much 'a part of him' as his original one does.

I asked Campbell: 'What would it take to make the myoelectric prosthesis really feel as if it were a part of you?'

His reply: 'Notice what you're doing, you're talking to me but using your hands to express yourself, you're probably not even aware you're doing it . . . until you are not aware you're doing it [gesticulating with a prosthesis], then you'll never achieve what was lost.'

(Gow *et al.* 2004).

This is a striking response because it brings the biomechanics of prosthetic development and the cognitive neuroscience of vision and proprioception back to our need to understand how a prosthesis can be integrated into the *whole-body experience of being human*; especially the emotional and expressive aspects of it. Through gesticulation we embody the language that conveys our thoughts and as such our body is the vehicle for our *being-in-the-world*. To be-in-a-prosthesis is different from being able to make a prosthesis do life-like things, or make the person momentarily believe it is in fact their limb. Referral of sensation to a visually compelling prosthesis may ultimately be achieved not through experimental 'trickery' but by integrating it directly into the nervous system, allowing for action to be mediated and touch receptors to provide feedback to a brain that affects action, because it is embodied.

If the next stage of development of myoelectrically powered limbs is their incorporation into the nervous system, then instead of micro switches, or pressure pads, being operated through fine movement of the remaining musculature, control could be achieved through directly wiring the prosthesis into the nervous system (see Popovic and Keller 2004 for an example of such a neuroprosthesis). If an arm can be moved not only 'at will', but also without awareness and expressively, and add to this the possibility of incorporating touch sense detection into the finger tips, at what point might the arm become a 'part of me' rather than an external appliance of a 'user'? We are now on the cusp of just such advances in biomedical engineering. If achieved, what then would be the difference between such a prosthesis and a 'real' arm?

Prosthetic embodiment

Chadderton (1983) asks: 'Is there any reason why the amputee should not regard his prosthesis in the same way as he regards other consumer (durable) goods such as automobiles?' I believe that a prosthesis may become more than a mechanical device, it may become psychologically invested into the self, and hence the person's relationship with it may symbolize how they relate to the world: the extent to which their prosthesis embodies their disability and to what extent it embodies their ability. Ramachandran and Blakeslee (1998) suggested that one could think of the whole body as a phantom, but, equally, the body may be construed as a prosthesis. Another participant in one of our studies, a young women who had to have both her legs amputated after she was caught in a fire, described her anguish at having to replace her prosthetic legs as being *more* disturbing than the loss of her own 'original' legs, because at least she didn't know in advance she was going to lose them. For some people, and no doubt to varying extents, a prosthesis can become a 'part of you'. This can be described as 'prosthetic embodiment' (Desmond and MacLachlan 2002).

Grosz (1994) notes that inanimate objects, if touched or if worn on the body for long enough, become extensions of the 'body image sensation'. Experience of amputation engenders disruption of the body image that is subsequently associated with varying degrees of body image alteration. Reconceptualization of body image following amputation requires the incorporation of the loss of the limb as well as probable phantom sensation of the limb, and in some instances the incorporation of prostheses, canes and crutches into the body image (Novotny 1991). This potential for the incorporation of inanimate objects into the body image again reflects the plasticity of the body image.

Perhaps some sense of embodiment could take the form of an emotional identification with, for instance, a wedding ring; or, on the other hand, a functional identification with, for instance, knowing that you will need a wheelchair to go shopping. The instances of 'prosthetic embodiment' described above in some ways incorporate both of these elements: there is a functional as well as an emotional 'attachment', and the boundaries of 'the self' are somewhat ambiguous. This ambiguity is of course salient to the body image.

Body imagery

Schilder (1964) believed that reluctance on the part of someone with an amputation to come to terms with a new body image may account for phantom experiences, and that there is an emotional investment in the missing limb. This, however, according to Schilder can be understood as a positive experience in that the construction of a phantom limb may serve an adaptive function in preserving the body image and the person's sense of self. In essence, a phantom limb minimizes the loss of bodily possibilities that accompany the loss of a limb. As Melzack (1992: 94) notes: 'The patient may try to step off a bed onto the phantom foot or lift a cup with a phantom hand.'

This idea of maintaining a previous bodily experience also fits in with reports of pain felt before the amputation continuing to be felt afterwards in the phantom limb. For instance, one man who had a sliver of wood caught under his fingernail also reported wood under the nail of his phantom finger (White and Sweet 1969). Such 'pain memories' or 'somatic memories' may be consistent with the 'wish' to preserve the last moments of their pre-amputated limb (although why such painful preservation should be sought is unclear to me). The 'body image intercourse' that exists between our ever changing body images would therefore see the fading of a phantom experience as being consistent with the construction (or updating) of a new body image. However, as we have seen above, these images must be very fluid and responsive indeed if influenced by brief experimental manipulations. For Schilder, phantom limbs may represent a more extreme form of what we all struggle with: the need to maintain a coherent body image in the face of our continually changing body and situation. Most profoundly, Schilder suggests that the body itself may be a phantom, a projection ready to materialize in any number of shapes or forms (Schilder 1964: 297).

When a phantom limb is 'seen' in the mirror, the tension between the body and the body image may be resolved. Weiss (1999) interprets Ramachandran's mirror work as

> using the visual image of the amputated limb to 'counter' the resistant body image and to motivate a new (imaginary) construction, one which will successfully negotiate the tension between the desire to get rid of the . . . phantom, and the equally powerful desire to maintain the coherence of the body image.

She goes on to suggest that if

> the phantom limb eventually does disappear . . . [this] should not be understood as the triumph of the body (or the specular image of the body) over the body image, but rather, as the construction of a *new morphological imaginary*, one that offers new sites of projection and identification and new bodily possibilities.
>
> (Weiss 1999: 37, emphasis added)

Identification with the rubber hand, as described above, would also support Schilder's theory that the body is ready to project itself into any number of shapes or forms: hiding the real hand may encourage the 'incorporation' of the prosthetic hand into the body image, in order to maintain the balance between the body and the body image. Of course this is what happens when a prosthesis is donned, and as we have described above, the body image may then realign itself with body appearance, through telescoping of the phantom into the length of the prosthesis. Henry Head in his classic 1920 neurology text stated that:

> It is to the existence of 'schemata' [in the brain] that we owe the power of projecting our recognition of posture, movement and locality beyond the limits of our bodies to the end of some instrument held in the hand. Without them we could not probe with a stick, nor use a spoon unless our eyes were fixed upon the plate. Anything which participates in the conscious movement of our bodies is added to the model of ourselves and becomes part of these schemata.
>
> (Head 1920: 606)

Such schemata may not, however, be permanent, but continuously reconstructed. We may be remaking our bodies, as we, each instant, choose from perhaps a few alternatives, which will only be lived through when the appropriate cues are present: for instance, the phantom limb extending down into the donned prosthetic leg.

Recognition of this phenomenon may have important therapeutic implications. Muraoka *et al.* (1996) reported a fascinating case of a man who had suffered phantom limb pain for 27 years, whom they treated with antidepressants (he also had longstanding PTSD) and hypnosis. During the hypnosis he was encouraged to imagine his phantom limb retracting into his stump. Within three months the phantom limb had contracted to the extent that only two toes and a foot, or at times only a foot-like image at the end of his stump, were experienced. Associated with this hypnotic-induced tele-scoping was a dramatic reduction in pain.

While body imagery clearly has a central role in illusory body experi-ences, its intricate role in people with an amputation has yet to be fully understood. For instance, Noble *et al.* (1954) reported that people judged to be poorly adjusted to their amputation drew their amputated limb either larger or more exaggeratedly on the projective 'draw-a-person test' than those who were judged to have adjusted well to their amputation. In another study, Rybarcyzk *et al.* (1995) found that people with amputations who, when asked to draw an image of their body, drew their body with all limbs intact were significantly more likely to experience PLP than those who drew their body with the amputated limb missing. In each of these studies there is some sense in which people who have had an amputation are representing their relevant limb in a non-veridical fashion, and this represen-tation is associated with greater phantom pain. Not only is the spatial repre-sentation of the limb important, so too may be the characteristics of the prosthesis worn in its place. Thus, Murray and Fox (2002) reported a nega-tive association between body image disturbance and prosthetic satisfaction, and Fisher and Hanspal (1998) have found an association between body image and anxiety, especially in younger people and those who had an amputation as a result of traumatic accidents rather than for vascular disorder (see also Breakey 1997). Panning back further from the conventional clinical neuroscience and body imagery of amputation and phantom experiences, we end by briefly considering the broader context and meaning of these phenomena.

Psychodynamic perspectives

Kolb (1954) suggested that although amputations aroused fantasies of per-sonal mutilation in the amputee, they were repressed because of the hostility and guilt they induced, and thus emotionality in relation to amputation was transformed into phantom limb experiences. Furthermore, the failure to experience such a phantom was seen to be a form of denial (personally, I think this is contrary to how one might expect a phantom to be inter-preted psychodynamically, i.e. perhaps as the 'embodiment' of denial). Sub-sequently Weiss (1958) suggested that when people have an amputation they narcissistically demand to have their limbs back. PLP was understood to serve the unconscious function of conveying the presence of their missing limb. Katz (1993) has argued that PLP cannot be accounted for by a denial mechanism as one does not need to lose a limb to experience a phantom limb (see Melzack and Loeser 1978) and many people who appear to have adapted well to having an amputation continue to report a phantom limb many years later (Simmel 1959; Desmond and MacLachlan, under review; Hill *et al*, 1995). Furthermore, in so far as emotionality is understood to convert psychodynamically into 'negative' bodily or mental states, not all phantoms are experienced negatively: some are not seen as a bother, some are seen as an advantage in learning to walk again for instance and, occasionally, they are experienced as positively pleasurable.

Socio-economic factors

The age at which one receives an amputation is an important factor (Gallagher and MacLachlan 2001). While for a young person a traumatic amputation (for instance, due to a road accident) resulting in limb loss and the accompanying loss of function may represent the loss of life opportunities, for an elderly person with peripheral vascular disorder amputation may offer increased mobility and/or an easing of physical distress (Williamson *et al.* 1994). Gender is another important factor; not only can men and women seek different attributes in a prosthesis (e.g. functionality versus cosmesis), but social reactions to a prosthesis may differ depending on gender (Michael and Bowker 1994). Furthermore, prosthetic provision has been found to vary across different cultural groups in Bosnia and Herzegovina (Burger *et al.* 2004). Weiss and Lindell (1996) reported that Caucasians with amputations had higher intensities of PLP than did non-Caucasians; while use of the 'stiff upper lip' has been described as a coping response among British people with amputations (Parkes 1975; Machin and Williams 1998). Beyond these few observations there has been very little consideration of cultural or contextual influences on the rehabilitation of people with amputations.

Richie *et al.* (2003), working with the Landmine Survivor's Network, investigated the factors that promote or hinder recovery from limb loss across different cultural, societal and economic backgrounds. They conducted open-ended in-depth interviews with participants in six landmined countries (Bosnia, El Salvador, Eritrea, Ethiopia, Jordan and Mozambique). Their sample included 33 survivors of limb loss and 25 immediate family members, as well as clinicians associated with their rehabilitation. The research was guided by the idea that recovery from limb loss depended on three interrelated domains: physical and emotional health, economic integration and social integration. They argued that a well fitting prosthesis was associated with less pain, fewer physical complications and greater 'emotional health', which in turn created the desire to work (economic integration) and to be a part of their community (social integration). Furthermore, being in a supportive family provided them not only with basic necessities for living but also with emotional support, which in turn gave a sense of hope and a stronger desire to integrate. While non-supportive families could also provide the basic necessities for living, they did not provide the necessary emotional support. This resulted in lower 'emotional health' (isolation, depression and suicidal ideation) and a lower desire to integrate socially. Ritchie et al. also found that peer support could facilitate a similar beneficial rehabilitation process to that found with an emotionally supportive family.

At a broader societal level they found that social barriers could result in both a lack of economic opportunity and a lack of accessible transport, each of which contributed to reduced physical and emotional health and thus prohibited the ability of people with amputations from being productive citizens. Ritchie et al. state that 'The ability to be productive and to provide for one's own basic needs and those of one's family was a central and core issue for many survivors.' This ongoing research project will, it is hoped, provide insights into the 'meaning' of limb loss in different cultures and how these social constructions relate to the practicalities of rehabilitation. One well known example of this is the study by French, who argues that 'even the most apparently subjective personal experience – the experience of one's own body – is shaped in important ways by the relations of power and domination in which the body is involved' (French 1994: 69). Working on the Thai–Cambodia border between 1989 and 1991, French was based in a site where amputations due to landmine explosions were ubiquitous. French wondered what the impact of living amidst so many mutilated bodies must be and how these bodies were 'read'. While initially looking to psychological and culturally constructed meanings to interpret what she observed, French found that such an interpretation could not be divorced from the political, economic, historical and spiritual context through which people with amputations lived.

French had also expected to find that people with amputations were an 'inexorable' reminder of the war and that their physical presence generated a compassionate Buddhist response. Instead she found that people with amputations did not elicit general anxiety about the war, but a specific anxiety about personal safety: 'people were afraid of them'. Particularly among the young males (mostly former soldiers) with limb loss, a reputation for violence, extortion and theft had been established, and they were invariably looked down upon; they were rarely regarded with compassion. Their own overriding sense was one of degradation and abandonment, by each of their families, leaders and society as a whole. At the crux of French's analysis, as it applies to our interest in embodiment here, is the idea that while we have personal experience as individuals, *what* we experience is socially and culturally mediated. To follow through this point, I can only abstract in the briefest manner from French's compelling, but lengthy, analysis. For instance, the Theravada Buddhist hierarchy of merit, or virtue, and its relationship to ideas of karma and reincarnation, were an important factor. Each being is believed to occupy a position in an order of merit that reflects the sum of their actions, stretching back across their previous reincarnations.

From earthworms up to the Buddha, we accumulate or lose merit according to our moral behaviour (or lack of it). Karmaric status therefore determines if we are rich or poor, crippled or able-bodied and so on. You and I are lucky to be born human, as this puts us fairly well 'up there', but of course within humanity there is a 'virtue pecking order', with the fully able-bodied being more perfect and having higher moral virtue than the disabled. To be born able-bodied and then to lose a limb is 'a drop in value', it reflects a 'rapid downturn in one's fortune, a sudden and inauspicious ripening of one's karma, or destiny. It does not bode well for the future' (French 1994: 81–2). While such a cultural interpretation effectively stigmatized those with amputations, French also argues that the reality of their context had much to do with the lack of compassion towards them:

> they were former soldiers with plenty of reason for anger and despair: their employment opportunities were limited but they had just as much need as anyone else for an income; they were likely to take what they needed if there was no other way to get it.
>
> (French 1994: 81–2)

We began this chapter by considering not only that pain is associated with amputation, a phenomenologically interesting experience, but also that the development of effective methods to treat such pain and associated disability is a clinical imperative. With something as 'sharp' and immediate as pain it is easy to assume that equally 'sharply focused' clinical interventions are the way forward. While these are welcome, it has been argued here that they are in fact insufficient, as the experience of amputation impacts much more broadly than on neural plasticity, pain-gating mechanisms or individualized psychological interventions. This is very clearly demonstrated in Husum et al.'s (2002) study on chronic pain in land mine accident survivors in Cambodia and Kurdistan. They found that pre-injury trauma exposure, the severity of the actual trauma experienced in the land mine injury (in terms of anatomical and physiological damage) and the quality of medical care (including amputation stump quality and wound infection) received following the trauma were *unrelated* to subsequent pain (both stump/residual pain and phantom pain). Only the *economic impact* of the injury was associated with the extent of chronic pain: only the consequences of the injury in terms of the person's ability to earn a living (for themselves and/or others) was associated with pain. This is a sobering reminder for us: while the gap between virtual limbs and 'virtue' limbs may seem great indeed, both high-tech and spiritual 'readings' of the body must remain grounded in our need to *live through* the body.

Chapter summary

1 Phantom sensations vary greatly across individuals. Although they are a relatively recent addition to 'respectable' scientific literature they have probably been experienced for many centuries and possibly thousands of years. Some of our earliest insights to phantom phenomenon come from prose.

2 Individuals' understanding of their phantom experiences, feelings about limb loss and relationship to their prosthetic limb are likely to change over time and constitute a dynamic of self–other identification and rejection.

3 Phantom pain incorporates all the mystery and paradox of pain in general, with the additional 'insult to injury' of its apparent impossibility. Contrary to what has been widely assumed, phantom pain may persist over many decades.

4 Research has clearly established a relationship between neural plasticity, in the form of somatosensory reorganization, and phantom pain. Whether this relationship has causal significance remains to be demonstrated but is a promising area of enquiry.

5 The use of the mirror box with people who have had an arm amputated has proved successful in diminishing phantom pain only in a minority of cases. Research on various techniques for inducing illusory body experiences has found that the degree of body plasticity is associated with the success of each of them.

6 Virtual and augmented reality versions of the mirror box may allow for a phenomenologically compelling and more therapeutically convincing test of the original hypothesis it was used to investigate: that the matching of visual and proprioceptive feedback would be helpful in reducing phantom pain.

7 Induction procedures not only produce subjective experience of, for instance, a rubber hand being one's own, but the 'peripersonal' space surrounding the rubber hand is also unwittingly treated similarly to that surrounding one's biological hand. Similarly, phantom experiences may change to correspond to the visual and tactile experience produced by wearing a prosthesis.

8 The development of myoelectrical limbs has allowed for much greater freedom of movement, but also requires greater conscious control. Embodiment through a prosthesis may be conceptualized as an ability to use the prosthesis expressively (as in gesticulation) without conscious awareness of its movement. Equally, however, embodiment may be apparent through some people's reluctance to part with their 'old prosthesis' because of an emotional attachment to it.

9 The body image of someone with an amputation may be ambiguous as they try to understand contradictory experiences of their body. Dissatisfaction with body image may be associated with significant distress. Body image may be frequently updated in the fully able-bodied with a

preparedness to 'project itself' on to any number of shapes and forms. For those who experience phantom sensations these experiences may be confusing.

10 While psychodynamic perspectives on phantom sensations have not been greatly illuminating they have often been the only psychosocially orientated explanations offered. Cultural factors indicate that the way in which limb loss is 'read' is likely to influence not just body image but general self-esteem, feelings of social value and opportunities for positive social roles. Some cultural/religious interpretations may further stigmatize those with amputations.

11 One of the greatest difficulties with phantom or stump pain is predicting who will experience it to a distressing extent. Recent research in post-conflict situations suggests that the economic consequences of limb loss are strongly associated with such pain. Such findings call for a synthesis of mechanistic, psychosocial and socio-economic perspectives on illusory bodily experiences.

Discussion points

1 To what extent may the human body be considered a prosthesis?
2 What other 'readings' of Colin's limb loss may be offered from the one outlined in this chapter?
3 Who is being 'tricked' in illusory body induction procedures and how can they best be explained?

Key reading

Farne, A., Pavani, F., Meneghello, F. and Ladavas, E. (2000) Left tactile extinction following visual stimulation of a rubber hand, *Brain*, 123: 2350–60.
French, L. (1994) The political economy of injury and compassion: amputees on the Thai–Cambodia border, in T. Csordas (ed.) *Embodiment and Experience: The Existential Ground of Culture and Self.* Cambridge: Cambridge University Press.
Gallagher, P. (2004) Psychological adjustment to amputation, *Disability and Rehabilitation*, Special Issue. Includes a substantial literature review by Horgan and MacLachlan giving more detail of areas covered in this chapter.
Gow, D., MacLachlan, M. and Aird, C. (2004) Reaching with electricity: externally powered prosthetics and embodiment, in M. MacLachlan and P. Gallagher (eds) *Enabling Technologies: Body Image and Body Function.* Edinburgh: Churchill Livingston.

Note

1 Prosthetic history page at Northwestern University: http://www.nupoc. nwu.edu/prosHistory.html

Enabling technologies

An impersonal and scientific knowledge of the structure of
our bodies is the surest safeguard against prurient curiosity
and lascivious gloating.

(Marie Stopes, *Married Love*, 1918)

Your heart lies at the centre of a 96,000 km (60,000
miles) network of blood vessels. If all these vessels were
laid out end to end, they would stretch almost two and a
half times around the earth's circumference . . . The human
heart pumps an amazing 7200 litres (1600 gallons) of
blood around the body each day – enough to fill a small
swimming pool.

(Reader's Digest, *The Heart and
Circulatory System*, 2001: 9, 12)

Our body is a machine for living. It is so organised for
that, it is its nature. Let life go on in it unhindered and
let it defend itself, it will more than if you paralyse it by
encumbering it with remedies.

(Lev Tolstoy, *War and Peace*, 1863–9)

The body as a machine

The minutiae of biological detail about the human body at once both
astound us and estrange us from those very bodies. How can it be that your
100 billion brain cells, each with about 1000 connections to other neurons,
are a part of the same self that you usually experience in an coherent,
integrated and continuous way? For that matter, how can you possibly
stretch yourself once around the world, never mind your entrails making it
around two and a half times? It is clear that not only is the human body
fantastically complex, but we in our everyday *being* are quite estranged from
its workings, at least when it is working. Indeed, it can be difficult not to see
the heart as simply a brilliant *machine*, albeit one that can embody our
palpitating emotions or our sense of physical exhaustion – 'I don't think I'm
going to manage all 7200 litres today folks.'

With the vast array of innovative technologies that can enable people to
overcome many difficulties it is tempting to think of the human body as a
sort of master computer, with numerous 'ports' that gadgets and gismos can
be plugged into, in series, or in parallel, in order to compensate for whatever
'you' are missing. Much of the technology used today in clinical settings is

beyond the ken of most of us using it. Technology, like the body, is taken as an act of faith, with converts 'linking-up' users and appliances. One could imagine a situation where to ask a patient how they feel about their dialysis machine could be almost as ridiculous as asking them how they feel about the 96,000 km of blood vessels busily at work inside of them. Sure, how would they know? Taken to extremes the person – 'you' – becomes only an interface between *a biological wonder* on the one hand and a *technological wonder* on the other hand.

Biotechnology can lead us to objectify and depersonalize those it is intended to benefit: recently a nurse walked into a patient's private room in a Dublin hospital, conscientiously and professionally checked the monitors above the bed and to each side of it, and strode towards the door; the patient, of whom these machines gave some impression, barked 'Hey, I'm fine too!' However, not only can technology lead us literally to overlook those it is intended to benefit, it can also lead us to think of people through the lowest common biological denominator – reductionism. Apparently there are more cell meeting points in the human brain (100,000 billion) than there are stars in the galaxy. This is certainly mind-boggling information, especially when it is presented without meaning. Of course, there is nothing wrong with reductionism *per se*, but it is insufficient to explain life, it is only partial. Perhaps what makes it *feel wrong* to many people is that it offers explanations at an explanatory level that do not coincide with people's experience of the world. So, for instance, if we take Donne's famous lines:

Do not ask for whom the bell tolls,
It tolls for you.

we could be astounded because the probability of each letter following the previous one in the sequence that they do is inconceivably small ($1/26 \times 1/26 \times 1/26 \times 1/26$ etc.) and I suppose we would end up somewhere in the billionths. However, to be impressed by such a statistic would indeed be folly, not because it is untrue, but because we live in a world of meaning, and we comprehend things because they appeal to that world of meaning. Perhaps it is often because the meanings we give to the biological world do not in fact accord with our conscious experience that we are estranged by its 'facts'.

In a *National Geographic* article on skin, Joel Swerdlow (2002) describes in fascinating detail how the skin 'works' and how it can be reworked in the case of people who suffer with burns or various skin disorders. In addition to this explication of the 'nanoscience' of the skin's structure and function, Swerdlow also sensitively and lovingly tells us of the visit he made to his 86-year-old mother who was in hospital after collapsing. The doctors had informed him that she might not be able to see or hear him:

I try to comfort her by talking, singing songs from my childhood, or just sitting quietly. I'm not sure what she can sense, but her skin feels warm and normal. I keep my fingers on her arm or cheek, anything to let her know that she is not alone and that she is loved. I realize that our only unbroken connection now is through touch. We are skin to skin, warmth to warmth. According to the textbooks, transduction within the skin is transforming physical energy to neural energy. But something far more important is occurring. Love and memory are flowing through my skin and into her dreams.

(Swerdlow 2002: 61)

These words nicely convey how a reductionist perspective on our biology is only partial, because biological existence has social meaning. Similarly with biotechnologies, a purely mechanistic rendering of their wonderment fails to convey their impact on the personal and social world of their users.

Technology for people

The Institute on Disability and Rehabilitation Research within the US Department of Education lists over 18,000 types of assistive technology that are currently available. However, Scherer and Galvin (1996) suggest that about one in three of all devices provided are abandoned by their intended users, primarily because there is a lack of consumer involvement in the selection of the technology. Scherer (2000) calls for a greater focus on the unique user of a particular device. If the twentieth century's ethos of technology was 'people-focused', meaning that it was directed at providing technology to meet the needs of people with different types of 'collective problems' (e.g. wheel chairs for immobility), then the twenty-first century's technology should be 'person-focused', where more attention is given to the unique circumstances and needs of particular users (Scherer 2002), to their social worlds.

'Professionals have tended to define goals achieved (e.g. independence) in terms of *physical functioning*, whereas consumers more often equate independence with *social and personal freedoms*' (Scherer 2002: 3, italics added). We are too used to thinking of biotechnology as 'fixing' physical problems, rather than as 'overcoming' social problems. As Craddock and McCormack (2002: 160) state:

The social model is concerned with how society responds to disability; the emphasis is not on the disability but on the barriers that exist in society that prevents the person from achieving his or her potential. This approach reverses the medical model focus from the disability to the client. Disability researchers have challenged this [medical] model, arguing that it does not usefully explain disability and that it has a profound effect on the self-identity of many people with disabilities who have considered themselves to be ill, rather than merely living with one or more functional limitations.

While it has been important to acknowledge the value of the consumer's perspective, with its emphasis on empowering those who are disabled, it is not the focus of this chapter.

Technology, disability and constructing meaning

Much has been written on the interface of technologies and the human body, but most of this has been with regard to bodies that are free of physical disability, with these 'techno-bodies' (Balsalmo 1995) representing enhanced functioning – super-bodies. We need to develop a greater understanding of how technology, intended to assist those who are disabled, affects people more broadly. Lupton and Seymour (2000) set out to explore the ways in which technologies contribute to the meanings and experiences of the 'lived body/self'. They argue that

> By augmenting or substituting particular bodily functions and transcending time and space, new technologies offer people with disabilities the possibility of facilitating entry and participation in previously inaccessible activities and domains . . . However, technologies also bear with them negative meanings and implications . . . technologies may be offensively represented as 'corrective' to or 'normalisation' of impairment, or as allowing people to 'overcome' their impairments.
>
> (Lupton and Seymour 2000: 1853)

The rationale for technology being used to 'make something better' is reasonable and this rationale may be applied to 'able-bodied' and 'disabled-bodied' people equally, whether it be wheelchairs or spectacles. However, it is when technology's role is cast as making up for a deficit (a deficient person), rather than achieving a goal, that the application of technologies can be disempowering.

The most commonly identified positive attributes of technology from the disabled user's perspective, reported in Lupton and Seymour's (2000) interviews, were communication with others, mobility, physical safety, personal autonomy, control over one's body and life, independence, competence, confidence, the ability to engage in the workforce and participation in the wider community. Magie, a 24-year-old woman with a visual disability, described how technology can give a sense of connectedness: 'It gives you a sense of, you're actually a real person and you actually have a brain yourself. It's a sense of reality, it gives you a sense that you're living in the real world. So it gives you that sense of first freedom from your isolation' (Lupton and Seymour 2000: 1856). Another participant, Tom, illustrated concern about how technology can work against its intentions by being stigmatizing and how alternative technology can overcome this:

I think its not so much technology as what the technology refers back to the user of the technology. That is, as soon as you pull out a long white cane, then people start making assumptions, sometimes right, sometimes wrong, about your level of vision, about your level of intelligence or sorts of things like that, sort of indirect associations that are formed. And you know, I think the best example is something where that does not happen, like the little [electronic] business memo that I use. I have to explain to people 'Look I'll just take a note of this. I'm going to speak into my business memo'. People think 'Gee, that's really cool', you know because anyone can use that, its not specially related to people with disability.

(Lupton and Seymour 2000: 1858)

This theme of wanting technology that has positive value for the person using it – because it is good to use such a thing – is important.

What could be called the 'negatively distinguishing' feature of, for instance, a wheelchair was raised as a concern by many people. Likewise, several people with cerebral palsy described the intrusiveness of using a communication board (where a pointing device selects letters in order to spell out words rather than speaking them). Ron argued that: 'I can go into a party [in a wheelchair] and I'm Ron, but if I took a computer in there or a communicator I'd be viewed as Ron and the computer, or Ron and the communicator' (Lupton and Seymour 2000: 1859). A further theme that arose from Lupton and Seymour's interviews with disabled people was the way in which breakdown of technology places users in a predicament, whereby the feelings of autonomy, self-control, independence and normality facilitated by technology are undermined by the reality of their dependence on the technology.

This sense of dependence on technology can foster resentment. Technology can thus both exacerbate disability and at the same time enhance feelings of self-worth and add to one's abilities. By being so useful, technology can accentuate how 'useless' you are without it. To use some technologies can therefore be experienced as becoming 'entrapped within a framework of meaning, that suggested helplessness, dependence, and above all, difference, try as the participants might to resist or reframe these meanings' (Lupton and Seymour 2000: 1861). Overall, in Lupton and Seymour's study, the two broad ways in which technology was conceptualized were as (a) being a tool that assisted bodily functioning and (b) being a means of experiencing and presenting the self to others.

Ways of being with technology

Biotechnologies create opportunities for the increased medicalization of problems because they offer more possibilities for expert interventions into the human body. Yet it is important to recognize that biotechnology is not synonymous with a single ideological stance and that it is necessary to reach beyond a simplistic technophilia versus technophobia clash:

> The celebratory rhetoric about biotechnology fits the "philia" slot: the confident hope that technologies will ameliorate the human condition and decrease pain and suffering. Unfortunately, the critique of ideology can easily slip into the phobia, that is, the dystopian fear that technology uniformly strengthens certain forms of domination and destroys the subject's autonomy.
>
> (Brodwin 2000: 5)

Brodwin goes on to suggest that those of us caught up in the 'biotechnological embrace' have some of our most implicit assumptions questioned: distinctions between humans and machines; between kin and non-kin; between male and female; and between nature and culture. Issues such as transplanting human and animal organs, the implantation of a wholly synthetic heart and the development of fully myoelectrically powered limbs are exciting, not just because of their description of technological innovations, but because they raise our natural anxieties over being able to distinguish what is 'me' from what is 'not me'; what is human from what is not human.

Enabling technologies also empower certain understandings of disabled experience. Nelson (2000) describes the case of a five and a half month old boy with nemaline rod myopathy – a rare and progressive neuromuscular disease that renders a person immobile. Breathing off a ventilator and being fed directly through a tube into his stomach, Michael had been transferred from the intensive care unit to the 'low tech' ward, where the idea was that the family would be trained in managing his home-ventilation unit. However, Michael's mother wanted him to be taken off the ventilator; she interpreted his tears as a sign of his suffering and the ventilator as 'something other than Michael: as a threat, as an invasion of his body, as something foreign' (Nelson 2000: 211). On the other hand, the staff on the ward saw his tears as a natural result of his inability to close his eyes and believed that there were other indications that he was able to experience pleasure and contentment.

The staff saw Michael as simultaneously body and machine and in refusing to turn it off, claimed greater authority over how to 'read' Michael's experience. This heart-wrenching example illustrates how enabling technologies may indeed privilege certain interpretations of experience and how the boundary between 'me-and-machine' can become obscured. It also sadly illustrates that technological capability may bring us no closer to 'truth', no more able to identify 'right' and 'wrong'. Indeed, enabling life often intensifies the anguish of its loss, symbolic or physical. People's experience of technology is not neutral; it can often be confusing, sometimes threatening and frequently emotional (see the section on ICU syndrome later). While all these technologies influence body functioning in some form or other (and this is obvious), what is perhaps less obvious is their influence over how we see ourselves. In offering alternative ways in which people can function or overcome different problems, enabling technologies offer different images of not just these issues, but also the people who encounter them.

Levels of technological engagement

MacLachlan and Gallagher (2004) have recently edited a volume that considers the relationship between body image and body function in the context of enabling technologies. We distinguish four ways in which people encounter technology within the rehabilitation field. *Interacting with technology* involves people using technology while retaining their bodily independence. The technology is an adjunct to their usual experience. *Listening to the body* concerns the use of technologies to monitor what is naturally going on in the body and then to use this activity for therapeutic advantage. *Technology of replacement* is concerned with the ways in which parts or functions of the body can be replaced and incorporated into a new body image. *Living through technology* is concerned with ways in which technology 'takes over' bodily functioning, where people have to, quite literally, 'live through' the technology. These four ways, or levels, of technological encounter are not meant to be either comprehensive or mutually exclusive, but are simply descriptive of the scope of technology in use.

An example of *interacting with technology* can be found in Stokes's (2004) description of the European *GENTLE/s* project concerned with robot-mediated therapy for the movement of the upper limb of people with stroke. The robot-mediated therapy delivers exercise-based interventions that enable the patient to carry out repetitive and meaningful movements individually tailored and set up in the robot by the therapist. Part of this technology is the use of virtual rooms where everyday tasks are simulated as a means of stimulating movement that mirrors everyday requirements. Preliminary results are favourable (see Stokes 2004) and given the high incidence of stroke and the associated acquired disability this is surely a worthwhile avenue to explore. None the less, the spectre of robot-mediated therapy may not be acceptable to all.

Perhaps one of the best known examples of technology *listening to the body* is the use of biofeedback. Sherman (2004) surveys the tools available to people to control their own physiology. Biofeedback enhances people's awareness of their psychophysiological functioning by recording what is going on inside the body and representing this outside the body, usually on a screen as visual feedback or as auditory feedback. Today biofeedback is used in a broad range of conditions from tension headaches to irritable bowel syndrome to drug addiction and alcoholism. It is a curious technology in that it at once makes us very familiar with our body's functioning and how this links to our thoughts and feelings, yet at the same time it can be seen to 'objectify' the body.

Technology of replacement describes the situation where body parts are replaced. Often this may be though some form of transplant, but recently developments in whole-organ replacement have spawned development of a viable artificial heart. Dowling (2004) describes the AbioCor implantable replacement heart system, currently undergoing clinical trials, which was first implanted in a human in 2001. Given the symbolism of the heart, how an individual responds to such a device and what affect, if any, it has on their body and self-image, research on this might provide fascinating insights into mind–body issues. Unlike with other artificial hearts there is no need for percutaneous lines or access, which can lead to infection and a negative impact on mobility and quality of life. Instead, energy transfer across the skin to power the device has been accomplished with inductive coupling, thus diminishing the sense of being 'linked up'.

Living through technology is exemplified by the development of a neuroprosthesis that applies short, low intensity electrical pulses to a paralysed muscle to cause the muscles to contract on demand. By stimulating a desired group of muscles and by properly sequencing their contractions, a neuroprosthesis can generate functions such as hand opening and closing, standing up and walking (Popovic and Keller 2004). Such technology is a lifeline of hope for people who experience paralysis, and significant research effort is currently being expended in the area. Popovic and Keller (2004) discuss their Complex Motion system, which is especially designed for rehabilitation treatments administered during early rehabilitation (for example, immediately after stroke or spinal cord injury). This technology quite literally brings the immobilized body back to life through electrical impulses that can be controlled by the user. If our sense of being is indeed so tied to the conduit of our body, what happens when the body is disabled and then re-enabled by technology?

To what extent do technologies that we interact with, listen with, use to replace our parts or actually live through ultimately become a 'concrete expression of an abstract idea', where that idea is the idea of self? Some technologies remain 'foreign' objects that the body is connected to like a computer with various 'ports', while other technologies become such a familiar part of the way in which we live, solve problems and communicate with each other that they effectively become a part of our *being-in-the-world?*

Technology can re-enable us and perhaps even *super-enable* us. However, the excitement and anxiety of such technological redefinition of the self should be guided by remembering that technologies, like skin, can be a barrier. Technologies, like skin, should not just be seen as a way of facilitating transduction when two people touch. We must aim for technologies that take us closer to Joel Swerdlow's experience with his mother: 'Love and memory are flowing through my skin and into her dreams'. Enabling technologies that allow people emotional and affectionate embodiment will allow them to feel, as the rest of us intuitively do, that they are more than the sum of their technological or biological marvels. Clearly a comprehensive review of the implications of technology for embodiment is beyond our scope here, so in the remainder of this chapter we will consider only a few select areas. We will consider technologies of reproduction, organ transplantation and virtual reality, and reflect on the idea of 'technological enframing'.

Perhaps one of the realms in which the application of modern technology has had the greatest impact on how we think about embodiment is that of reproduction. Louise Brown, the world's first 'test tube' baby, born in England in 1978, arrived despite concerns about the morality of conception outside the body, and calls to have the technology banned. IVF (*in vitro* fertilization) has since that time spawned close to a million babies (Trefil 2001). It involves removing eggs from a woman's ovaries and fertilizing them with sperm in a laboratory. After cell division the resulting embryos are then inserted into the woman's uterus, where, it is hoped, one of them will grow into a baby. If, for some people, this marvellous technological feat questions the morality of procreation, then with more recent advances it also questions the notion of parenthood: as many as five adults can claim 'parenthood' in the IVF scenario. These could include the sperm donor, the egg donor, a surrogate who carries the foetus and the couple who wish for such a baby (Trefil 2001). No matter how wonderful the technological achievement, technology is rarely neutral in its effects on people: if it represents a gain for someone in some way, it often also represents a loss for others, in different ways.

One of the most challenging issues in the technology of our reproduction is what these technologies mean for how we understand the human body, particularly the *female body*. Historically in Western cultures child labour and things obstetrical were the domain of women: men would be ushered out of the room in the house that was to be used to give birth, doors firmly closed, as if with 'Women at Work' signs dangling from the door knob. This has all changed with the medicalization and technologicalization of pregnancy, gestation and labour – now that sign is much more likely to read 'Men at Work' and perhaps implicit in much of this is even an attempt to usher the woman's body out the door.

Monitoring the production line

Taylor (2000) undertook an ethnographic study of obstetrical ultrasound in a hospital clinic in Chicago and she has argued for how this extensively used prenatal diagnostic technology creates a context where the relationship between mother, foetus and doctor is subtly, but dramatically, reorientated. Ultrasound uses high frequency sound waves to create visual images of internal body structures. In obstetrics it can be used to visualize the ovaries, cervix, foetus, placenta, umbilical cord etc. Feminists have long argued that, as the male-dominated medical profession has subsumed the reproductive area, the natural process of gestation and birth has become akin to the world of industrial production. For instance, doctors have positioned themselves as 'managers', the foetus as a 'product' and women in labour as the 'workers'. Taylor argues that the routine use of ultrasound and other prenatal diagnostic technologies actually reinforces the implicit 'industrial production' metaphor in our hospitals.

Similarly, Martin (1987: 63) sees technologies such as ultrasound presenting images of the uterus as a machine and the woman as the labourer producing the baby, with the doctor a sort of 'foreman of the labour process'. For the obstetrician, ultrasound can be seen as a relatively inexpensive, safe and non-invasive way of obtaining important information about the foetus that would not otherwise be available. However, it also effectively allows clinicians to by-pass the mother as a knowledgeable source and cast her in the role of 'a someone' to be informed about her condition; a condition related to, but distinct from, that of the foetus. Indeed, in the Republic of Ireland, where I am writing this, the distinct state of being of the mother and the foetus is enshrined in our constitution, giving each an *equal* right to life. Such imagery therefore also helps to delineate the independence of the foetus's *being*, a representation some pro-abortion feminists are uncomfortable with (because *it's my body*).

Taylor (2000), scrutinizing this 'foreman–worker–product' analogy, asks 'Who are the consumers?', and her answer is as penetrating as the technology she examines. She asked women having ultrasound, among other things, if they wanted to know the sex of their baby and if so, why. 'So I can start buying things for the baby' was the predominant theme of their answers. In short, women are the consumers of the production process, and no doubt so are their assorted men-folk. The North American tradition of the Baby Shower (buying of presents for the baby (mother) before the baby is due) celebrates the sophistication of ultrasound for its ability to indicate whether to buy pink or blue. But through the process of pregnancy, mothers-to-be also consume special diets, and have to make choices about what sort of healthcare to consume, even what crèches to consume and so on. Pregnancy, then, moves the woman from production to consumption, aided – and abetted – by the technology of ultrasound.

Nesting babies

It is somehow ironic that perhaps the ultimate achievement in terms of biotechnology and reproduction, aside from cloning, is a woman's capability to give birth to a child that is not her own. *Mother* nature, it would seem, is the ultimate enabling technology when she is used to overcome another's thwarted desires to nurture. Goslinga-Roy (2000) has described the case of Julie, a 25-year-old woman with a ten-month-old son, who agreed to become a gestational surrogate mother. Since the mid-1980s when it has become possible to implant successfully a fertilized egg into a woman who has not produced that egg, the 'unified' cycle of reproduction within one person's body has been unnecessary. Jokingly Julie described herself as a 'cow', 'incubator', 'oven', 'breeder', 'vessel'; she chose surrogacy over egg donation because this way she would 'just be nesting the baby' (Goslinga-Roy 2000: 125) rather than being tied to it by a genetic relationship. Such conceptions question just what status the associated technology confers on women and their reproductive potential. Does it liberate women from the gendered and often oppressive politics of reproduction, allowing them to realize the emotional or market value of their physiology; or does it further disempower them and represent them as 'only breeders' of, or incubators for, other people's (men's or women's) seed? There is, of course, no easy answer to this, but returning to ultrasound, we can see how technology textures the issues.

We have already noted how ultrasound can effectively separate a mother from her foetus by imaging its independent agency: 'It's kicking but you can't feel it' (Nurse). 'I didn't realize it was so active at this stage' (Mother). 'Oh yea, they work away on their own, even at that stage' (Nurse). This discussion of the antics of my second daughter, Tess, at ten weeks into her 'being', occurred with myself positioned observing the observers (the nurse and my wife), and fulfilling that awkward, disconnected, but totally enthralling, 'ultrasound-father' role.

Ultrasound also provides the mother (and father) with a thrilling opportunity for 'visual bonding' (Goslinga-Roy 2000). In the case of Julie, the ultrasound allows the surrogate mother to objectify the foetus *outside* of her own body, i.e. on the screen. On the other hand, the genetic mother of the child, Pamela, who also attended Julie's ultrasound screening, was able to experience the visual thrill and emotional bonding; in fact, placed in a somewhat similar position to that which I have described for myself. Gosling-Roy (2000: 137) describes the different perspectives of the two mothers in poignant terms: Julie experiencing 'being two in one body' and Pamela feeling that her child was 'alone and amongst strangers, "away from her parents who want to love her and hold her" '.

These different perspectives induced by the technology of reproduction, subsequently produce heart-arching tensions as people failed to conform to the script of their neo-biological roles. For instance, Julie, in her desire to attend Pamela's baby shower, exemplified her wanting to be more than 'just a womb', an event which Pamela saw as being the 'only day during the pregnancy when she could be a mother' (Goslinga-Roy 2000: 138). While Julie wanted to know Pamela's home address in order to send the baby gifts, Pamela didn't want to give this for fear that after the birth she might call at their house. The identification of Pamela as the child's birth mother (on the birth certificate) is just one way in which one particular narrative of these competing experiences is privileged over another. Perhaps the key point here is that while the technology involved in this process is not itself biased to one interpretation or another, neither is it 'innocent' (Haraway 1991).

Sadly, the video that Goslinga-Roy produced from this study, which included Julie's narrative and gave recognition of her role, has, should it be distributed, been threatened with a lawsuit for libel and fraud by Pamela and her husband. Goslinga-Roy (2000: 142) concludes that 'We urgently need to problematize oversimplistic, abstracting, and unitary representations of embodiment, power, and technology.' Whether, in the instance described here, Julie's body should be seen as one that simply 'stops at her skin' (Haraway 1991) or whether it should be seen more as a 'collective body' (Goslinga-Roy 2000), where others' aspirations can be realized, is probably ultimately a value judgement, no doubt influenced by any reasons one may have for needing to make such a judgement.

New developments in reproductive technologies have been greatly advantageous in many ways but they have also presented us with increasingly more complex choices and opportunities, particularly for feminists (Wolf 2001). The pro-choice movement (i.e. the right of women to choose whether to carry their pregnancy to full term or to have a termination) has been a central plank of the feminist agenda. Wolf, after seeing her own baby at three months gestation, realized that she could never abort the child. When she subsequently had a blood test that showed her foetus to be at risk for spina bifida, she declined to have amniocentesis (extracting some fluid from the womb), a test that would have given a definitive result. In one sense, technology can be seen here as giving an informed choice, which might be thought of as the essence of feminist empowerment, yet perhaps there is an assumption of cold blooded rationality here, a rationality that may not be equal to the emotional attachment facilitated by ultrasound. Wolf also describes the tragic case of a friend who conceived *in vitro*, resulting in three foetuses. She was given the choice of selectively aborting one of them, thus increasing the chance of having two healthy children. She decided against selective abortion, placed her faith in God and lost all three of them. Technology presents use with improbable opportunities, choices, tragedies and joys. Yet it also often depersonalizes us. However, recently, through the medium of birth plans, some individuals have tried to 'individualize' their experience of giving birth.

Birth plans have become people's way of reasserting their role in bringing children into the world. Sometimes these plans can be seen as attempts to neutralize, or even contradict, the sterile clinical environment of hospital delivery rooms. Bernstein (2002), in her wonderfully entitled article 'It ain't over 'til the fat lady sings', describes the plan that Tina Vervane, from Michigan, USA, came up with for her second child: no drugs, a warm shower during contractions, her husband videotaping the birth, and, oh yes, just one other thing – her five-year-old daughter to deliver the baby, while dressed in her favourite Scooby-Doo sundress. Other requests range from live violin duets at the appropriate point to bringing home 'placenta prints'. Consumerism, patients' rights and much sought after maternity revenue have dawned a new age of permissiveness, at least in some delivery rooms in the USA. While the Vanderbilt University Medical Centre in Nashville, Tennessee, offers a packing service for placentas 'to go' as it were, the Mountainside Hospital, Mountclair, New Jersey, will facilitate 'birthday parties' in the delivery room and has recently purchased a $12,000 labour pool for water births. On the other hand, those of a more traditional inclination will be pleased to know that the Parkland Health and Hospital System, in Dallas, Texas, with 16,000 births per annum, allows no videotaping at all, with one of its administrators saying 'We're a bit like an assembly line'.

Hello Dolly!

Perhaps the ultimate in embodiment – giving physical expression to an abstract idea – and perhaps consumerism too – giving people what they want – is the advent of cloning, where, at least according to popular media portrayals, people will be able to reproduce themselves. In fact, the reality is far from this, regardless of the ethical considerations. If cloning humans follows the same process as developed by Ian Wilmut of the Roslin Institute in Scotland when he cloned the now famous Dolly in 1996, then it will involve several distinct stages: (a) eggs would be harvested from donors given fertility drugs; (b) cells would then be taken from the person to be cloned; (c) the nuclei from the donor's eggs would be removed by sucking them out with a fine needle; (d) the DNA-free donor eggs and the donor cells would then be placed next to one another and fused by applying an electric current to them; (e) some of the resulting reconfigured eggs would be divided to produce embryos; (f) several of these embryos would be implanted into gestational surrogate mothers. Through such a process, up to 50 surrogates could be needed to produce one baby, as many of the pregnancies would terminate by miscarriage or be aborted due to abnormalities (Gibbs 2001).

Time magazine reported a telephone poll of 1015 adult Americans conducted by Yankelovich Partners Inc. and asked which of a range of circumstances justified creating a human clone. Unfortunately the 'don't know' responses were omitted (so 'yes' and 'no' sum to 100 per cent) and in descending order the following 'yes' responses were reported: to produce clones whose vital organs can be used to save others (28 per cent), to save the life of the person being cloned (21 per cent), to help infertile couples to have children (20 per cent), to allow parents to have a twin child later (10 per cent), to allow parents to create a clone of a child they lost (10 per cent), to allow gay couples to have children (10 per cent), to create genetically superior beings (6 per cent). Interestingly, only 10 per cent of the sample thought that a clone of a dead person would have the same personality as the person they were cloned from, and only 5 per cent said they would clone themselves, if they had a chance. However, even at 5 per cent, in North America alone, that would constitute over 15 million clones. While there is insufficient detail in this survey to judge how representative its sample might be, it does at least give some indication of how some people think about cloning.

I suspect that those who wish themselves to be cloned have a fairly poor understanding of the relative roles of nature and nurture – and if I was in the 'to create a superior being' camp, then I would suggest that anyone who wants to be cloned is a pretty poor candidate. There is ample evidence – in the form of monozygotic twins (i.e. from the same egg and therefore having exactly the same DNA) – that identical genes do not produce identical people. There are often notable physical differences and always psychological differences. Furthermore, despite the fact that a clone would have identical DNA to its 'parent', it would grow in a different womb, experience a different relative mix of chemicals during gestation and experience these at different times; it would also be born decades later and so not just have a different familial environment but also have a world of different experiences. Therefore, while the blueprint for brain development can be copied, the experiences that stimulate dendritic growth will necessarily differ, create different associations, memories, thought patterns, hopes, anxieties and so on. A clone can never have the same brain as its 'parent'. Identical twins thus have much more in common than a clone will ever have in common with its 'parent'. One thing that we have learnt from the advent of cloning is that *simply having a body (no matter how similar it may be to your own) is not sufficient for establishing an alternative, or additional, sense of your own embodiment.* If the human genome project has given us a staggeringly detailed map of the human body, then from the perspective of embodiment, it may indeed be a map that can help us to find our way around, but through cloning we will find no one that we know.

When do people begin?

Related to cloning are the equally intriguing advances in stem cell research. Each of the millions of cells that comprise our body has the same DNA (deoxyribonucleic acid), the molecule providing our genetic code, yet only a small portion of this DNA is used for the specific task any given cell must perform. This ability to perform any task within the body – called pluripotency – is lost after the second week of fertilization. Stem cells are cells that are only partially differentiated. Another source of stem cells is the human embryo, the so-called embryonic stem cells, composed of just a few dozen cells (Trefil 2001). These cells hold great potential for the development of treatments that would allow us to replace tissue damaged by disease or injury; for instance, growing a new kidney, which, because it grew from the person with the kidney failure, would not be rejected by their immune system when implanted. However, because embryonic stem cells have the potential to develop into human beings some feel that experimentation on them is immoral and should be banned.

The further science and technology delves into what has been thought impossible the more it rattles our social constructions of right and wrong, of God's will, of humanitarianism, of just who or what we are. In the context of embodiment, embryonic stem cell research begs the question 'When do people begin?' If a few dozen cells in an embryo do not constitute human life, and are not seen as 'a person', then at what stage along the biological continuum of development do we confer 'personhood'. Perversely, one could ask at what stage of cell loss, or cell death, due to Alzheimer's disease, for instance, does a person stop being a person. It will be immediately obvious that while this may, on the one hand, appear to be somewhat abstract philosophical musing – albeit of great relevance to the concept of embodiment – it is, on the other hand, salient to the morality of selective abortion

If consideration of 'When does a person begin?' is intellectually complex, that is nothing to the emotional despair that many women (and men) must go though when contemplating a termination. Whatever the biological or intellectual rationality of the matter, the phenomenological fact is that many women experience a foetus as a *being*, and are loath to make the decision that it should *cease to be*. Whether a foetus at 24 weeks has a person projected on to it by others, or is a person embodied by flesh, and eyes and arms etc., is ultimately a value judgement, not a scientific one. We now move from technologies of creating bodies to technologies of swapping body parts.

Organ transplantation

Whole organ transplantation was one of the 'biological wonders' of the twentieth century, saving and improving the quality of countless lives. Our concern here is only to consider the implications of organ transplantation from the perspective of embodiment, while recognizing the great benefit recipients derive from transplanted organs. For instance, when Tim Heidler was 22 he lost the power of speech after riding his motorcycle into a wire stretched across a road. His throat was slashed and his larynx irreparably damaged. After 19 years of being able to speak only through a hand held electronic device, that gave him a buzzing monotonic voice, he had the world's first larynx transplant. Now 46, Heidler speaks again. His voice has the deeper pitch of the organ's donor, while his original accent has been retained. His new voice gradually improved as his own nerves grew into the transplanted tissue and the donated larynx actually shrank to suit the body of its new user (Dobson 2001).

Organ transplant is big business. PPL Therapeutics, which recently cloned five piglets from an adult female as part of their programme to transplant pig organs into humans, estimates the market for 'solid' organs to be worth US$6 billion. They estimate that cellular therapies, such as transplantable cells for insulin production in people with diabetes, to be worth another $6 billion. Of the approximately 180,000 people around the world awaiting organ transplants, only about a third will receive one, due to their shortage and the increasing demand for transplants. Xenotransplantation – transplanting organs across species – is seen as an answer to this problem and pig organs seem to be especially suitable for human implantation (Dobson 2001). Xenografting (cross-species transplantation) is one way of addressing the shortage of donor organs and would also allow transplantation to occur before people became critically ill. As well as pig organs being transplanted, two people have received baboon-to-human liver transplants and one person received a porcupine liver transplant. However, these xenografts have largely been unsuccessful due to the vigorous responses mounted by the human host's immune system (Martin 2000). Regardless of the biological efficacy of xenografts, they raise important ethical issues about abuse of animals, as well as profound concerns about incorporating non-human biology into the human body.

Pillage of the body

Human-to-human organ transplant also creates all too human ethical dilemmas. For instance, people from poor countries may be paid to sell their kidney and this is often justified on the grounds that everybody gains: it benefits recipients by increasing the supply of organs, and it benefits donors by improving their economic circumstances. Goyal *et al.* (2002) studied 305 people who had sold a kidney in Chennai, India. As the selling of organs in Chennai is illegal, the survey had to be conducted in a clandestine fashion. Nephrectomy was verified by the presence of scars. Ninety-six per cent of those reporting having a nephrectomy sold their kidney to pay off debts; however, the average family income had subsequently declined by one third after they had sold their kidney. The survey took place on average six years after selling a kidney, at which time three-quarters of the participants were still in debt. Eighty-six per cent reported deterioration in their health after selling their kidney. Thus, for the majority of those surveyed, selling their kidney did not result in long-term economic benefit and was associated with worsening of their own health. Scheper-Hughes (2003) has also described how the new technologies of transplantation have created a world trade in human organs, one that is largely resistant to regulation, and which is unjust in the sense that the rich sack the poor of their body parts. To highlight this exploitation Organ Watch has been established.

The Organ Watch project grew out of the work of the Bellagio Task Force on Securing Bodily Integrity for the Socially Disadvantaged in

Transplant Surgery (1994–96). This task force documented many abuses that result from the traffic in organs, such as the sale of organs in India and the use of organs from executed prisoners in China. It also noted the complex sources of rumours regarding organ theft, which although not documented, 'nevertheless point to the pervasive fears of a loss of bodily integrity by vulnerable populations' (Organ Watch website, 20–03–03). Scheper-Hughes and Cohen conducted ethnographic research in Brazil, India and South Africa during 1997–98, which they claim has revealed:

1 Strong and persistent race, class and gender inequalities and injustices in the acquisition, harvesting and distribution of organs.
2 Violation of national laws prohibiting the sale of organs.
3 The collapse of cultural and religious sanctions against body dismemberment and commercial use in the face of the enormous market pressures in the transplant industry.
4 The appearance of new forms of traditional debt peonage in which the commodified kidney occupies a critical space.
5 Persistent and flagrant human rights violations of cadavers in public morgues, with organs and tissues removed without any consent for international sale.
6 The spread and persistence of narratives of terror concerning the theft and disappearance of bodies and body parts globally.

Body organs are not considered surplus to requirement by all. For at least some, body organs are too strongly identified with the present and future health of a person to be simply sold off. However, in addition to the sense of 'body integrity' that might be associated with resisting the temptation to 'sell bits off' (out of economic despair), perhaps resisting the market value of the organs is related to the psychological value of retaining them; that is, of them *embodying the value of the person*. As such, the biological integrity of the body may be seen as integral to the value of self, at least for some.

Brain dead?

Organ transplant is not a straightforward grafting of small inert 'pieces' of flesh on to larger unreflective 'bits' of flesh. A striking instance of how having a piece of another person attached to you can have a transformative effect beyond one's biological functioning is cited by Daar (2000). A white supremacist Ku Klux Klan member became an advocate for black rights after receiving the kidney of a black cadaveric donor. As Daar notes, this is a welcome contrast to a recent case in the UK where a family consented to donation on the condition that their deceased relative's organs not be transplanted into a black person. Clearly, much more than flesh is being transplanted here, and much more than flesh can be gained, or lost. Gillet

(2000) cautions against uncritically adopting a utilitarian approach. To illustrate this he asks: if five seriously ill patients could be saved by transplanting organs into each of them from a healthy person, should we do that?

When is somebody actually dead? The criterion for brain death – 'irreversible loss of the capacity for consciousness combined with irreversible loss of the capacity to breathe' (Pallis 1982) – suggests the the loss of capacity to breathe (but we have ventilators) and essentially the loss of personhood (but people are maintained in a persistent vegetative state for long periods) are key criteria. Yet is a person in a persistent vegetative state or an anencephalic infant (child born without the cerebral functions to support mental functioning) really a 'completely depersonalised biological larva, where nothing remains' (Thielicke 1970, quoted in Gillet 2000) or not? What is it that is embodied there and is it OK for us to take out their organs for use by 'higher beings'?

Masterson (2000) has argued that physicians share the public's prejudice against people with mental health problems. For instance, Levenson and Oldbrisch (1993), in a survey of US organ transplant centres, found that 'active schizophrenia' was an 'absolute contraindication' to transplantation in 92 per cent of cardiac, 73 per cent of renal and 67 per cent of liver units. Even when schizophrenia was diagnosed as 'controlled', it was still seen as a contraindication in 51, 62 and 65 per cent respectively. While contraindication for organ transplant on the grounds of mental health is highly questionable, its justification is likely to be in terms of the influence that organ rejection may have on somebody who is already experiencing difficulties coping, along with the likelihood of the organ recipient adhering to the requirements of the transplant and rehabilitation team in terms of subsequent drug regimes, immunosupressants and so on. However, it is also likely that, for some surgeons at least, there is a disinclination to transplant healthy body parts to be under the governership of 'unhealthy minds'.

On keeping others' hands to yourself

A review of the literature, even the psychological literature, on organ transplantation is beyond our scope or purpose here, but it will be instructive to consider one type of transplant, hand transplant, in more detail. In exploring the psychological impact of arm/hand amputation, Klapheke et al. (2000) reported that most people who wished to have such a transplant commented on the great sense of loss with regard to human touch, especially in close loving relationships. Klapheke (1999) and Klapheke et al. argue that the hand plays an important role in 'ego maturation, body image, and sense of identity' (Klapheke et al., 2000: 453) and note that Freud considered that the ego is 'first and foremost a bodily ego' (quoted in Klapheke et al. 2000). Loss of a hand through amputation can result in conflicts concerning loss of autonomy, guilt/punishment and potency. Possibly to a greater extent than with organ transplants within the body, the visible hand graft with distinctive skin texture and hair patterning, stitching and swelling, 'forces the issue' of psychological integration. Such integration, it is suggested, is influenced not simply by the recipient's psychological state, but also by the cathexis – 'or psychological valuation' – of the hand and by how the recipient 'anthropomorphizes' the hand – 'that is, how the hand is felt to symbolise the donor and additional traits received (in fantasy) from the donor along with the hand' (Klapheke *et al.* 2000: 454). Hand grafting also presents the certainty that the grafted hand will lack immediate functionality and may take many months to approach the functionality of a prosthetic hand. Furthermore, the graft may be physically rejected, necessitating a higher and less functional amputation subsequently. Whether this is the case or not, it is clear that the re-experiencing of much of what is associated with the initial hand loss may be very traumatic and regressive.

Burloux and Bachman (2004) describe the case of the first double hand graft (transplantation of two lower arms with hands), performed in Lyon in 2000. Burloux and Bachman were both psychiatrists attached to the transplant team, and write from a psychodynamic perspective. In the period immediately following the grafts, GH displayed a confused state in which he experienced hands flying above his head. Later, however, in a more lucid state, when he was able to see the ends of his grafted fingers which appeared at the edge of the dressings, he believed that his *own* hands had, in fact, been put back on. He insisted on this being the case, even when told that they were a donor's hands. Other than this assertion, his behaviour was perfectly rational. However,

> the first dressing caused major anxiety, all the more since he could then see the demarcation between his forearms and the donor's hands. The grafted hands were lifeless and the donor's skin colour was slightly different . . . the limit between the two bodies is obvious as a result of the stitches, swells and seams. At this stage the patient's anxiety was never verbally expressed. It showed through abundant sweats, some agitation, somatic complaints about difficulties swallowing, and the obvious refusal to verbally express what he felt.
>
> (Burloux and Bachman 2004: 170–1)

A few days later he did express his anxiety that the hands might come 'unstitched' and the fear of losing the newly grafted hands was associated with a return of traumatic dreams about the explosion that caused him to lose his hands originally, and acute reliving of the trauma previously experienced.

About three months after receiving the grafts, on his first returning home, GH's two-year-old son immediately noticed the difference between the grafted hands and the prostheses he had previously worn; he caressed his father's hands saying 'hands, daddy', kissing them with delight and amazement. While the significance of such an event cannot be underestimated for the psychological integration of the grafted hands, GH himself, even at this stage, still insisted that the hands were his own. Later GH said 'I am not sure Professor Dubernard grafted my hands on me'. GH was not, at least on one level, unaware of the origin of the hands, as media coverage and indeed some close family members conveyed to him that he had 'dead man's hands'. GH preferred not to talk about this 'as though verbally discussing those difficult moments would reactive the anxiety. At this point we respected his denial and tried to reassure him by emphasizing how unique and shocking such an experience was for any human being' (Burloux and Bachman 2004: 171).

The recovery of movement in the grafted hands (progressing slowly from the third through to the ninth month postoperatively) was obviously an important element in their psychological integration into 'the self'. A fascinating element in this was the use of MRI (magnetic resonance imaging) to provide a high resolution image of the functioning of the brain areas associated with hand movement. As Burloux and Bachman (2004: 6) note: 'the patient uses the imagery as a sign that the hands are becoming his own since his brain activates them'. Thus the MRI is inadvertently used as a form of biofeedback and self-integration. Ten months after the operation GH could spontaneously discuss the donor and publicly thank the donor's family.

Burloux and Bachman (2004: 19) address the issue of how a hand graft recipient, and their family, who wish for full functionality of the hand, deal with the 'new hand, which is dead, strange and alien, slowly coming back to life in such an odd way'. Burloux and Bachman consider various psychological processes that may be invoked. Anxiety may arise from the explicit physical boundary between the donor's hand and recipient's arm, which may symbolize the troublesome coexistence between the familiar and the unfamiliar; between the living and the dead. Such juxtapositioning of life and death may implicitly undermine and weaken the defensive functions that social order and cultural values provide (Becker 1962; see Chapters 1 and 7). The distinctions above are reinforced by the patient's references to 'my' hand and the medical team's references to 'the' hand, but there are various reasons why the defence of denial is necessary, at least early on.

What will the grafted hand do? Will it try to take control? Will it do something unmentionable? Will the recipient be affected by the qualities of its previous owner? The fantasy of the donor somehow taking control is common in all types of grafts (Burloux and Bachman 2004) but is possibly especially strong in hand grafts because of their 'in your face' quality. Another fantasy that occurs is the (illogical but none the less experienced) sense of having killed the donor to get their organ(s) or other body parts, and perhaps related to this may be the desire to erase any donor characteristics (skin or hair colour, nails, etc.) that remain. Such concerns may be signs of possible psychological rejection of the grafts. Of course, other people's reactions to hand grafts may be problematic: for instance, in a sexual relationship how comfortable may either partner feel with 'another person's' hand touching intimate parts?

In Klapheke *et al.*'s (2000) study people's motivation for hand transplantation was often reported as a sense of not being 'whole' or 'complete'. Klapheke *et al.* asked people seeking hand transplants how they felt about receiving a cadaver hand (that is, a hand from someone who had died). While few voiced concerns about specific aspects of donor selection (for example, race or gender – but this may be because these were assumed), typical responses were to dismiss its 'not-me' quality: 'It wouldn't be considered as someone else's hand – I would think of it as the limb growing again', or 'If it's on, it's yours'. An interesting illustration of a wish for ownership yet recognition of a transplanted hand not fully 'belonging' but almost being in one's 'care' was also reported: 'When it's attached, it's mine – my blood will be going through it – I'd be the one responsible for it, and *I'd take care of it*' (Klapheke *et al.* 2000: 456, italics added). Alternatively, and somewhat more brashly: 'I don't care if it's big, green and fuzzy . . . once it's on, it's mine!' Ultimately, Klapheke *et al.* (2000: 457) conclude:

> Hand transplantation appeared to offer those who seek it the potential psychological benefits of improvement of body image and sense of body integrity, increased sense of autonomy and potency/effectiveness, potential restoration or enhancement of human touch (which several longed for, especially in their close relationships), improved job satisfaction and fulfilment, and thus mastery over the physical and psychological trauma of hand loss.

The prospect of forthcoming 'face transplantations' draws into focus even more acutely the complex, intersecting and perhaps uncomfortable issues of psychological identity and altered physical embodiment (Furness 2003).

Giving and receiving

For all the psychological dynamics that may be encompassed in the experience of donor and recipient during transplantation, recently the immunological dynamics of what has been called 'chimerism' – 'the mixing of host cells with those of the donor genome' (Martin 2000) – has been a focus of excitement and optimism for improving the success of organ transplants. In following up kidney and liver recipients some 30 years after their transplants it was found that donor leukocytes had migrated from the donated organs and 'survived ubiquitously'. These cells, it seems, had been assimilated into the much more vast immunological network of the host. This remarkable finding is most poignantly expressed by Starzl (2000: 10)

The discovery was instinctively understood by most patients to whom it was explained, and it had a surprisingly great emotional impact. The point was not lost that the physical intimacy of the donor to the recipient was greater than anyone had imagined. It was closer and more lasting than that of a gestational fetus with its mother. The woman applying lipstick in the morning was touching that unknown cadaveric male donor of 30 years ago whose live cells were everywhere in her own tissue. She was not the recipient of an organ only. The realization was usually moving, and it was invariably sobering.

The notion of an immunological confrontation between donor and recipient in whole-organ transplantation, where either the recipient's immune system would kill the donated organ or the donated organ would kill the host's immune system, has now given way. Over the past ten years, there has developed a conception of a David (donor) and Goliath (recipient) exchange where neither has to prevail, but each could prosper by tolerating the other, exchanging emissaries, albeit under the protective umbrella of a 'United Nations' of immunosupressant drugs, equally protecting both cells' lines. Some romantic, sometime, somewhere, must surely have said: 'That gift was no gift – you are my gift'. As devious as a jilted Greek god, as subtle as a Freudian repression, as sensational as a 'whodunnit' without a body; the implications of chimerism for a sense of singular or collective embodiment are apparent. The chimeristic Trojan horse of transplantation, in keeping with the subtlety of the postmodern ethos, does not 'take over' the citadel body, but blends in: lives in you, through you, becomes you and you become it.

Fox (1999: 85) contrasts care as a vigil and care as a gift. 'The *vigil* of care is the disciplinary technology which, through professionalism and theory, fabricates and inscribes those who are cared for' (original italics). Thus the vigil of care implies a surveillance of almost depersonalized despair and a channelling of 'its' modes of expression and our treatment of 'it'. Warning against gifts as power-plays or with expectations of reciprocity, Fox (1999: 87) states that 'in the realm of the gift, those who give do not expect gratefulness or even an acknowledgement of their effort'. The 'gift' is thus a true *giving-by*-oneself, and perhaps in the realm of live-organ donation a *giving-of*-oneself.

Technological enframing

Haemodialysis has been used to treat end stage renal failure since the 1960s and is one of our most enduring and 'invasive' health-related technologies. Yet 'invasive' is not really the right description of it, and possibly 'exvasive' would be more appropriate: blood leaves the body, is essentially cleansed and then returned in a purified, and life-saving, state. Haemodialysis has undoubtedly added 'years to life' for those with end stage renal failure, and 'life to years' through its facilitation of greatly enhanced *quality* of life. Yet there is a cost attached: the regular and frequent interactions that the person has with the technology, the physiological and psychosocial manifestations of the treatment, and the culture of the haemodialysis unit in the hospital, may *enframe* the person in the technology.

Moran and Gallagher (2004) describe how when the technology of haemodialysis is introduced for the treatment of renal disease the patient must 'stand reserve' (Heidegger 1977) or 'put their life on hold' in order to cope with the demands of the haemodialysis. Heidegger also argues that the challenges and demands of the technological framework engulf the individual, binding their life to the demands of the technology, in this case the treatment regime, thus 'technologically enframing' the individual (Moran and Gallagher 2004). The physical and psychosocial manifestations of the technology of haemodialysis enframe the individual; even though these may not be explicitly technological in themselves, they act as continuous reminders of the technological frame in which the individual now lives and on which he or she depends. These include, in the physical realm, acute reactions such as hypotension, cramps, nausea and vomiting, and in the longer term complications in gastrointestinal, cardiovascular, neurological, ocular, reproductive, haematological and dermatological functioning. The prevention, or at least reduction, of these longer-term problems requires compliance with a specific treatment regime, often including attending the haemodialysis unit three times a week, self-administering many medications and adhering to a strict diet and fluid restrictions.

There are also various psychosocial manifestations arising from haemo-dialysis that contribute to a sense of becoming enframed in technology. The uncertainty about the illness trajectory, an inability to achieve life goals and changes in roles and responsibilities, and the development of explicit dependence on machinery and 'powerful' others all contribute to this. In the haemodialysis centre, where the demand for dialysis units outstrips their avail-ability, people are scheduled, and sometimes have to queue, to 'link up'. Nagle (1998) has described initial encounters with haemodialysis as disturbing and surreal in relation to the shock and horror of initial encounters with the technological environment. Patients experienced a loss of their sense of self because of the dehumanizing effects of haemodialysis and the associated physical deterioration; they strived to remain embodied in an environment which threatened to disembody them (Nagle 1998). In reality, in dialysis, the life-blood leaves you and goes somewhere else, and then is returned. Without the blood being returned you die. Machines bleep and pulses race (at first anyway) when faults occur. To be in a dialysis unit and to see machines being continuously fed by people's blood, first one, then another, is, at times, to become confused as to the direction of the flow of life: 'I'm keeping this bloody machine going'. . .

If an embodied phenomenological perspective is one that takes all parts of the body as integral to a sense of 'being-in-the-world' then surely it is impossible for individuals to separate themselves from the technology of haemodialysis that sustains them. More than that, the dialysis experience cultivates in the individual a new language (technical terms), relationships of cooperation (between staff and patients) and the need for compliance with other's requirements: all essential aspects of a distinctive cultural subsystem, where the person simply becomes an extension of the technology that resides in the culture. As Moran and Gallagher (2004) conclude, people face great difficulties when adjusting to haemodialysis because the technology threatens the 'shared skills and practices' of the world that the individual depends on for meaning and identity.

ICU are trying to kill me . . .

Perhaps one of the most dramatic examples of how this sense of identity can go astray in high technology environments is the case of the, continuingly controversial, intensive care unit (ICU) syndrome. Dyer (1995a) describes how during the 1950s, when intensive care developed as a speciality, short-term psychological problems became apparent in ICU patients. It is a matter of controversy to what extent ICU syndrome is attributable to the illnesses that justify admission to the ICU, the toxic nature of the physical treatments that patients receive, the environment, routine and type of care provided by staff, or some combination of these (Dyer 1995a, b; McGuire et al. 2000; Bennun 2001, 2003; Ely et al. 2001). ICUs are highly specialized treatment facilities, usually for a small number of patients with acute life-threatening conditions. Usually busy, with a variety of clinicians milling around, they are quite different from the normal hospital setting: with numerous monitors, bleeps, alarms and the hum of technology dominating the atmosphere, invariant with time of day. Here, the lives of both staff and patients become 'entwined with the technology' (Walters 1995: 338).

Bennun (2004) vividly describes the experience of Clifford in an ICU who required respiratory support, monitoring of tissue oxygenation, fluid administration, cardiovascular monitoring, nutritional feed and intravenous drug lines following surgery for the removal of two aneurysms. Such technology assumes an omnipotence that effectively detracts from the person, the patient's progress being ascertained from the machinery, which speaks on the patient's behalf, both in a visual and auditory fashion. It is widely accepted that the physical environment of most ICUs is a source of stress for patients, family and staff alike (Jastremski 2000). Dyer (1995a: 130) quotes Hopkinson and Freeman (1998):

> Many patients in ITU [intensive treatment units] are quietly delusional and will report hallucinations if they survive the experience. Little

notice is taken of this unless the patient becomes overtly agitated and deluded, causing disruption to the care of both themselves and other patients.

While our interest here is in exploring psychological aspects of the technological environment of the ICU and its implications for embodiment, there are clearly many physical factors that can contribute to ICU syndrome, including cerebral hypoxia, metabolic imbalance and effects of the plethora of drugs administered. However, the fact that a syndrome may have at least some physical causes doesn't mean that we should ignore psychological factors, for these may at least cause distress, and quite probably interact with physical imbalances, if they do not directly produce such effects themselves.

The ICU syndrome may be defined as a 'constellation of clinical signs that include fluctuating levels of consciousness, poor orientation, hallucinations, delusions and a number of behavioral anomalies such as aggression and passivity' (Bennun 2004: 247). Hallucinations and delusions may include persecutory themes, including the idea that staff are actually out to harm them, indeed to kill them. In Laitenen's (1996) study of patients following cardiac surgery it was found that many people reported dreams of being imprisoned, tortured and dehumanized in various ways, both during and after their ICU experience. Other studies conducted in Sweden (Bergbom-Engberg and Haljamae 1988; Granberg et al. 1998) found that ICU patients felt they could not trust the machinery surrounding their bed, fearing that it might break down and they would die. The various tubes and monitoring lines restricted their movement and made them feel insecure. They also felt as if they could not trust the staff caring for them; they developed perceptions of body distortion and changed self-concept. Altered self-concept particularly occurred when nurses appeared to pay more attention to the technology than to the patients. Bennun (2004) points out that limited mobility within the ICU environment causes patients to feel isolated and fearful, and that in these circumstances there is a risk that they lose their integrity, body sensations and functions: 'Gradually, the patient may feel that their body does not exist or they develop a perceptual distortion so that they do not know where their body begins and ends' (Bennun 2004: 243).

Torturing patients

It is important to note that not all patients in ICUs have the sort of experiences described above, and to acknowledge that their dire circumstances may require an oppressive level of technical control which, none the less, may hugely benefit them. However, in a provocative article entitled 'Preventing the ITU syndrome or how not to torture an ITU patient!', the suitably pronounced Dyer (1995a) draws out parallels in the sort of environment created in ICUs and the various categories of torture, as outlined by Amnesty International (1973). For instance, for the category of 'isolation' it is important to appreciate that physical isolation is not necessary for effective isolation; being in a new and strange environment, having difficulties initiating communication or in sensing touch can be isolating. This difficulty in 'representing oneself' can result in the experience of depersonalization. Dyer (1995a: 133) quotes one ICU sister: 'if they've got an endotracheal tube and they are asleep you tend to think that they are not even a person really'.

In addition to isolation, the monopolization of perception is another 'torture' category where people experience a lack of *meaningful* stimuli. Thus, beyond the general monotony and lack of stimulation produced by a constant (day and night) environment, sight, hearing and even taste and smell can be affected (for instance, by intubation or tracheostomy). Interestingly, Keep *et al.* (1980) have found that patients in ICUs that have windows report half the rate of hallucinations and delusions of patients in windowless ICUs. Other categories of 'torture' that may be relevant to ICUs include debility and exhaustion, feeling under threat, feeling degraded and experiencing others' demonstrations of omnipotence (see Dyer 1995a for a full discussion of these; and Dyer 1995b and Bennun 2004 for a discussion of how to minimize these factors).

Two contrasting paradigms of patient care have been described: 'touch' and 'technology' (Gadow 1984). Technology may diminish human dignity by reducing people to objects. Furthermore, by inducing this experience of distance and 'otherness', technology resists being assimilated into a person's individuality and thus objectifies human life. However, moving beyond this dichotomy Jastremski (2000) calls for ICU bedside environments of the future to combine 'high tech' and 'high touch' components of care in the same setting, thus creating a more humane and healing environment. As Bennun notes, in the ICU people are simultaneously exposed to life threatening illnesses, the awe of medical procedures and technology, as well as an inability to communicate needs, and the loss of personal control in a new and threatening environment. Regardless of the extent to which ICU syndrome, or associated delirium, may be caused by organic factors, it is surely important to address those environmental and psychological components that may threaten further to disembody and derange the person entwined in the technology of an ICU.

Virtual realities

In virtual realities a sense of self may be also challenged; sometimes with therapeutic effect, at other times by creating a nauseating contrast between the experience of a virtual embodiment and the biological embodiment. Although virtual reality is a relatively new technology it has already being used in a range of therapeutic endeavours, including: pain management in burn wound care, dental procedures and chemotherapy; the treatment of phobias, post-traumatic stress disorder, eating and other body disorders; the assessment and rehabilitation of cognitive processes, such a visual perception and executive functions; rehabilitative training for the use of public transport and meal preparation; training of surgical procedures and the education of patients and medical students (Scultheis and Rizzo 2001).

Garcia-Palacios *et al.* (2004) outline an innovative use of *virtual reality* as a psychological analgesic for burn patients. The analgesic effect is achieved by blocking the person's view of the real world though immersing them in a computer generated virtual three-dimensional world (e.g. Spiderworld or Snow World). This attention grabbing experience reduces their attention to processing the excruciating pain usually engendered by wound care and physical therapy, the adherence to both of which is essential for successful rehabilitation. Garcia-Palacios *et al.* describe a man who suffered burns on 42 per cent of his body surface area and who experienced a reduction in pain while immersed in Snow World (see also Hoffman *et al.* 2000a, b).

In the work of Hoffman and colleagues, it would seem that the psychological analgesic effects of virtual reality act as an invaluable supplement to opioids, which are often unable to control adequately the level of acute pain experienced during wound care. In effect, the 'spotlight' of attention that is usually given to the physical experience of pain is redirected into a compelling virtual world with the result that wound care becomes more of an annoyance – a distraction from the virtual world the person is immersed in – than a focus for distress. Using virtual reality techniques the Seattle group has demonstrated a 50 per cent reduction in subjective pain for burn patients. One of the great attractions of virtual reality (VR) from a clinical and research perspective is that it is very flexible; one can present a great variety of controlled stimuli, measure and monitor responses made by the participant/patient and alter characteristics of the environment they are experiencing (Riva 2000).

While virtual reality can be conveyed through imagery presented on a computer screen, a more compelling 'immersion', or sense of 'presence', may be achieved through using a head mounted display (so that the point of view in the virtual environment changes in accordance with head movements) and the incorporation of other senses, such as sound, touch (mediated through a data glove), motion (mediated through a treadmill) and vestibular information (via motion platforms). The most compelling VR experiences are probably achieved by successfully 'enveloping' as many aspects of embodied experience as possible, and at the same time diminishing as much 'real world' experience as possible. However, this perspective may seem to challenge the rootedness of embodied experience, and Murray and Sixsmith (1999: 318) suggest:

Dominant discourses around virtual reality treat it as a disembodying medium. Such discourses talk of leaving the body behind at the computer terminal, of projecting a wandering mind into space. The body, the story goes, remains docked, immobile at the interface, while the mind wanders the pixelled delights of the computer programmer's creation.

Mindful demise of the body

Citing Stone (1992: 20) to the effect that 'No reconfigured virtual body . . . no matter how beautiful, will slow the death of a cyberpunk with AIDS', Murray and Sixsmith agree with Stone that the virtual experience is an embodied experience. They also cite Fisher's (1973) description of the psychiatrist John C. Lilly submerging himself in a tank of water, where the water was the same temperature as his body. Floating in this tank, isolated from any light or sound, Lilly felt 'merged and indistinguishable' from his surroundings, unable to tell where his 'body left off and the water began' (Fisher 1973: 22). Here the temperature of his body did not 'frame' him against that of the surrounding environment's temperature. If there is an analogy to VR here it is that perhaps it works through a trade-off between sensory deprivation on the one hand, and sensory augmentation on the other.

Murray and Sixsmith note that we effectively neglect the body when we are unaware of it, which is most of the time. Only when there is something wrong with it do we pay it attention. This slipping in and out of our attention

reveals that the body in the world is *both foreground and background*. It constitutes our locus, so that we are 'here', rather than 'there'. Yet, at the same time, the body recedes from conscious reflection. At once a holistic sense organ, and yet an assemblage of sense apparatus, the body recedes from awareness in its perceptual activity. It is the very disclosure of the world the sense organs provide that leads to their mindful demise.

(Murray and Sixsmith 1999: 323–4, emphasis added)

It therefore follows that if the 'sense organs' can be engaged sufficiently then there are infinite possibilities for the sorts of objects in which people can feel embodied in a virtual environment. While it may seem more natural to represent a person in a human body anthropomorphically, if the actual body can be 'surpassed' in the everyday functioning sense then alternative identities, such as birds or pigs or fish, become possible. In this scenario the person is 'using' two identities, their 'real world' physical identity and their 'virtual world' chosen identity.

If it becomes possible to experience 'physical expression' in a virtual world then such a world may offer opportunities denied to many – for instance, people who are quadriplegic – in the real world. In the virtual world we all use prosthetic devices and are enabled through them. There is also great scope for combining the physical embodiment of the real world with fantasy identification in a virtual world, and using the interplay between these to therapeutic ends. McDarby *et al.* (2004) present an innovative application of biofeedback technology that they refer to as *affective feedback*. This involves using biofeedback in combination with sensory immersion, novel signal processing and compelling computer game playing. They incorporate narrative and intelligent technology into the biofeedback loop from which people can learn about their responses. They describe the case of Peter, a 9-year-old boy disabled by anxiety attacks who, as part of his therapy, was taught to relax by playing the 'Relax to Win' game. In this game your dragon races against another dragon (either another person or your previous best time). What is intriguing about this game is that while competitive racing is intuitively associated with tension – both physical and psychological – to win here you have to be the most relaxed competitor. The speed of the dragon, presented on an engrossing screen with impressive graphics, is determined through galvanic skin response (GSR): the more relaxed you are the lower the GSR and the *faster* your dragon goes. It is hard to describe the calm satisfaction derived from watching your dragon take flight and glide to the finishing line, over the head of the other poor fella, who is simply trying too hard!

Cybersickness

As if to remind us that people do not just slot into machinery, at least not all in the same way, Riva (2000) notes that during and after immersion in VR environments, some people develop unpleasant 'side effects'. Such 'simulator sickness' includes ocular problems (eye strain, blurred vision and fatigue), disorientation and balance disturbances and nausea; and these effects can occur with less than ten minutes' immersion in VR. However, not everybody experiences them (Regan and Price 1994; see also the Simulator Sickness Questionnaire (SSQ), Kennedy *et al.* 1993). Nichols and Patel (2002) report a comprehensive literature review of 35 studies concerned with health and safety issues in VR environments. 'Cybersickness' was the effect most frequently reported across these studies and is thought to occur because of conflicting input to the visual and vestibular senses. The sensory conflict occurs because different sensory systems are registering different types of experience: the visual system may be presented with simulated movement, but as far as the vestibular system is concerned, everything is static. Nichols and Patel (2002: 252–3) note that 'simulator sickness' is polysymptomatic – no one symptom predominates in all people – and that it is polygenic – 'equipment, simulator usage and variables associated with participant characteristics may all have an influence on the type and severity of symptoms experienced'. They note that a large proportion of the population report some increase in sickness symptoms after experiencing VR.

It seems that an illusory feeling of self-motion – termed *vection* – is a precursor to feeling of sickness in VR. Such vection may increase the sense of presence in the virtual environment, but at the cost of inducing simulator sickness (McCauley and Sharkey 1992; I should say I experienced no such symptoms in the 'Relax to Win' game). Nichols and Patel (2002) also note that susceptibility to motion sickness predicts simulator sickness in VR environments, and this association has now been found in several studies. Interestingly, Reason and Brand (1975) reported that susceptibility to motion sickness is greatest between 2 and 12 years of age and decreases rapidly from 12 to 21 years of age, and then decreases more gradually after that.

Perhaps individual variability between the occurrence of 'cybersickness' and 'presence' is mediated by people's experience of embodiment. For instance, those with a strong sense of 'rootedness' to their bodies may feel the contradiction between presence achieved through vection and their static body as sickness, while those with a lesser degree of 'rootedness' to their body, experience presence without sickness. The more compelling a 'photorealistic' environment in VR is, the more its induced sense of 'presence' tugs at the rootedness of one's embodiment. Those 'less embodied' may be less susceptible to simulator sickness. Another way of thinking about the extent of embodiment may be to consider it in terms of how bounded one is by the skin of one's body. Just as the concept of culture-bound syndromes refers to the idea that certain forms of distress are encapsulated within and through a particular cultural context (MacLachlan 1997), experiences of embodiment may be constrained to the body we have. On the other hand, as we have shown in our research on illusory bodily experiences (MacLachlan *et al.* 2003), this may not be the case, and a greater sense of body plasticity may in fact have therapeutic value (see Chapter 5).

Chapter summary

1 Biological reductionism presents us with a wonderfully complex image of the human body as a sophisticated mechanical being. Biotechnology tends to interface with this mechanical image and has the potential to objectify and depersonalize subjective experience.

2 Biological and psychological interpretations of experience have different levels of meaning and the potential of enabling technologies will only be fully realized when they facilitate *personal* meaning, overcome dependence and foster self-respect.

3 Enabling technologies create opportunities for expert interventions in others' bodies. Due to the emotional significance of such possibilities it is important to avoid extreme technophilic or technophobic

perspectives, and to recognize that the interpretations of disabled experience that technologies may suggest are not the only ones.

4 Technology can be used to interact with the body, to listen to the body, to replace parts of it or to even act as a means for the rest of the body to live through it. The uses of technology are rarely neutral. Ultrasound, for instance, gives agency and identity to a foetus that has traditionally been bounded within a women's body, and bounded by her wishes for it.

5 The technologies of IVF and surrogacy challenge the notion of a child being the product of two parents and scrambles our ideas of what parental and child rights should be observed. Cloning may offer a biological replica but not an identical experience of embodiment.

6 Embryonic stem cell research forces us to consider when people 'begin', and what we may legitimately do with them. Ultimately such considerations lead back to wondering about the morality of terminations.

7 Organ transplantation may represent the ultimate 'gift' of life from one person to another. The 'Trojan horse-like' persistence of the 'other', in the biological systems of the organ recipient, alerts us to a more diffuse and systemic embodiment of the donor.

8 Charitable donation, or donation from a cadaver, must be contrasted with the situation where people caught in poverty resort to selling off parts of themselves in order to sustain their families. In the latter case the transplant also embodies the shameful social inequalities that are plundered for the benefit of the rich.

9 Whatever the biological or moral dimensions of transplant, there may also be profound psychological dimensions, especially when it involves 'external' body parts, such as hands. Recipients may struggle to form an identity with the hands and an acceptance of their cadaver origins. While the motivation for such a transplant may be functional, it may also relate to ideas of feeling 'whole' again.

10 Technological enframing of people's distress is often an inevitable consequence of certain interventions, such as haemodialysis. It may be that the demands of the machinery eschew the legitimacy of subjective experience.

11 For some people in intensive care units, their apparent subjugation by technology can be associated with beliefs that the care staff are actually out to harm them, and that they are victims of the technology, rather than being assisted by it.

12 The use of virtual reality may help to diminish some aspects of a distressing experience. Virtual reality technology also has the potential to offer people different forms of embodiment and to match this to their own psychophysiological processes. Cybersickness, experienced by some using virtual reality, may be a marker of the tension between virtual and biological embodiments.

Discussion points

1 Are there psychological implications of chimerism?
2 How can different levels of meaning about bodily experience be integrated?
3 How could people with quadriplegia be liberated from their physical state through the use of virtual reality.

Key reading

Brodwin, P. E. (ed.) (2000) *Biotechnology and Culture: Bodies, Anxieties, Ethics*. Bloomington: Indiana University Press.

Burloux, G. and Bachman, D. (2004) Psychology and hand transplantation: clinical experiences, in M. MacLachlan and P. Gallagher (eds) *Enabling Technologies: Body Image and Body Function*. Edinburgh: Churchill Livingstone.

Lupton, D. and Seymour, W. (2000) Technology, selfhood and physical disability, *Social Science and Medicine*, 50: 1851–62.

CHAPTER 7

Forms of embodiment

It's seven whole days since I
have seen my lover. A sickness
Pervades me. My limbs are lead
I barely sense my body

(From B. H. Fowler's *Love Lyrics of Ancient Egypt*,
1994, cited in Carr 2003)

The human mind perceives the world in symbolic terms
and never stops exercising the imagination. As a result,
much of culture consists of fictions that endow natural
processes with symbolic importance . . . Every part and
function of the body plays its symbolic role.

(Sims 2003: 5–6)

In this concluding chapter I do not attempt to synthesize the many strands
of embodiment into one coherent whole – one body, as it were. I hope that
the preceding chapters have made clear that there are many forms of
embodiment, some interlocking, some quite distinct. To allow for this
multiplicity we need a fairly permissive and pluralistic conception of just
what embodiment is, or how it may play out. In this chapter I briefly
recollect some of the themes previously discussed, revisit a couple and intro-
duce some others that I see as being critical for a broader understanding of
embodiment from a clinical, critical and cultural perspective.

Recently the concept of neural plasticity has challenged, nay contradicted, what we had been taught for many years: that regeneration of the
central nervous system was impossible. The significance, and reality, of
neural plasticity, however, goes beyond simply showing that 'scientific
fact' was wrong (could not, in fact, have been, 'fact'), it has also required a
loosening up, an opening up, of thinking in neuroscience. The margins are
more blurred, the limits are unclear, and this uncertainty is being seen as
exciting. I have argued that a similar process has been occurring in
people's ideas about the body. While once gene-machines produced
'what you get is what you see' bodies, now this need not be so. Our
memes (Dawkins 1976), our cultural ideas and values, have usurped the
pre-eminence of their genetic masters. Now ideas change genes, change
hearts, change faces, breasts, penises; and that which cannot yet be
changed is on the 'to do' list. In an age of amazing biotechnologies 'what
you get' (genetically) can be endlessly revised, enabled and improved
upon, according to cultural standards. Of course, culture has always left its

mark on the body, whether by tattooing or other 'superficial' embellishments; but now culture has pierced the skin, scanning through layers of epidermis to reveal tumours, blockages and indeed people, that previously only broke the surface at biologically determined times. In some respects our ideas of biological modification have transmuted into living possibilities and raced ahead of our understanding of their ethical, moral and spiritual meaning.

The traditional mechanistic explanation of people in terms of their constituent neurons or cells, while very worthy and necessary, will never be adequate, or indeed satisfying, for people motivated to find meaning in life and their struggle through life. Whatever other levels of explanation we may have we will always need an explanation that makes sense at the level through which we experience the world. This level is one where it is important to make meaning out of our experiences (Frankl 1984). The need to try to form coherent Gestalts (or actually 'sub-Gestalts') out of life is arguably at the root of objectifying representations of the self presented in Cartesian dualism, the notion of the Foucauldian 'gaze', Lacan's 'specular image' and so on. The possibility, indeed the promise, of Merleau-Ponty's concept of embodiment is to recognize the 'perceiving percept' as a mindful body. An important element of this is the construction (and continual reconstruction) of the self though language and the biological work that is associated with this. The concept of 'self' is not only a psychological construction, it is underpinned by a biology of the self. In chronic pain we see the struggle to distinguish a psychological self from 'another' (biological) one, and the difficulties that ensue. Only the ill, or disabled, body is within our awareness; the well body is, like a familiar friend, too taken for granted to give it such courteous attention.

Sims's (2003) recent book *Adam's Navel* is a fascinating exploration of how the cultural history of the body shadows its natural history, and how all aspects of the body's surface are imbued with symbolic cultural significance. While the body may be a canvas to write upon it is also a messenger, and often one that reaches beyond itself: conveying personal, interpersonal, group or societal concerns, and sometimes in forms that are difficult to decipher. The old idea of some physical illnesses being caused by psychological factors (psychosomatics) has now been broadly abandoned with the realization that in fact all physical illnesses are influenced by psychosocial factors. The advent of psychoneuroimmunology has effectively undermined simplistic sequential notions of mind–body cause–effect. Furthermore, even those conditions with clearly the heaviest biological burden in their aetiology can be shaped by the personal, social and cultural avenues that constitute their broader environment.

Our everyday embodiment is evidenced most clearly in a metaphorical psychophysiological reaction to stress. This atavistic and symbolic reaction, when chronic, produces channels for serious illnesses. As well as explicit psychological factors, such as the anger–hostility–aggression aspect of the type A personality, more implicit (and perhaps unconscious) factors, such as degree of social inequity, or people's place in the social hierarchy, have a physical imprint on the health of the body. Additionally, forms of somatization, despite their myriad diagnoses, may be grouped into 'fatigue pain' and 'cardiorespiratory' categories. Like conversion reactions, their creation and their half-life may be determined by their cultural utility. On the other hand, a range of neurological conditions vividly conveys how brain damage mediates anomalous representations of the body: how the personal meaning of body parts can be 'lost', or how an inanimate object can be taken as a person. The coordination of action and intention, so clearly a part of our individualized embodiment, provides us with agency. The lack of such agency, explicit in some forms of disability, may be seen as diminishing the person who is disabled, some bodily functions being absent, and through that absence, ever present. Such difference, in drawing us away from cultural ideals, becomes stigmatized and frightening, and seen as embodying 'the other'. By being defined not by limitations, but by abilities and aspirations, a confident disembodiment (as opposed to disowning of the body) may be a useful perspective for some physically disabled people.

The supposed link between physicality and personality has led us to sculpture body shapes imbued with the self-esteem we seek. By conforming to culturally sanctioned bodily forms we reap assurance of our worth. Today, like the Greek gods of old, our air-brushed digitized celeb-somas are fables. This does not stop us trying to acquire such forms of embodiment, for like the ancients, in a world of myth (and biotechnological wonderment) we can imagine that just about anything is possible. However, at a time when bodies can be nipped, tucked, sucked and so on, more and more of them are, in fact, becoming obese, and ironically such excess is most prevalent among those with least money. In the rich world of the industrialized West obesity is increasingly becoming the embodiment of relative scarcity. While we may validly question the attractiveness of cultural ideals of the body, these ideals remain responsible for propelling at least some people into the desperate grasp of eating disorders, where cultural preoccupations produce a channel for personal distress to become embodied in a painfully diminished form. Equally worrying can be the striving of the 'reverse anorexic' to achieve the disproportional super-hero steroid-pumped musculature that some men and boys (and a few women) now seek. If the body, like the veil, can hide the self, then the somas being touted to our children and tweenagers must surely also have implications for their sense of self. Ambiguities between gender identification and biological sex, and ambiguities raised by intersexuality and by paraphilias, continue to question the rigid assumptions we have of the physical body.

Such assumptions are nowhere more questioned than in illusory body experiences. Phantom phenomena only became scientifically respectable once explanations were available for their occurrence. Yet explanations that appeal to neural plasticity offer only a partial understanding. Individuals' negotiation with their body image and their sense of 'lost limbs' may be an ongoing experience over many years, with some people reporting phantom pain more than 50 years after amputation. Bodily illusions are also to be found in the fully able-bodied and appear, at least to some extent, to interact with people's sense of 'body plasticity'. In addition to this, 'body-space' illusions in peripersonal space may also reflect a sense of embodiment in inanimate objects. Perhaps equally interesting is what *does not* appear to be 'me', when it might be expected to. For instance, sophisticated myoelectric limbs that allow for the incorporation of intention and action in a 'life-like' manner may not embody the self. Such an experience may be achieved in time when prostheses are wired into the nervous system and when they can be used for emotional and declarative expression, such as in gesticulation. Again, here, it is suggested that a sense of embodiment may be achieved only when there is a lack of awareness of the body part in question. This spotlight of attention may be considered individually and 'close up', or socially and more 'distantly'. Culture determines how disability is to be read and thus initially illuminates the ground of possible experience and foci of attention. Ultimately the social meaning and implications of a bodily injury, such as amputation, may feed back into the biological mechanisms that influence their occurrence.

The reading of bodily experience is also in contention when enabling technologies offer objectifying representations that differ from subjective feelings: biomedical and personal meaning may collide, and whether by design or by practice, the use of technology is rarely neutral. Technologies can listen to the body, interact with it, replace parts of it or allow the rest of the body to live through it. Ultrasound, IVF, surrogacy and stem cell research are just some of the reproductive technologies that question our previously biologically restricted constructions of personhood and parenthood: issues that will continue to feed into the debate on termination, abortion and human rights. Ironically, the 'absolutism' of cloning may ultimately have extinguished to mythology the notion of individual immortality. Yet chimerism, as the engine of organ transplantation, does offer a 'Trojan horse' entrance into the body of another, when the organ's owner has passed away. In the transplanting of limbs the integration of 'foreign' body parts may challenge the psychological integrity of the body, of who and what is embodied. Indeed, the technological enframing of the body may undermine its agency on the one hand, while offering it new possibilities for existence in virtual worlds on the other hand. As ever, technological possibilities live in a world of social, economic and political disparity, and the worldwide trade in organs – from rich to poor – represents perhaps the most exploitative form of embodiment.

Embodiment emerges not simply as 'the concrete expression of an abstract idea', when that expression is through the soma, but as a sort of collage of superimposed forms. These include:

♦ *Body social*: where the social spectre of the body is obvious to the person, such as in the case of cosmetic surgery, or where a disabled person feels that only their body is seen, and not 'them'.

♦ *Body emotion*: where the immediacy of emotional experience produces physical reaction beyond the ability of rational reflection; for instance, an otherwise paralysed limb responding by movement to music.

♦ *Body expression*: where the body conveys distress though symbolism, as in anorexia nervosa.

♦ *Body unawareness*: where physical or social agents inscribe their effects upon the body without conscious awareness; for instance, viral infections or socio-economic gradients.

♦ *Body memory*: where the immune systems 'learns' how to respond to environmental threats, or becomes hypersensitive to them, without conscious mediation.

♦ *Body anomaly*: where through either brain damage or illusory induction procedures people ascribe human embodiment to inanimate objects, or treat others or the self as an inanimate object.

♦ *Body delusion*: where an extreme and false belief is held about some aspect of the body, such as in body dysmorphic disorder.

♦ *Body contagion*: where, perhaps through a process of social contagion, one body reproduces the symptoms of another body.

♦ *Body agency*: where a sense of being-a-body is created by the coordination of intention and motor action.

♦ *Body sensation*: where the boundaries of the body are known through the rim of its felt sensation, as in the case of Siamese twins.

♦ *Body absence*: where a lack of awareness of the body is taken for granted because functionally it is unproblematic.

♦ *Body plasticity*: where a sense of the self is not necessarily restricted to aspects of biological inheritance, but may extend to include identification with transplanted organs or limbs, belongings worn on the person or distinct inanimate objects.

♦ *Body indifference*: where the body, its appearance and functioning seem of little consequence to a person who may be invested in ideas, abstract concepts or ideals.

This is not an exhaustive range of forms of embodiment, and it certainly is not exclusive either. It is intended simply to be illustrative of how the body is used as the vehicle of a sense of being-in-the-world. For instance, often body awareness is combined with a lack of awareness, when some regions are focused on and others therefore ignored. Body anomaly may be combined with body agency, body plasticity, body expression and so on. These different facets of embodiment represent various ways in which we can relate to, and through, our bodies. It is this flexibility of our 'perceiving perceptible' (Merleau-Ponty 1962) that offers alternative forms of embodiment, that may be most therapeutic in the clinical context as we strive to find better ways for people to 'live their bodies'. I conclude now by considering some fundamental issues regarding embodiment that I have not previously dealt with sufficiently.

The cultural body

We concluded Chapter 1 by considering Terror Management Theory (TMT), which was based on the work of Ernest Becker and others, and hinted that it might apply to the realm of embodiment. Recent developments in TMT that have linked cultural identity to bodily concerns, and to embodiment, consider some of the implications of seeing the body as a cultural object. An obvious question is: 'Why make the body a cultural object?' One of the implications of Darwinian theory is that if there is little that sets us apart from animals then the justification for a distinct soul, or divine beginning, or afterlife, is questionable. There is thus a need for us to distinguish ourselves from the 'baseness' of our everyday animal functions. Our symbolic identities achieve this, but precariously, since we can never escape our biological needs. As noted earlier, Becker (1973: 51) says we are 'gods with anuses', and Goldenberg et al. (2000) argue that the reason our animal nature is a problem is because it reminds us that we are finite, that we will, like all animals, arrive at death. The consequence of this is that cultures cultivate ideas about the body that distinguish it from animals and in doing so, at an unconscious level, present the possibility of at least symbolic immortality. Cultures may differ in their rule of dress, practices of hygiene and norms of sexuality, in defining what is attractive and what is not, but they all, none the less, provide such rules.

Sexuality may present a special problem for a sanitized symbolic body, because (as quoted in Goldenberg et al. 2000) 'Sex is of the body, and the body is death' (Becker 1973: 162). While romanticism may be one strategy for diminishing the animality of sex, the glamorization of sexual success may also allow for the attainment of self-esteem therein. Aside from concerns about sex, TMT argues that the drive to make beautiful the body is so important 'because it allows humans to transform the most threatening aspect of the self, the animal body, into a symbol through which one can acquire value by living up to cultural standards and thereby ward off our fear of death' (Goldenberg et al. 2000: 210). Self-esteem is traded for mortality, and even poor self-esteem, it may be argued, is better than being transfixed on certain death. 'In other worlds, people buy into the cultural value system and become absorbed in meeting cultural standards of the body so they do not have to view themselves as mere ambulatory conglomerates of flesh and guts doomed to decay and death' (Goldenberg et al. 2000: 211). Again quoting Becker, Goldenberg et al. note that the civilizing process 'is one in which we exchange a natural animal sense of our basic worth, for a contrived, symbolic one'.

A long series of clever experimental manipulations (for reviews see Solomon *et al.* 1991, 1998) have shown that when people are indirectly reminded of their mortality (for instance, by writing about what happens to a body after the person dies) they show greater belief in the cultural world views they hold, compared to those given a 'non-mortality salience' intervention (for instance, writing about TV). Applying this to the context of the body being portrayed as a cultural symbol of beauty, Goldenberg *et al.* (2000) divided college students into high and low body esteem groups, gave then a mortality (or non-mortality) salience exercise and then asked them how central to their sense of self were various bodily and non-body characteristics. They found that people with high body esteem, when given the mortality salience manipulation, identified more strongly with their bodily selves. In a subsequent experiment they found that after mortality salience manipulation, those with high body esteem also showed increased interest in physical sex.

Thus, it seems that the body, and indeed sexual activity, can be used as a buffer against the anxiety aroused by indirect contemplation of one's own mortality. Of course, the body may only be a good anxiety buffer to the extent that it is judged to be a 'good body' by 'its owner', and these judgements are influenced by cultural norms. I find results, such as those described above, exciting and intriguing. Unfortunately it is beyond our scope to examine this research further, as my primary purpose for mentioning it is to develop a line of argument more strongly related to our current concern.

The objectified body

In distinct, but related, work Fredrickson and Robert's (1997) Objectification Theory argues that – in North American culture – females' assessment of their self-worth is strongly influenced by the extent to which their physical appearance accords to sexually objectifying and unrealistic standards of beauty. 'Sexualized gazing' serves to objectify the body, where a person's body (its parts and sexual functions) is separated from their self. This sexual objectification is more common for women than for men, suggesting the cultural presumption that a woman's body is more able to represent her than a man's body is able to represent him. Objectification theory argues that socialization into these norms particularly leads girls to internalize an objectifying observer's perspective on their own body (Fredrickson *et al.* 1998). However, increasing objectification of men's bodies has also been discussed for some time now (see, for instance, Van Zoonen 1994).

A powerful biological exemplar of the influence of gaze is found in Darwin's (1872: 325) observation relating to shame: 'It is not the simple act of reflecting on our own appearance, but the thinking of what others think of us, which excites a blush.' Ironically, by standing back from our self and considering the perspective of others, we induce an intimate biological rush of shame in the very body we are escaping through our objectification. Shame is the entwinement of negative self-evaluations and the fear of this being made public, and this is exactly what our betraying body does when it pushes through a blush. Shame (and its anticipation through an ever-present Foucauldian gaze) motivates compliance with social norms for appearance, where 'body ideals are taken as moral ideals' (Fredrickson *et al.* 1998: 272).

Fredrickson *et al.* (1998), in their wonderfully entitled paper 'That swimsuit becomes you', set out to test the predictions that self-objectification in women produces shame, which leads to restrained eating (the cultural ideal being thin), and also consumes attentional resources, thus interfering with performing on a maths test (because if you are thinking about your body it is harder to do maths). In their first experiment, participants tried on either a swimsuit or a sweater in front of a mirror (unaware of the other condition). They were then given cookies to eat (as part of another sham market research procedure). Those women in the swimsuit condition, who had high (trait) self-objectification, reduced their subsequent intake of cookies, relative to those in the sweater condition. In a subsequent experiment comparing men and women, the effect was replicated for women but not found for men. Subsequent ability on a maths test (replacing the cookies) was also diminished for women in the swimsuit condition but not for men. This latter finding was interpreted as women's experience of shame interfering with their ability to do cognitively demanding tasks, such as maths.

Assuming a third-person perspective on one's own body diminishes that body's inclinations (consuming cookies) and performance (maths test). The objectification of the body seems at once to distance the self from it yet also to accept it as a symbol of, or metaphor for, self-worth. This sort of what might be called 'proximate distancing' makes the body an inescapable projection of the self. Fredrickson *et al.*'s studies also, however, indicate that there is considerable individual variability in the extent of body objectification. There is also variation in the extent to which people will project 'themselves' into physical entities other than their biological body. Certain situations may promote these responses more than others, and it would seem that Fredrickson *et al.*'s swimsuit condition 'reduced participants to feeling "I am a body" – in effect, that the swimsuit becomes you'. Increasingly the sexual objectification of girls and women is also applying to boys and men (see Chapter 4) and so the processes alluded to above are becoming a more pervasive and probably more destructive cultural norm, at least in the North-Western world.

Transitional objects

Winnicott (1971) coined the term transitional object (TO) to refer to the child's 'first not-me possession'. Examples include a teddy bear or a blanket, and such TOs can be seen as a normal part of healthy development occurring around six months. The TO was understood to represent the breast, or mother, and its use protected against the anxiety associated with the process of individuation – the child recognizing that he or she is a 'separate' person. Although there is little empirical research in the area, Arthern and Madill (1999, 2002) suggest that TOs continue to be used by some throughout adolescence and indeed into adulthood.

I believe that the ethos of Western science, with its historical emphasis on the primacy of the 'mind', has in effect created a *context* for the body itself to become a transitional object. Moreover, increasing Western cultural objectification of the body has provided a *mechanism* for this to happen and the creation of the body as an iconic cultural object has provided a *reason* for it to happen. So how do TOs work in practice? Arthern and Madill (1999a) asked therapists to describe the way in which transitional objects came into being as a part of adult psychotherapy, and what they believed their function was. Based on interviews with the therapists, they derived a four-level theory based on the process of embodiment and stated that: 'The TO literally "embodied" (gave body to) the [therapeutic] relationship in the absence of the actual presence of the therapist' (Arthern and Madill 1999a: 16).

Just as a physical object can represent and give comfort regarding the absence of an idealized figure (the therapist, or mother), so too can the human body be sculptured into an idealized form, the possession of which, it is assumed, will be comforting because of its association with idealized *figures*: actors, singers, models; cultural icons; the 'beautiful people'. In essence, the human body can act as a TO, *but in reverse*. Conventionally the TO is identified with in order to alleviate anxiety associated with *loss of*, or *removal from*, an idealized object (mother). However, the transitional object in reverse (TOR), in the form of the human body, is a mechanism for the person to *approach* an idealized object, it is an acquisitive project. Thus rather than the significance of the TO reducing over time, it increases over time, as the person is able to shape and mould their body increasingly in the image of their idealized object. Sugarman and Kurash (1982: 59) also argued that the body acted as a transitional object in bulimia nervosa, and noted that 'the body of the infant is the first transitional object, a precursor of the later external transitional objects'. We have already noted, however, that in objectifying the body it came to be viewed from the third person, to be externalized. Sugarman and Krush (1982: 62) saw the bulimic's feeding of her body as being to 'lose herself in the experience of being one with mother' in terms of reuniting her with the physical sensation of satisfaction. However, this maladaptive use of the body as a TO is not necessarily the case.

Sugarman and Kurash (1982: 62) note the increasing importance of TOs during adolescence:

transitional objects can become more diverse during adolescence than they were in childhood. Clothing, living space, and their culture's concept of art replace the blanket or teddy bear, but in a more symbolic sense. It is what they stand for, the symbol of the adolescent member-ship in his peer group, rather than their tactile or sensory qualities which imbue them with transitional qualities for the adolescent.

Although we have noted previously that the ideal celeb-soma is, realistically, unobtainable, at the same time our contemporary technologies, surgeries and medicines allow fewer reasons not to try. Indeed, our increasing secular-ism demands alternative world-views, views that are crammed with the apparent pleasures of consumption and celebrity. Through making our bodies transitional objects in reverse we consume the trail to bodily perfection, achieving two goals in one.

We are all affected to some extent by the reach of Western cultures, but their reach may be particularly unfortunate for those combating physical distress, disease or disability. For such an ethos literally adds insult to injury: loss of self-esteem to prospects of mortality. It is the omnipotence of the contemporary body that has made the concept of embodiment so relevant for understanding the experience of alternative physical beings. Ultimately, however, one may well ask how such a constructivist view of the human body, how any transitional object-like status it may have, relates back to the hard wiring of the brain, which it must do. How can a socially constructed consciousness and a biologically inherited neurology be reconciled?

The conscious body

In trying to develop a constructivist perspective on chronic pain, Chapman et al. (1999) note two key aspects of research on consciousness. First they note that:

Biology offers thousands of examples of how organisms, ranging from colonies of bacteria to herds of caribou, organise themselves as a leader-less collective in the course of adapting to an environment. The behaviour of a flock of birds is a common example. One can argue that crowd behaviour, traffic jams, and culture itself are human aspects of this process.

(Chapman et al. 1999: 44).

Their key point here is that seemingly chaotic phenomena can in fact be considered as complex systems.

A second aspect of much consciousness research is the concept of emergence; that is, of consciousness being an emergent property, something that exists but is not present in its constituent parts, or predictable from them. This resonates with the notion of a Gestalt where the whole is taken as being greater than the sum of its parts. As Chapman *et al.* (1999: 44) state, 'the concept of emergent property helps one escape from the constrained thinking of Cartesian clockwork mechanics'.

Combining these, Chapman *et al.* (1999: 44) understand consciousness as a 'dynamical self-organising process operating in a distributed neural network', with some on/off aspects (coma, sleep, anaesthesia) but generally varying with degree of arousal. An essential point is that the brain deals not with reality, but with an *internal representation* of reality, and this representation is *subjective* and continually being *reconstructed* (updated). The 'drivers' of this revisioning include sensory stimuli, emotions, cognitions and it 'always has a point of view. The point of view is the sense of self, which is closely tied to the sense of body-self' (Chapman *et al.* 1999: 45). Chapman *et al.* go on to describe how pain is both an event that produces biological events and one that calls for a meaning to be made of it; consciousness seeks to 'form meaningful wholes' of both internal and external events, of both biological and social representations of the self.

The spotlight of consciousness is always 'about something' and often patterned by emotions. Chapman *et al.* (1999: 46) note that the biological processing of pain involves not simply sequential processing along single pathways, but, in fact, massive parallel and distributed processing in the cerebral cortex, which 'integrates, produces coherence, and sets the stage for the individual's construction of immediate experience and meaning'. Such a conception of consciousness is enthralling and encouraging from the point of view of embodiment, yet it does not, I believe, go far enough; for it locates the conscious 'mind' only on top of the shoulders. Yet the mind is not only of the brain; I believe that the essence of embodiment implies that it is also *of the body*. Organs are emotional.

In Chapter 1, I quoted Carey (2000: 38) to the effect that 'because the cells of the body, not just the brain, receive and secrete information-bearing chemicals, the whole body is an intelligence-bearing organism'. My heart, as it beats with excitement, passion or anxiety, is not only providing signals to a cerebral relay station, it is also living a meaning. How my heart reacts tells me how I feel about things, just as my eyes and ears tell me how things look and sound. Not only my heart is at once a sensory and reactive organ, so too are my many organs innervated by the autonomic nervous system, which prepares me for fight or flight (Chapter 2). If a 'chicken might be an egg's way of making another egg', then might a brain be a heart's way of responding to another's heart?

We can take the concept of emergence and apply it beyond the confines of cerebral neurology, to include all aspects of the human body. Merleau-Ponty argues for a perception of the world that is *particular* because of the being that one is embodied in. However, this body does not just *constitute* a point of view (as in astride a mountain or down a valley), it also *constructs* a point of view. Furthermore, bodies react differently to similar stimuli and similarly to different stimuli. Our body has a place in what we think, and *is* the place of what we think. Our brain is an integral part of our bodily processes, but the emergent property of mind has somatic as well as neuro-logical elements. I have quoted, with approval, Schweder's phrase that 'culture and mind make each other up', yet this too can be extended: 'culture and mind *and body* make each other up'. Our culture's construction of what the body is about, and our individual ideas concerning body shape and function, each intrude upon the body, inject it, take bits off and add others on. And all this both constitutes and determines our embodied point of view.

Questions

1 Is the essence of embodiment to be found in a lack of awareness of the body or in enhanced awareness of it?
2 Can the body be considered as a cultural object?
3 Is the body a transitional object?

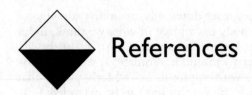

References

Adler, N.E., Boyce, T., Chesney, M.A. et al. (1994) Socioeconomic status and health: the challenge of the gradient. *American Psychologist*, 49: 15–24.

Amnesty International (1973) *Report on Torture*. London: Duckworth.

Anderson, A.E. (2002) Eating disorders in males, in C.G. Fairburn and K.D. Brownell (eds) *Eating Disorders and Obesity* (2nd edn). New York: The Guilford Press.

Arthern, J. and Madill, A. (1999) How do transitional objects work? The therapist's view. *British Journal of Medical Psychology*, 72: 1–21.

Arthern, J. and Madill, A. (1999) How do transitional objects work? The client's view. *Psychotherapy Research*, 12: 369–88.

Balsalmo, A. (1995) Forms of technological embodiment: reading the body in contemporary culture. *Body and Society*, 1: 215–38.

Barber, N. (1998). Secular changes in standards of bodily attractiveness in American women: different masculine and feminine ideals. *Journal of Psychology*, 132: 87–94.

Barefoot, J.C., Dahlstrom, W.C. and Williams, R.B. (1983) Hostility, CHD incidence, and total mortality: a 25-year follow-up study of 255 physicians. *Psychosomatic Medicine*, 45: 59–63.

Bass, E. and Davis, L. (1988) *The Courage to Heal*. New York: Harper and Row.

Bauby, J.D. (1998) *The Diving-Bell and The Butterfly* (translated by Jeremy Leggatt). London: Fourth Estate.

Becker, E. (1962) *The Birth and Death of Meaning*. New York: Braziller.

Becker, E. (1973) *The Denial of Death*. New York: Free Press.

Bendelow, G.A. and Williams, S.J. (1995) Transcending the dualisms – towards a sociology of pain. *Sociology of Health and Illness*, 17: 139–65.

Bennun, I. (2001) Intensive care unit syndrome: a consideration of psychological interventions. *British Journal of Medical Psychology*, 74: 369–77.

Bennun. I. (2004) Critical care in high technology environments, in M. MacLachlan and P. Gallagher (eds) *Enabling Technologies: Body image and body function*. Edinburgh: Churchill Livingstone.

Benson, C. (2001) *The Cultural Psychology of Self: Place, Morality and Art in Human Worlds*. London: Routledge.

Bergbom-Engberg I. and Haljamae H. (1988) A retrospective study of patient's recall of respirator treatment: nursing care factors and feelings of security/insecurity. *Intensive Care Nursing*, 4: 95–101.

Berlucchi, G. and Aglioti, S. (1997) The body in the brain: neural basis of corporeal awareness. *Trends in Neurosciences*, 20: 560–4.

Bernstein, E. (2002) It Ain't Over 'Til the Fat Lady Sings. *The Asian Wall Street Journal*, 6th–8th December, p. 3.

Biderman, A., Yeheskel, A. and Herman, J. (2003) Somatic fixation: the harm of healing. *Social Science and Medicine*, 56: 1135–8.

Birbaumer, N., Lutzenberger, W., Montoya, P. et al. (1997). Effects of regional anaesthesia on phantom limb pain are mirrored in changes in cortical reorganisation. *The Journal of Neuroscience*, 17: 5503–8.

Bisiach, E., Rusconi, M.L. and Vallar, G. (1991) Remission of somatoparaphrenic delusion through vestibular stimulation. *Neuropsychologia*, 29: 1029–31.

Blackford, K.M.H. and Newcomb, A. (1915) *The Job, the Man, the Boss*. New York: Doubleday.

Blanke, O., Ortigue, S., Landis, T. and Seeck, M. (2002) Stimulating illusory own-body perceptions. *Nature*, 419: 269.

Bogin, B. and Loucky, J. (1997) Plasticity, political economy, and physical growth status of Guatemala Maya children living in the United States. *American Journal of Physical Anthropology*, 102: 17–32.

Botvinick, M. and Cohen, J. (1998) Rubber hands 'feel' touch that eyes see. *Nature*, 391: 756.

Breakey, J.W. (1997) Body image: the lower-limb amputee. *Journal of Prosthetics and Orthotics*, 9: 58–66.

Brodwin, P.E. (2000) Introduction, in P.E. Brodwin (ed.) *Biotechnology and Culture: Bodies, anxieties, ethics*. Bloomington: Indiana University Press (pp. 3–23).

Buckley, W.A., Yesalis, C.E., Friedl, K.E. et al. (1988) Estimated prevalence of anabolic steroid use among male high school seniors. *Journal of the American Medical Association*, 260: 3441–5.

Burger, H., Marincek, C. and Jaeger, R.L. (2004) Prosthetic device provision in landmine survivors in Bosnia and Herzegovina: outcomes in three ethnic groups. *Archives of Physical Medicine and Rehabilitation*, 85: 19–28.

Burloux, G. and Bachmann, D. (2004) Psychology and hand transplantation: clinical experiences, in M. MacLachlan and P. Gallagher (eds) *Enabling Technologies: Body image and body function*. Edinburgh: Churchill Livingstone.

Bushfield, J. (2000) *Men, Woman and Madness: Understanding gender and mental disorder*. London: Macmillan.

Cannon, W.B. (1935) Stress and strains of homeostasis. *American Journal of Medical Science*, 189: 1–14.

Carey, S. (2000) Cultivating ethos through the body. *Human Studies*, 23: 23–42.

Carr, S.C. (2003) *Social Psychology: Context, Communication and Culture*. Sydney: Wiley.

Cash, T.F. and Pruzinsky, T. (1990) (eds). *Body Images: Development, deviance and change*. New York: The Guilford Press.

Cash, T.F. and Pruzinsky, T. (eds) (2002) *Body Images: A handbook of theory, research, and clinical practice*. New York: The Guilford Press.

Cash, T.F. (1989) Body-image affect: gestalt versus summing the parts. *Perceptual and Motor Skills*, 69: 17–18.

Cash, T.F. and Deagle, E.A. (1997) The nature and extent of body–image disturbance in anorexia nervosa and bulimia nervosa: a meta-analysis. *International Journal of Eating Disorders*, 22: 107–25.

Casper, R.C. (1982) Treatment principles in anorexia nervosa. *Adolescent Psychiatry*, 10: 86–100.

Cassell, E.J. (1976) Disease as an 'it': concepts of disease revealed by patients' representations of symptoms. *Social Science and Medicine*, 10: 143–6.

Cassidy, T. (1999) *Stress, Cognition and Health*. London: Routledge.

Cavallaro, D. and Vago, C. (1997) *The Body for Beginners*. New York: Writers and Readers Publishing Inc.

Chadderton, H.C. (1983) Consumer concerns in prosthetics. *Prosthetics and Orthotics International*, 7: 15–16.

Channel 4 (2003) 'Skinny Kids', screened on 13th January.

Chapman, C.R., Nakamura, Y. and Flores, L.Y. (1999) Chronic pain and consciousness: a constructivist perspective, in R.J. Gatchel and D.C. Turk (eds) *Psychosocial Factors in Pain: Critical Perspectives*. New York: The Guildford Press.

Cheng, S.T. (1994) A critical review of the Chinese koro. International Congress of Applied Psychology, Madrid, July 17–22.

Childress, D.S. (1985) Historical aspects of powered limb prostheses. *Clinical Prosthetics and Orthotics*, 9: 2–13.

Chomsky, N. (1965) *Aspects of a Theory of Syntax*. Cambridge, MA: MIT Press.

Church, R.B., Ayman-Nolley, S. and Gordon, E. (2002) Levels of embodiment and learning: 'Do as I do, not what I say'. Paper presented at 23rd Jean Piaget Society Conference: *The Embodied Mind and Consciousness: Developmental perspectives*, Philadelphia, 6–8 June.

Clare, A. (2001) *On Men: Masculinity in Crisis*. London: Arrow Books.

Cohn, L.D., and Adler, N.E. (1992). Female and male perceptions of ideal body shapes: distorted views among Caucasian college students. *Psychology of Women Quarterly*, 16(1): 69–79.

Corbin, J. and Strauss, A.L. (1987) Accompaniments of chronic illness: changes in body, self, biography and biographical time. *Research in Sociology and Health Care*, 6: 249–81.

Corson, P.W. and Andersen, A.E. (2002) Body image issues among boys and men, in T.F. Cash and T. Pruzinsky (eds) *Body Image: A handbook of theory, research, and practice*. New York: The Guilford Press.

Craddock, G. and McCormack, L. (2002) Delivering an AT service: client-focused, social and participatory service delivery model in assistive technology in Ireland. *Disability and Rehabilitation*, 24(1/2/3): 160–70.

Crisp, A.H. (1997) Anorexia nervosa as flight from growth: assessment and treatment based on the model, in D.M. Garner and P.E. Garfinkel (eds) *Handbook of Treatment for Eating Disorders* (2nd edn). New York: Guilford.

Critser, G. (2003) *Fat Land: How Americans Became the Fattest People in the World*. London: Penguin.

Cutting, J. (1990) *The Right Cerebral Hemisphere and Psychiatric Disorders*. Oxford: Oxford University Press.

Daar, A.S. (2000) Cultural and societal issues in organ transplantation: examples from different cultures. *Transplantation Proceedings*, 32: 1480–1.

Damasio, A. (1999) *The Feeling of What Happens: Body and Emotion in the Making of Consciousness*. New York: Harcourt Brace.

Damasio, A. (2002) Rethinking emotion. Paper presented at 23rd Jean Piaget Society Conference: *The Embodied Mind and Consciousness: Developmental perspectives*, Philadelphia, 6–8 June.

Darwin, C. (1782/1965) *The Expression of Emotion in Man and Animals*. Chicago: University of Chicago Press.

Davis, F. (1961) Deviance disavowal: the management of strained interaction by the visibly handicapped. *Social Problems*, 9: 120–32.

Dawkins, R. (1976) *The Selfish Gene*. Oxford: Oxford University Press.

Day, H.J.B. (1998) Amputee rehabilitation – finding the niche. *Prosthetics and Orthotics International*, 22: 92–101.

Delahanty, D.L., Dougall, A.L., Hawken, L. et al. (1996) Time course of natural killer cell activity and lymphocyte proliferation in response to two acute stressors in healthy men. *Health Psychology*, 15: 48–55.

Desmond, D., Horgan, O. and MacLachlan, M. (2001) Body boundary appraisals and the measurement of plasticity: development of the Trinity Assessment of Body Plasticity (TABP). Paper presented at the 10th World Congress of the International Society for Prosthetics and Orthotics, Glasgow, July 2001.

Desmond, D. and MacLachlan, M. (2002) Psychosocial issues in the field of prosthetics and orthotics. *Journal of Prosthetics and Orthotics*, 12(2): 12–24.

Desmond, D. and MacLachlan, M. (2004) Psychosocial perspectives on postamputation rehabilitation: a review of disease-, trauma-, and war-related literature. *Critical Reviews in Rehabilitation and Physical Medicine*, 16: 77–93.

Desmond, D. and MacLachlan, M. (submitted) Phantom Pain Persists.

Diamond, M. and Sigmundson, H.K. (1997) Sex reassignment at birth: long-term review and clinical implications. *Archives of Paediatric and Adolescent Medicine*, 151: 298–304.

Dijkstra, P.U., Geertzen, J.H.B., Stewart, R. and van der Schans, C.P. (2002) Phantom pain and risk factors: a multivariate analysis. *Journal of Pain and Symptom Management*, 24: 578–85.

Dittmar, H., Lloyd, B., Dugan, S. et al. (2000). The 'body beautiful': English adolescents' images of ideal bodies. *Sex Roles*, 42(9–10): 887–915.

Dobson, R. (2000) Cloning of pigs bring xenotransplants closer. *British Medical Journal*, 320: 862.

Dobson, R. (2001) Larynx patient sings praises of transplant. *The Sunday Times*, 9th September, p. 4.

Docter, R.F. (1988) *Transvestites and Transsexuals: Towards a theory of cross-gender behaviour*. New York: Plenum.

Dowling, R.D. (2004) Implantable replacement hearts, in M. MacLachlan and P. Gallagher (eds) *Enabling Technologies: Body image and body function*. Edinburgh: Churchill Livingstone.

Doyal, L. (2001) Sex, gender and health: the need for a new approach. *British Medical Journal*, 323: 1061–3.

Driscoll, M. (2003) Stealthily stealing their innocence. *The Sunday Times*, 19th January, pp. 5–7.

Dyer, C. (2000) Surgeon amputated healthy legs. *British Medical Journal*, 320: 332.

Dyer, I. (1995a) Preventing the ITU syndrome or how not to torture an ITU patient! Part 1. *Intensive and Critical Care Nursing*, 11: 223–32.

Dyer, I. (1995b) Preventing the ITU syndrome or how not to torture an ITU patient! Part 2. *Intensive and Critical Care Nursing*, 12: 132–9.

Easterling, B.A., Kiecolt-Glaser, J.K. and Glaser, R. (1996) Psychological modulation of cytokine-induced natural killer cell activity in older adults. *Psychosomatic Medicine*, 58: 264–72.

Eddy, K.T., Keel, P.K., Dorer, D.J. et al. (2002) Longitudinal comparison of anorexia nervosa subtypes. *International Journal of Eating Disorders*, 31: 191–201.

Edelman, G.M. (2002) From brain dynamics to consciousness: how matter becomes imagination. Paper presented at 23rd Jean Piaget Society Conference: *The Embodied Mind and Consciousness: Developmental perspectives*, Philadelphia, 6–8 June.

Elliot, C. (2003) Magic way to true self. *The Times Higher Educational Supplement*, 30th May, p. 14.

Ellis, H.D., Quayle, A.H., de Pauw, K.W. et al. (1996) Delusional misidentification of inanimate objects: a literature review and neuropsychological analysis of cognitive deficits in two cases. *Cognitive Neuropsychiatry*, 1: 27–40.

Ely, E.W., Siegel, M.D. and Inouye, S.K. (2001) Delirium in the intensive care unit: an under-recognized syndrome of organ dysfunction. *Seminars in Respiratory and Critical Care Medicine*, 22: 115–26.

Etard, O., Mellet, E., Papathanassiou, D., Benali, K. and Houde, O. (2000) Picture naming without Broca's and Wernicke's areas. *NeuroReport*, 11: 617–22.

Fadiga, L., Fogassi, L., Pavesi, G. and Rizzolatti, G. (1995) Motor facilitation during action observation: a magnetic stimulation study. *Journal of Neuropsychology*, 73: 2608–11.

Fallon, A.E., and Rozin, P. (1985). Sex differences in perceptions of desirable body shape. *Journal of Abnormal Psychology*, 94(1): 102–5.

Fallon, P. and Ackard, D.M. (2002) Sexual abuse and body image, in T.F. Cash and T. Pruzinsky (eds). *Body Images: A handbook of theory, research, and clinical practice*. New York: The Guilford Press.

Farne, A., Pavani, F., Meneghello, F. and Ladavas, E. (2000). Left tactile extinction following visual stimulation of a rubber hand. *Brain*, 123: 2350–60.

Flor, H., Elbert, T., Knecht, S. et al. (1995). Phantom limb pain as a perceptual correlate of cortical reorganization following arm amputation. *Nature*, 375: 482–4.

Featherstone, M. (1991) *Consumer Culture and Postmodernism*. London: Sage.

Ferriar, J. (1795) *Medical Histories and Reflections*. Volume 2. London: Cadell and Davies.

Fisher, S. (1973) *Body Consciousness*. London: Galder and Boyars.

Fisher, K. and Hanspal, R. (1998) Body image and patients with amputations: does the prosthesis maintain the balance? *International Journal of Rehabilitation Research*, 21: 355–63.

Fitzpatrick, M.C. (1999) The psychologic assessment and psychosocial recovery of the patient with an amputation. *Clinical Orthopaedics and Related Research*, 361: 98–107.

Foucault, M. (1979) *Discipline and Punishment: The birth of the prison*. New York: Random House.

Foucault, M. (1990) *The Birth of the Clinic: An archaeology of medical perception*. New York: Random House.

Fox, N.J. (1999) *Beyond Health: Postmodernism and embodiment*. London: Free Association Books.

Frankl, V.E. (1984) *Man's Search for Meaning*. London: Pocket Books.

Frazier, S.H. and Kolb, L.C. (1970) Psychiatric aspects of pain and phantom limb pain. *Orthopedic Clinics of North America*, 1: 481–95.

Fredrickson, B.L. and Roberts, T. (1997) Objectification theory: toward understanding women's lived experiences and mental health risks. *Psychology of Women Quarterly*, 21: 173–206.

Fredrickson, B.L., Roberts, T., Noll, S.M., Quinn, D.M. and Twenge, J.M. (1998) That swimsuit becomes you: sex differences in self-objectification, restrained eating, and math performance. *Journal of Personality and Social Psychology*, 75: 269–84.

French, L. (1994) The political economy of injury and compassion: amputees on the Thai–Cambodia border, in T. Csordas (ed.) *Embodiment and Experience: The existential ground of culture and self.* Cambridge: Cambridge University Press.

Friedmann, L.W. (1978) *The Psychological Rehabilitation of the Amputee*. Springfield, Illinois: C.C. Thomas.

Furness, P.J. (2003) Facing the future. *The Psychologist*, 16: 538–40.

Furnham, A. and Alibhai, N. (1983) Cross-cultural differences in the perception of male and female body shapes. *Psychological Medicine*, 13: 829–37.

Futterman, A.D., Kemeny, M.E., Shapiro, D. and Fahey, J.L. (1994) Immunological and physiological changes associated with induced positive and negative mood. *Psychosomatic Medicine*, 56: 499–511.

Gadow, S. (1984) Touch and technology: two paradigms of patient care. *Journal of Religious Health*, 23: 63–9.

Gallagher, P. and MacLachlan, M. (1999) Psychological adjustment and coping in adults with prosthetic limbs. *Behavioral Medicine*, 25: 117–24.

Gallagher, P. and MacLachlan, M. (2000a.) Positive meaning in amputation and thoughts about the amputated limb. *Prosthetics and Orthotic International*, 24: 196–204.

Gallagher, P. and MacLachlan, M. (2000b.) Development and psychometric evaluation of the Trinity Amputation and Prosthesis Experience Scales (TAPES). *Rehabilitation Psychology*, 45: 130–54.

Gallagher, P. and MacLachlan, M. (2001) Adjustment to an artificial limb, a qualitative perspective. *Journal of Health Psychology*, 6(1): 85–100.

Gallagher, P. and MacLachlan, M. (2002) Application of the emotional disclosure paradigm to lower limb amputees: a study in clinical practice. *Archives of Physical Medicine and Rehabilitation*, 83: 1464–6.

Gallagher, P. and MacLachlan, M. (2000) The development and psychometric evaluation of the Trinity Amputation and Prosthesis Experience Scales (TAPES). *Rehabilitation Psychology*, 45(2): 130–54.

Gallagher, P., Allen, D. and MacLachlan, M. (2001) Phantom limb pain and stump pain: a comparative analysis. *Disability and Rehabilitation*, 23: 522–30.

Galloway, M. (producer and director) (1995) *Network First: Eilish – life without Katie.* Manchester, England: ITV.

Garcia-Campayo, J., Campos, R., Marcos, G. et al (1996) Somatisation in primary care in Spain II: differences between somatisers and psychologisers. *British Journal of Psychiatry*, 168: 348–53.

Garcia-Palacios, A., Hoffman, H.G., Cain, V. et al. (2003) Using Virtual Reality to help reduce pain during severe burn wound care procedures, in M. MacLachlan and P. Gallagher (eds) *Enabling Technologies: Body image and body function.* Edinburgh: Churchill Livingstone.

Garner, D.M. (2002) Body image and anorexia nervosa, in T.F. Cash and T. Pruzinsky (eds) *Body Image: A handbook of theory, research, and practice.* New York: The Guilford Press.

Garner, D.M., Garfinkel, P.E., Schwartz, D. and Thompson, M. (1980). Cultural expectations of thinness in women. *Psychological Reports*, 47: 483–91.

Gething, L. (1991) Generality versus specificity of attitudes towards people with disabilities. *British Journal of Medical Psychology*, 64: 55–64.

Gibbs, N. (2001) Baby, It's You! And You, and You . . . *Time Magazine*, 19th February, pp. 36–47.

Gillet, G. (2000) Ethics and images in organ transplantation, in P. Trzepacz and A. Dimartini (eds) *The Transplant Patient: Biological, psychiatric and ethical issues in organ transplantation.* Cambridge: Cambridge University Press.

Goffman, E. (1993) *Stigma: Notes on the management of spoiled identity.* Englewood Cliffs, NJ: Prentice-Hall.

Goldberg, D. (1978) *Manual of the General Health Questionnaire.* Windsor: NFER-Nelson, 1978.

Goldenberg, J.L., Pyszczynski, T., Greenberg, J. and Solomon, S. (2000) Fleeing the body: a terror management perspective on the problem of human corporality. *Personality and Social Psychology Review*, 4: 200–18.

Goldin-Meadow, S. and Butcher, C. (2003) Pointing toward two-word speech in young children, in S. Kita (ed.) *Pointing: Where language, culture and cognition meet.* Mahwah, NJ: Lawrence Erlbaum Associates.

Gomel, E. and Weninger, S. (2003) Cronenberg, Greenway and the ideologies of twinship. *Body and Society*, 9: 19–36.

Gordon, R.A. (2000) *Eating Disorders: Anatomy of a social epidemic* (2nd edn). Oxford: Blackwell.

Gordon, R.A. (2002) Eating disorders East and West: a culture-bound syndrome unbound, in M. Nasser, M.A. Katzman and R.A, Gordon (eds) *Eating Disorders and Cultures in Transition.* Hove, UK: Brunner-Routledge.

Goslinga-Roy, G.M. (2000) Body boundaries, fiction of the female self: an ethnographic perspective on power, feminism, and the reproductive technologies, in P.E. Brodwin, (ed.) *Biotechnology and Culture: Bodies, anxieties, ethics.* Bloomington: Indiana University Press.

Gow, D., MacLachlan, M. and Aird, C. (2004) Reaching with electricity: externally-powered prosthetics and embodiment, in M. MacLachlan and P. Gallagher (eds) *Enabling Technologies: Body image and body function.* Edinburgh: Churchill Livingstone.

Gow, D.J., Douglas, W., Geggie, C., Monteith, F. and Stewart, D. (2001) The development of the Edinburgh modular arm system. *Proceedings of the Institute of Mechanical Engineers*, 215(H): 291–8.

Goyal, M., Mehta, R.L., Schneidermann, L.J. and Sehgal, A.R. (2002) Economic and health consequences of selling a kidney in India. *Journal of the American Medical Association*, 288: 1589–93.

Gralink, A. (1942) *Folie a deux*: the psychosis of association: a review of 103 cases and the entire English literature. *Psychiatric Quarterly*, 16: 230–63.

Granberg, A., Engberg, I.B. and Lundberg, D. (1998) Patients' experience of being critically ill or severely injured and cared for in an intensive care unit in relation to the ICU syndrome. Part 1. *Intensive Critical Care Nursing*, 14: 294–307.

Graziano, M.S.A., Yap, G.S., Gregory, S. and Gross, C.G. (1994). Coding of visual space by premotor neurons. *Science*, 266: 1054–6.

Grogan, S. (1999) *Body Image: Understanding body dissatisfaction in men, woman and children*. London: Routledge.

Grosz, E. (1994) *Volatile Bodies: Toward a corporeal feminism*. Sydney: Allen and Unwin.

Grusser, S.M., Winter, C., Muhlnickel, W. et al. (2001a) The relationship of perceptual phenomena and cortical reorganization in upper extremity amputees. *Neuroscience*, 102(2): 263–72.

Grusser, S.M., Winter, C., Schaefer, M. et al. (2001b) Perceptual phenomena after unilateral arm amputation: a pre-post surgical comparison. *Neuroscience Letters*, 302: 13–16.

Guggenbuhl-Craig, A. and Micklem, N. (1988) No answer to Job: reflections on the limitations of meaning in illness, in M. Kidel and S. Rowe-Leete (eds) *The Meaning of Illness*. London: Routledge.

Habermans, T. (1996) In defense of weight phobia as the central organizing motive in anorexia nervosa: historical and cultural arguments for a culture-sensitive psychological conception. *International Journal of Eating Disorders*, 19: 317–34.

Halbert, J., Crotty, M. and Cameron, I.D. (2002) Evidence for the optimal management of acute chronic phantom limb pain: a systematic review. *The Clinical Journal of Pain*, 18: 84–92.

Halligan, P.W., Zeman, A. and Berger, A. (1999) Phantoms in the brain. *British Medical Journal*, 319: 587–8.

Harenstam, A., Theorell, T. and Kaijser, L. (2000) Coping with anger-provoking situations, psychosocial working conditions, and the ECG-detected signs of coronary heart disease. *Journal of Occupational Health Psychology*, 5: 191–203.

Head, H. (1920) *Studies in Neurology*. Oxford: Oxford University Press.

Heidegger M.(1977) The question concerning technology, in D.F. Krell (ed.). *Basic Writings*. London: Sage (pp. 307–43).

Hill, A., Niven, C.A., Knussen, C. and McCreath, S.W. (1995) Rehabilitation outcome in long-term amputees. *British Journal of Therapy and Rehabilitation*, 2: 593–8.

Helman, C.G. (2001) *Culture, Illness and Health*. London: Arnold.

Herman, J. (1998) Phantom limb: from medical knowledge to folk wisdom and back. *Annals of Internal Medicine*, 128: 76–8.

Hoffman, H.G., Doctor, J.N., Patterson, D.R., Carrougher, G.J. and Furnesss, T.A. (2000) Use of virtual reality for adjunctive treatment of adolescent burn pain during wound care: a case report. *Pain*, 85: 305–9.

Hoffman, H.G., Patterson, D.R. and Carrougher, G.J. (2000) Use of virtual reality for adjunctive treatment of adult burn pain during physical therapy. *Clinical Journal of Pain*, 16: 244–50.

Horgan, O. and MacLachlan, M. (2004) Psychosocial adjustment to amputation: a review. *Disability and Rehabilitation*.

Horgan, O. and MacLachlan, M. (submitted) A longitudinal study of psychosocial rehabilitation of people with amputations.

Houston, V. and Bull, R. (1994) Do people avoid sitting next to someone who is facially disfigured? *European Journal of Social Psychology*, 24: 279–84.

Howell, P. (2003) A stroke of genius. *The Sunday Times Magazine*, 5th October, pp. 32–5.

Husum, H., Resell, K., Vorren, G. et al. (2002) Chronic pain in land mine accident survivors in Cambodia and Kurdistan. *Social Science and Medicine*; 55: 1813–16.

Iverson, J.M. and Goldin-Meadow, S. (1998) Why people gesture when they speak. *Nature*, 396: 228.

Jackson, L.A. (2002) Physical attractiveness: a sociocultural perspective, in T.F. Cash and T. Pruzinsky (eds) *Body Image: A handbook of theory, research, and practice*. New York: The Guilford Press.

James, K. (2001) Individualism and immune function: are asthma and allergies partly a function of an overly constricted self? *Journal of Health Psychology*, 6: 241–5.

Jastremski, C.A. (2000) ICU bedside environment – a nursing perspective. *Critical Care Clinics*, 16: 273.

Jensen, T.S. and Rasmussen, P. (1994) Phantom pain and other phenomena after amputation, in P.D. Wall and R. Melzack (eds) *Textbook of Pain* (3rd edn). Edinburgh: Churchill Livingstone.

Joon, L. (2002) Meanings of representation and discourse of the body in visual art, in *Bodyscape*. Seoul: Rodin Gallery (www.rodingallery.org).

Kalp, C. (1999) Our quest to be perfect. *Newsweek*, 16th August.

Katz, J. (1993) Reality of phantom limbs. *Motivation and Emotion*, 17: 147–79.

Kawachi, I., Sparrow, D., Vonkonas, P.S. and Weiss, S.T. (1994) Symptoms of anxiety and risk of coronary heart disease: The Normative Aging Study. *Circulation*, 90: 2225–9.

Kaye, J.A. and Jick, H. (2003) Incidence of erectile dysfunction and characteristics of patients before and after the introduction of sildenafil in the United Kingdom: cross sectional study with comparison patients. *British Medical Journal*, 326: 424–5.

Keel, P.K. and Klump, K.L (2003) Are eating disorders culture-bound syndromes? *Psychological Bulletin*, 125: 747–69.

Keep, P.J., James, J. and Inman, M. (1980) Windows in the intensive therapy unit. *Anaesthesia*, 35: 257–62.

Kelly, S.D., Iverson, J.M., Terranova, J. et al. (2004) Putting language back in the body: speech and gesture in three timeframes. *Developmental Neuropsychology*, 22: 323–49.

Kennedy, R.S., Lano, N.E., Berbaum, K.S. and Lilienthal, M.G. (1993) Simulator Sickness Questionnaire: an enhanced method for quantifying simulator sickness. *International Journal of Aviation Psychology*, 3: 203–22.

Kenny, M.G. (1985) Paradox lost: the Latah problem revisited, in R.C. Simon and C.C. Hughes, *The Culture-Bound Syndromes: Folk illnesses of psychiatric and anthropological interest*. Dordrecht: D. Reidel.

Kidel. M. (1988) Introduction, in M. Kidel and S. Rowe-Leete (eds) *The Meaning of Illness*. London: Routledge.

Kiecolt-Glaser, J.K., Dura, J.R., Speicher, C.E., Trask, O.J. and Glaser, R. (1991) Spousal caregivers of dementia victims: longitudinal changes in immunity and health. *Psychosomatic Medicine*, 53: 345–62.

Kierkegaard, S. (1849/1954) *The Sickness Unto Death* (translation, W. Lowrie). New York: Princeton University Press.

Kinsbourne, M. (2002) The brain and body awareness, in T.F. Cash. and T. Pruzinsky (eds) *Body Images: A handbook of theory, research, and clinical practice*. New York: The Guilford Press.

Kirmayer, L.J. and Santhanam, R. (2001) The anthropology of hysteria, in P.W. Halligan, C. Bass and J.C. Marshal, *Contemporary Approaches to the Study of Hysteria*. Oxford: Oxford University Press.

Kirmayer, L.J. and Young, A. (1998) Culture and somatisation: clinical, epidemiological and ethnographic perspectives. *Psychosomatic Medicine*, 60: 420–30.

Klapheke, M. (1999) Transplantation of the human hand: psychiatric considerations. *Bulletin of the Menninger Clinic*, 63: 159–73.

Klapheke, M., Marcell, C., Taliaferro, G. and Creamer, B. (2000) Psychiatric assessment of candidates for hand transplantation. *Microsurgery*, 20: 453–7.

Kleinman, A. (1980) *Patients and Healers in the Context of Culture*. Berkeley: University of California Press.

Klerk, R. (1969) Physical stigma and task orientated interactions. *Human Relations*, 22: 53–60.

Klerk, R., Ono, H. and Hastorf, A.H. (1966) The effects of physical deviance upon face-to-face interaction. *Human Relations*, 19: 425–36.

Knecht, S., Soros, P., Gurtler, S. et al. (1998) Phantom sensations following acute pain. *Pain*, 77: 209–13.

Kolb, L.C. (1954) *The Painful Phantom: Psychology, Physiology and Treatment*. Springfield, Illinois: C.C. Thomas.

Kosambi, D.D. (1967) Living prehistory in India. *Scientific American*, 216: 105–14.

Kroenke, K., Spitzer, R.I., deGruy, F.V. et al. (1997) Multisomatoform disorder: an alternative to undifferentiated somatoform disorder for the somatizing patient in primary care. *Archives of General Psychiatry*, 54: 352–8.

Lacan, J. (1966) (1997 translation) *Ecrits: A Selection*. London: Routledge.

Lacan, J. (1981) *The Four Fundamental Concepts of Psycho-Analysis*. New York: Norton.

Laitenen H. (1996) Patients' experience of confusion in the intensive care unit following cardiac surgery. *Intensive Critical Care Nursing*, 12: 79–83.

LaPiere, R.T. and Farnsworth, P.R. (1949) *Social Psychology* (3rd edn), New York: McGraw-Hill.

Lavater, J.K. (1878) *Essays on Physiognomy*. London: Tegg.

Leader, D. (1995) *Lacan for Beginners*. Cambridge: Icon Books.

Lechte, J. (1994) *Fifty Key Contemporary Thinkers*. London: Routledge.

Leder, D. (1990) *The Absent Body*. Chicago: University of Chicago Press.

Lee, A.M. and Lee, S. (1999) Disordered eating in three communities in China: A comparative study of high school students in Hong Kong, Shenzhen and rural Hunan. *International Journal of Eating Disorders*, 27: 312–16.

Legro, M.W., Reiber, G.D., Smith, D.G. et al. (1998) Prosthesis evaluation questionnaire for persons with lower limb amputations: assessing prosthesis-related quality of life. *Archives of Physical Medicine and Rehabilitation*, 79: 931–8.

Leit, A., Pope, H.G. and Gray, J.J. (2001) Cultural expectations of muscularity in men: the evolution of Playgirl centerfolds. *International Journal of Eating Disorders*, 29: 90–3.

Levenson, J.L. and Oldbrisch, M.E. (1993) Psychosocial evaluation of organ transplant candidates. *Psychosomatics*, 29: 388–95.

Leventhal, H., Idler, E.L. and Leventhal, E.A. (1999) The impact of chronic illness on the self system, in R.J. Contrada and R.D. Ashmore (eds) *Self, Social Identity and Physical Health: Interdisciplinary explorations*. New York: Oxford University Press.

Lindsay, S.J.E. (1994) Fears and anxiety: treatment, in S.J.E. Linsay and G.E. Powell (eds) *The Handbook of Clinical Adult Psychology* (2nd edn). Routledge: London.

Lishman, W.A. (1987) *Organic Psychiatry: The psychological consequences of cerebral disorder* (2nd edn). Oxford: Blackwell Scientific Publications.

Lobo, A., Garcia-Campayo, J. and Campos, R. et al (1996) Somatisation in primary care in Spain. I: Estimates of prevalence and clinical characteristics. *British Journal of Psychiatry*, 168: 344–53.

Lupton, D. (2003) *Medicine as Culture* (2nd edn). London: Sage.

Lupton, D. and Seymour, W. (2000) Technology, selfhood and physical disability. *Social Science and Medicine*, 50: 1851–62.

Luria, A.R. (1966) *Higher Cortical Functions in Man*. New York: Basic Books.

Luria, A.R. (1972) *The Man with the Shattered World*. New York: Basic Books.

Lynch, J.W. and Kaplan, G.A. (1997) Understanding how inequality in the distribution of income affects health. *Journal of Health Psychology*, 2: 297–314.

Lyons, A.C. and Farquhar, C. (2002) Past disclosure and conversational experience: effects of cardiovascular functioning while woman talk. *Journal of Applied Social Psychology*, 32: 2043–66.

Lyons, A.C., Spicer, J., Tuffin, K. and Chamberlain, K. (2000) Does cardiovascular reactivity during speech reflect self-construction processes? *Psychology and Health*, 14: 1123–40.

Machin, P. and Williams, A. (1998) Stiff upper lip: coping strategies of World War II veterans with phantom limp pain. *The Clinical Journal of Pain*, 14: 290–4.

MacLachlan, M. (1997) *Culture and Health*. Chichester: Wiley.

MacLachlan, M. (2001) Cultivating Health, in M. MacLachlan (ed.) *Cultivating Health: Cultural perspectives on promoting health*. Chichester: Wiley.

MacLachlan, M. (in press) *Culture and Health: A Critical Perspective towards Global Health* (2nd edn). Chichester: Wiley.

MacLachlan, M. and Gallagher, P. (2004) (eds) *Enabling Technologies: Body image and body function*. Edinburgh: Churchill Livingstone.

MacLachlan, M. and Smyth, C.A. (2004) (eds) *Binge Drinking and Youth Culture: Reasons, Ramifications and Remedies*. Dublin: Liffey Press.

MacLachlan, M., Banda, D.M. and McAuliffe, E. (1995) Epidemic psychological disturbance in a Malawian secondary school: a case study in social change. *Psychology and Developing Societies*, 7: 79–90.

MacLachlan, M., de Paor, H., McDarby, G., Halligan, P. and Stone, B. (2002) *Development and Evaluation of Augmented Reality Technology for the Treatment of Phantom Limb Pain and to Facilitate Adaptation to use of a Prosthesis*. Trinity Psychoprosthetics Group, Trinity College Dublin.

MacLachlan, M., Desmond, D. and Horgan, O. (2003) Psychological correlates of illusory body experiences. *Journal of Rehabilitation Research and Development*, 40: 59–66.

MacLachlan, M., Allen, D., Desmond, D. et al. (2004) Virtual reality, phantom limb pain and prosthetic embodiment: the development of phenomenologically authentic virtual reality technology for treatment of phantom limb pain and adaptation to a prosthetic limb. Thrandhart Lecture, Annual Conference of the American Academy of Orthotists and Prosthetists, New Orleans, USA.

MacLachlan, M., Smyth, C.A., Breen, F. and Madden, T. (2004) Acculturation and mental health in modern Ireland. *International Journal of Social Psychiatry* (in press).

Malatesta, V.J. and Adams, H.E. (2001) Sexual Dysfunctions, in P.B. Sutker and H.E.

Adams, *Comprehensive Handbook of Psychopathology* (3rd edn). New York: Kluwer Academic/Plenum Publishers.

Martin, E. (1987) *The Woman in the Body: A cultural analysis of reproduction*. Boston: Beacon.

Martin, M. (2000) Current trends and new developments in transplantation, in P. Trzepacz and A. Dimartini (eds) *The Transplant Patient: Biological, psychiatric and ethical issues in organ transplantation*. Cambridge: Cambridge University Press.

Masters, W.H. and Johnson, V.E. (1966) *Human Sexual Response*. Boston: Little Brown.

Masters, W.H. and Johnson, V.E. (1970) *Human Sexual Inadequacy*. Boston: Little Brown.

Masterson, G. (2000) Psychosocial factors in selection for liver transplantation. *British Medical Journal*, 320: 263–4.

Mathews, E. (2002) *The Philosophy of Merleau-Ponty*. Chesham, Bucks: Acumen.

McCarroll, J.E., Ursano, R.J., Fullerton, C.S., Liu, X. and Lundy, A. (2002) Somatic symptoms in Gulf War mortuary workers. *Psychosomatic Medicine*, 64: 29–33.

McCauley, M.E. and Sharkey, T.J. (1992) Cybersickness: perception of motion in virtual environments. *Presence: Teleoperators virtual environments*, 1: 311–18.

McCormick, E.W. (1988) Heart abuse, in M. Kidel and S. Rowe-Leete (eds) *The Meaning of Illness*. London: Routledge.

McDarby, G., Condron, J., Hughes, D., Augenblick, N. and Sharry, J. (2004) Affective feedback, in M. MacLachlan and P. Gallagher (eds) *Enabling Technologies: Body image and body function*. Edinburgh: Churchill Livingstone.

McGrath, M.H. and Mukerji, S. (2000) Plastic surgery and the teenage patient. *Journal of Pediatric and Adolescent Gynecology*, 13: 105–18.

McGuire, B.E., Basten, C.J., Ryan, C.J. and Gallagher, J. (2000) Intensive care unit syndrome – a dangerous misnomer. *Archives of Internal Medicine*, 160: 906–9.

McNeill, D. (1992) *Hand and Mind: What gesture reveals about thoughts*. Chicago: University of Chicago Press.

Meltzoff, A.N. (1990) Towards a developmental cognitive science – the implications of cross modal matching and imitation for the development of representation and memory in infancy. *Annals of the New York Academy of Science*, 608: 1–37.

Melville, H. (1942) *Moby Dick*. New York: Dodd, Mead (as cited in Herman, 1998).

Melzack, R. (1990) Phantom limbs and the concept of a neuromatrix. *Trends in Neuroscience*, 13: 88–92.

Melzack, R. (1992) Phantom limbs. *Scientific American*, 266: 90–6.

Melzack, R. (1995) Phantom limb pain and the brain, in B. Bromm and J.E. Desmedt (eds) *Pain and the Brain: From nociception to cognition*. New York: Raven Press.

Melzack, R. and Loeser J.D. (1978) Phantom body pain in paraplegics: evidence for a central 'pattern generating mechanism' for pain. *Pain*, 4: 195–210.

Melzack, R. and Wall, P.D. (1965) Pain mechanisms: a new theory. *Science*, 150: 971–9.

Melzack, R. and Wall, P.D. (1982) *The Challenge of Pain*. London: Penguin Books.

Merleau-Ponty, M. (1962) *Phenomenology of Perception* (translation, C. Smith) London: Routledge.

Merleau-Ponty, M. (1964) The child's relation with others, in J. Edie and C. Dallery, *The Primacy of Perception* (translation, W. Cobb). Evanston: Northwestern University Press.

Micheal, J.W. and Bowker, J.H. (1994) Prosthetics/orthotics research for the twenty-first century: Summary 1992 Conference Proceedings. *Journal of Prosthetics and Orthotics*, 6(4): 100–7.

Milgram, S. (1963) Behavioural study of obedience. *Journal of Abnormal and Social Psychology*, 67: 371–8.

Minchom, P.E., Ellis, N.C., Appleton, P.L. et al. (1995) Impact of functional severity on self concept in young people with spina bifida. *Archives of Disease in Childhood*, 73: 48–52.

Mogilner, A., Grosman, J.A., Ribary, U. et al. (1993) Somatosensory cortical plasticity in adult humans revealed by magnetoencephalography. *Proceedings of the National Academy of Sciences*, 90: 3593–7.

Money, J. (1975) Ablatio penis: normal male infant sex-reassigned as a girl. *Archives of Sexual Behaviour*, 4: 65–71.

Moran, A. and Gallagher, P. (2004) Technological enframing in the hemodialysis patient, in M. MacLachlan and P. Gallagher (eds) *Enabling Technologies: Body image and body function*. Edinburgh: Churchill Livingstone.

Morse, J.M. and Mitcham, C. (1998) The experience of agonising pain and signals of disembodiment. *Journal of Psychosomatic Research*, 44: 667–80.

Morse, J.M. (1997) Responding to threats to integrity of self. *Advances in Nursing Science*, 19: 21–36.

Muraoka, M., Komiyama, H., Hosoi, M., Mine, K. and Kubo, C. (1996) Psychosomatic treatment of phantom limb pain with post-traumatic stress disorder: a case report. *Pain*, 66: 385–8.

Murphy, R. (1995) Encounters: the body silent in America, in B. Ingstad (ed.) *Disability and Culture*. Berkeley: University of California Press.

Murray, C.D. (2001) The experience of body boundaries by Siamese twins. *New Ideas in Psychology*, 19: 117–30.

Murray, C.D. and Fox, J. (2002) Body image and prosthesis satisfaction in the lower limb amputee. *Disability and Rehabilitation*, 24: 925–31.

Murray, C.D. and Sixsmith, J. (1999) The corporeal body in virtual reality. *Ethos*, 27: 315–43.

Nagel, T. (1986) *The View from Nowhere*. Oxford: Oxford University Press.

Nagle L.M. (1998) Meaning of technology for people with chronic renal disease. *Holistic Nursing Practice*, 12(4): 78–92.

Nasser, M. (1999) The new veiling phenomenon – is it an anorexic equivalent? A Polemic. *Journal of Community and Applied Social Psychology*, 9: 407–12.

Nasser, M. and Di Nicola, V. (2001) Changing bodies, changing cultures: an intercultural dialogue on the body as the final frontier, in M. Nasser, M. Katzman and R. A. Gordon (eds) *Eating Disorders and Cultures in Transition*. Hove, UK: Brunner-Routledge.

Nelson, R.M. (2000) The ventilator/baby as cyborg, in P.E. Brodwin (ed.) *Biotechnology and Culture: Bodies, anxieties, ethics*. Bloomington: Indiana University Press (pp. 3–23).

Newell, R. (2000) *Body Image and Disfigurement Care*. London: Routledge.

Nichols, S. and Patel, H. (2002) Health and safety implications of virtual reality: a review of empirical evidence. *Applied Ergonomics*, 33: 251–71.

Nimnuan, C., Rabe-Hesketh, S., Wessely, S. and Hotopf, M. (2001) How many functional somatic symptoms? *Journal of Psychosomatic Research*, 51: 549–57.

Noble, D., Price, D. and Gilder, R. (1954) Psychiatric disturbance following amputation. *American Journal of Psychiatry*, 110: 609.

Norris, J., Kunes-Connell, M. and Stockard-Spelic, S. (1998) A grounded theory of reimaging. *Advances in Nursing Science*, 20: 1–12.

Novotny, M. (1991) Psychosocial issues affecting rehabilitation. *Prosthetics*, 2: 373–93.

O'Shaughnessy, B. (1973) Trying (as the mental 'pineal gland'). *Journal of Philosophy*, 70: 365–86.

Olivardia, R. (2002) Body image and muscularity, in T.F. Cash and T. Pruzinsky (eds) *Body Image: A handbook of theory, research, and practice*. New York: The Guilford Press.

Oliver, M. (1990) The *Politics of Disablement*. London: Macmillan.

Oltmanns, T.F. and Emery, R.E. (2004) *Abnormal Psychology* (4th edn). New Jersey: Prentice Hall.

Osborn, M. (2002) The personal experience of chronic benign low back pain: an interpretive phenomenological analysis. Unpublished PhD thesis, University of Sheffield (52–14187).

Osborn, M. and Smith, J.A. (1998) The personal experience of chronic benign lower back pain: an interpretative phenomenological analysis. *British Journal of Health Psychology*, 3: 65–83.

Pallis, C. (1982) ABC of brain stem death. *British Medical Journal*, 285: 1409–12.

Pape, T.L.B., Kim, J. and Weiner, B. (2002) The shaping of individual meanings assigned to assistive technology: a review of personal factors. *Disability and Rehabilitation*, 24(1/2/3): 5–20.

Parkes, C.M. (1975) Psycho-social transitions: comparison between reactions to loss of a limb and loss of a spouse. *British Journal of Psychiatry*, 127: 204–10.

Penfield, W. and Rasmussen, T. (1950) *The Cerebral Cortex of Man: A clinical study of localisation of function*. New York: McMillan.

Penninex, B.W., Beekman, A.T.F., Honig, A. et al (2001) Depression and cardiac mortality: results from a community-based longitudinal study. *Archives of General Psychiatry*, 58: 221–7.

Pert, C.B. (1997) *Molecules of Emotion*. New York: Scribner.

Phillips, H. (2001) Boy meets girl. *New Scientist*, 2290 (12 May): 29–35.

Phillips, H. (2001) The gender police. *New Scientist*, 2290 (12 May): 38–41.

Phillips, K. (2002) Body image and body dysmorphic disorder, in T.F. Cash and T. Pruzinsky (eds) *Body Images: A handbook of theory, research, and clinical practice*. New York: The Guilford Press.

Phillips, K. and Diaz, S. (1997) Gender differences in body dysmorphic disorder. *Journal of Nervous and Mental Disease*, 185: 570–7.

Piaget, J. (1958) *The Child's Construction of Reality*. London: Routledge.

Pinel, J.P.J. (2003) *Biopsychology* (5th edn). Boston: Allyn and Bacon.

Pinker, S. (1995) *The Language Instinct: How the mind creates language*. New York: HarperCollins.

Plugge, H. (1970) Man and his body, in S.F. Spiker (ed.) *The Philosophy of the Body*. New York: Quadrangle.

Polhenus, T. (ed.) (1978) *Social Aspects of the Human Body*. Harmondsworth: Penguin.

Pope, H.G., Olivardia, R., Gruber, A. and Borowiecki, J. (1999). Evolving ideals of male body image as seen through action toys. *International Journal of Eating Disorders*, 26: 65–72.

Pope, H.G., Phillips, K.A. and Olivardia, R. (2000) *The Adonis Complex: The secret crises of male body obsession*. New York: Free Press.

Popovic, M.R. and Keller, T. (2004) Complex motion: neuroprosthesis for grasping applications, in M. MacLachlan and P. Gallagher (eds) *Enabling Technologies: Body image and body function*. Edinburgh: Churchill Livingstone (pp. 197–216).

Porter, R. (1993) The body and the mind, the doctor and the patient: negotiating hysteria, in S. Gilman, H. King, R. Porter, G.S. Rousseau and E. Showalter, *Hysteria Beyond Freud*. Berkley, CA: University of California Press.

Price, M. (1957) *The Dissociation of Personality*. New York: Meridian Books.

Pruzinsky, T. (2002) Body image disturbances in psychotic disorders, in T.F. Cash and T. Pruzinsky (eds) *Body Images: A handbook of theory, research, and clinical practice*. New York: The Guilford Press.

Pucher, I., Kickinger, W. and Frischenschlager, O. (1999) Coping with amputation and phantom limb pain. *Journal of Psychosomatic Research*, 46: 379–83.

Pulvermuller, F., Hearle, M. and Hummel, F. (2001) Walking or talking? Behavioral and neurophysiological correlates of action verb processing. *Brain and Language*, 78: 143–68.

Quebec Rehabilitation Institute. *Prosthetics and Orthotics International*, 25: 119–31.

Ramachandran, V.S. and Blakeslee, S. (1998) *Phantom in the Brain*. London: Fourth Estate.

Ramachandran, V.S., Rogers-Ramachandran, D. (1996) Synaesthesia in phantom limbs induced with mirrors. *Proceedings of the Royal Society of London, B*, 263: 377–86.

Reason, T.J. and Brand, J.J. (1975) *Motion Sickness*. London: Academic Press.

Regan, E.C. and Price, K.R. (1994) The frequency of occurrence and severity of side-effects of immersion virtual reality. *Aviation, Space and Environmental Medicine*, 65: 527–530.

Richards, J.C., Alvarenga, M. and Hof, A. (2000) Serum lipids and their relationships with hostility and angry affect and behaviors in men. *Health Psychology*, 19: 393–8.

Richie, B.S., Ferguson, A., El-Khoury, D., Gomez, M. and Adamaly, Z. (2003) Physical rehabilitation is not enough: comprehensive and coordinated care for landmine survivors. Paper presented at 2nd Congress of the International Society for Psychical and Rehabilitation Medicine, Prague, May.

Riddoch, G. (1941) Phantom limb and body shape. *Brain*, 64: 197–222.

Riria, K.T. and Simmons, D. ((1999) *Moko Rangatira: Maori Tattoo*. Auckland: Reed Books.

Riva, G. (2000) Virtual reality in rehabilitation of spinal cord injuries: a case report. *Rehabilitation Psychology*, 45: 81–8.

Rizzolatti, G. and Arbib, M.A. (1998) Language within our grasp. *Trends in Neuroscience*, 21: 188–94.

Robert, S.A. and J.S. (2000) Socioeconomic inequalities in health: integrating individual-, community-, and societal-level theory and research, in G.L. Albrecht, R. Fitzpatrick and S.C. Scrimshaw (eds) *Handbook of Social Studies in Health and Medicine*. London: Sage.

Robertson, I. (1999) *Mind Sculpture*. London: Bantam Books.

Rorden, C., Heutink, J., Greenfield, G. and Robertson, I. (1999) When a rubber hand 'feels' what the real hand cannot. *NeuroReport*, 10: 135–8.

Rousso, H. (1982) Special considerations in counselling clients with cerebral palsy. *Sexuality and Disability*, 5: 78–88.

Routhier, F., Vincent, C., Morissette, M.-J., and Desaulniers, L. (2001) Clinical results of an investigation of paediatric upper limb myoelectric prosthesis fitting at the Quebec Rehabilitation Institute. *Prosthetics and Orthotics International*, 25: 119–31.

Ryarczyk, B., Nyenhuis, D.L. Nicholas, J.J., Cash, S.M. and Kaiser, J. (1995) Body image, perceived social stigma, and the prediction of psychosocial adjustment to leg amputation. *Rehabilitation Psychology*, 49: 95–110.

Ryarczyk, B., Nicholas, J.J., and Nyenhuis, D.L. (1997) Coping with a leg amputation: integrating research and clinical practice. *Rehabilitation Psychology*. 42(3): 241–56.

Sacks, O. (1984) *A Leg to Stand On*. London: Picador.

Sacks, O. (1985) *The Man Who Mistook His Wife for a Hat*. London: Picador.

Sacks, O. (2002) Embodiment and phantom pain. Paper presented at 23rd Jean Piaget Society Conference: *The Embodied Mind and Consciousness: Developmental perspectives*, Philadelphia, 6–8 June.

Sampson, E.E. (1998) Life as an embodied art: the second stage – beyond constructionism, in B.M. Bayer and J. Shotter (eds) *Reconstructing the Psychological Subject: Bodies, practices and technologies*. London: Sage (pp. 21–32).

Sarwer, B.D. (2002) Cosmetic surgery and changes in the body image, in T.F. Cash and T. Pruzinsky (eds) *Body Image: A Handbook of Theory, Research, and Practice*. New York: The Guilford Press.

Sarwer, B.D., Wadden, T.A. and Whitaker, L.A. (2002) An investigation of changes in body image following cosmetic surgery. *Plastic and Reconstructive Surgery*, 109: 363–9.

Sarwer, B.D., Wadden, T.A., Pertschuk, M.J. and Whitaker, L.A. (1998) The psychology of cosmetic surgery: a review and reconceptualisation. *Clinical Psychology Review*, 18: 1–22.

Sarwer, D.B., Wadden, T.A., Pertschuk, M.J. and Witaker, L.A. (1998) The psychology of cosmetic surgery: a review and reconceptualization. *Clinical Psychology Review*, 18: 1–22.

Scheper-Hughes, N. (2003) Human kidneys: the new cash crop. *New Internationalist*, 354: 6–7.

Scherer, M.J. and Galvin, J.C. (1996) An outcomes perspective of quality pathways to the most appropriate technology, in J.C. Galvin and M.J. Scherer (eds) *Evaluating, Selecting and Using Appropriate Assistive Technology*. Gathersburg, MD: Aspen (pp. 1–26).

Scherer, M.J. (2000) *Living in the State of Stuck: How assistive technology impacts the lives of people with disabilities* (3rd edn). Cambridge, M.A.: Brookline Books.

Scherer, M.J. (2002) The change in emphasis from people to person: introduction to the special issue on assistive technology. *Disability and Rehabilitation*, 24(1/2/3): 1–4.

Schilder, P. (1964/1935) *Image and Appearance of the Human Body*. London: Kegan Paul.

Schilling, C. (1993) *The Body and Social Theory*. London: Sage.

Schulteis, M.T. and Rizzo, A.A. (2001) The application of virtual reality technology in rehabilitation. *Rehabilitation Psychology*, 46: 296–311.

Schwenkreis, P., Witscher, K., Jannsen, F. et al. (2001) Assessment of cortical reorganisation in the sensorimotor cortex after upper limb amputation. *Clinical Neurophysiology*, 112: 627–35.

Sharpe, M. and Carson, A. (2001) 'Unexplained' somatic symptoms, functional syndromes, and somatization: do we need a paradigm shift? *Annal of Internal Medicine*, 134(2 suppl.): 926–30.

Sheldon, W.H., Stevens, S.S. and Tucker, W.B. (1940) *The Varieties of Human Physique*. New York: Harper.

Sherman, R. and Sherman, C.J. (1983). Prevalence and characteristics of chronic phantom limb pain among American veterans. *American Journal of Physical Medicine*, 62(5): 227–38.

Sherman, R.C. (ed.) (1997) *Phantom Limb Pain*. New York: Plenum.

Sherman, R.C. (2004) Psychophysiological recording and biofeedback: tools enabling people to control their own physiology, in M. MacLachlan and P. Gallagher (eds) *Enabling Technologies: Body image and body function*. Edinburgh: Churchill Livingstone.

Shorter, E. (1994) The reinvention of hysteria. *Times Literary Supplement*, 17th June, p. 26.

Showalter, E. (1997) *Hystories: Hysterical Epidemics and Modern Culture*. London: Picador.

Shweder, R.A. (1991) *Thinking Through Cultures: Expeditions in cultural psychology*. Cambridge, MA: Harvard University Press.

Simmel, M.L. (1959) Phantoms, phantom pain and 'denial'. *American Journal of Psychotherapy*, 13: 603–13.

Simpson, D.C. (1968) An externally powered prosthesis for the complete arm. *Proceedings of the Institute of Mechanical Engineers*, 183(J): 11–17.

Sims, A. (1988) *Symptoms in the Mind*. London: Bailliere Tindall.

Sims, M. (2003) *Adam's Navel: A natural and cultural history of the human body*. London: Allen Lane.

Smith, J.A., Jarman, M. and Osborn, M. (1999) Doing interpretive phenomenological analysis, in M. Murray and K. Chamberlain (eds) *Qualitative Health Psychology: Theories and methods*. London: Sage.

Smyth, C.A., MacLachlan, M. and Clare, A. (2003) *Cultivating Suicide? The destruction of self in modern Ireland*. Dublin: Liffey Press.

Solomon, S., Greenberg, J. and Pyszczynski, T. (1991) A terror management theory of social behaviour: the psychological functions of self-esteem and cultural worldviews. *Advances in Experimental Social Psychology*, 24: 93–159.

Solomon, S., Greenberg, J. and Pyszczynski, T. (1998) Tales from the crypt: on the role of death in life. *Zygon*, 33: 9–43.

Spitzer, R.L. (2003) Can some Gay men and Lesbians change their sexual orientation? 200 participants reporting a change from homosexual to heterosexual orientation. *Archives of Sexual Behaviour*, 32, 403–417.

Starzl, T.E. (2000) The mystique of transplantation: biologic and psychiatric considerations, in P. Trzepacz and A. Dimartini (eds) *The Transplant Patient: Biological, psychiatric and ethical issues in organ transplantation*. Cambridge: Cambridge University Press.

Stirling, J. (2002) *Introducing Neuropsychology*. London: Psychology Press.

Stokes, E.K. (2004) Robotics and rehabilitation: the role of robot mediated therapy post stroke, in M. MacLachlan and P. Gallagher (eds) *Enabling Technologies: Body image and body function*. Edinburgh: Churchill Livingstone.

Stone, A.R. (1992) Will the real body please stand up?: boundary stories with virtual cultures, in M. Benediktt (ed.) *Cyberspace: First steps.* Cambridge, MA: MIT Press (pp. 81–118).

Struther, C. (2002) The illness industry. *Health and Fitness*, August: 82–3.

Sugarman, A. and Kurash, C. (1982) The body as a transitional object. *International Journal of Eating Disorders*, 1: 57–67.

Suminski, R.R., Poston, W.S., Jackson, A.S. and Foreyt, J.P. (1999) Early identification of Mexican American children who are at risk for becoming obese. *International Journal of Obesity-Related Metabolic Disorders*, 23: 823–9.

Swerdlow, J.L. (2002) Unmasking skin. *National Geographic*, November: 36–63.

Taleporos, G. and McCabe, M.P. (2002) Body image and physical disability – personal perspectives. *Social Science and Medicine*, 54: 971–80.

Taylor, J.S. (2000) An all-consuming experience: obstetrical ultrasound and the commodification of pregnancy, in P. Brodwin *Biotechnology and culture: bodies, anxieties, ethics.* Bloomington: Indiana University Press.

Thayer, H.S. (ed.) *Pragmatism: The Classical Writings.* New York: The New American Library.

Trefil, J. (2001) Brave New World. *Smithsonian*, 32: 38–46.

Trimble, M. (1982) Functional disease. *British Medical Journal*, 285: 1768–70.

Tseng, W. and Hsu, J. (1980) Minor psychological disturbances of everyday life, in H.C. Triandis and J.G. Draguns (eds) *Handbook of Cross-Cultural Psychology: Psychopathology* (vol. 6). Boston: Allyn and Bacon, Inc.

Turner, B.S. (2001) Disability and the sociology of the body, in G.L. Albrecht, K.D. Seelman and M. Bury (eds) *Handbook of Disability Studies.* Thousand Oaks, CA: Sage.

Turner, B.S. (1984) *The Body and Society: Explorations in social theory.* Oxford: Blackwell.

Turner, B.S. (1997) From government to risk: some reflections on Foucault's contribution to medical sociology, in A. Peterson and R. Bunton (eds) *Foucault, Health and Medicine.* London: Routledge (pp. ix-xxi).

Van Zoonen, L. (1994) *Feminist Media Studies.* London: Sage.

Voracek, M. and Fisher, M.L. (2002) Shapely centerfolds? Temporal change in body measures: trend analysis. *British Medical Journal*, 325: 1447–8.

Waitzkin, H. and Magana, H. (1997) The Black Box in somatization: unexplained physical symptoms, culture, and narratives of trauma. *Social Science and Medicine*, 45: 811–25.

Wallace, I. and Wallace, A. (1978) *The Two.* New York: Simon and Schuster.

Walters A.J. (1995) Technology and the lifeworld of critical care nursing. *Journal of Advanced Nursing*, 22: 338–46.

Wasserstein, A.G. (1988) Towards a romantic science: the work of Oliver Sacks. *Annals of Internal Medicine*, September: 440–4.

Weiss, G. (1999) *Body Images:Eembodiment as intercorporeality.* London: Routledge.

Weiss, M.G., Raguram, R. and Channabasavanna, S.M. (1995) Cultural dimensions of psychiatric diagnosis: a comparison of DSM-III-R and illness explanatory models in South India. *British Journal of Psychiatry*, 166: 353–9.

Weiss S.A. (1958) The body image as related to phantom sensations: a hypothetical conceptualization of seemingly isolated findings. *Annals of the New York Academy of Science*, 74: 25–9.

Weiss, S.A. and Lindell, B. (1996) Phantom limb pain and etiology of amputation in unilateral lower extremity amputees. *Journal of Pain and Symptom Management*, 11: 3–17.

White, J.C. and Sweet, W.H. (1969) *Pain and the Neurosurgeon*. Springfield, IL: C.C. Thomas.

Wilde, M.H. (1999) Why Embodiment Now? *Advanced Nursing Sciience*, 22: 25–38.

Wilkinson, R.G. (1996) *Unhealthy Societies: The afflictions of inequality*. New York: Routledge.

Williamson, D.A., Zucker, N.L., Martin, C.K. and Smeets, M.A.M. (2001) Etiology and management of eating disorders, in P.B. Strucker and H.E. Adams (eds) *Comprehensive Handbook of Psychopathology* (3rd edn). New York: Kluwer/ Plenum.

Williamson, G.M., Schulz, R., Bridges, M.W. and Behan, A.M. (1994) Social and psychological factors in adjustment to limb amputation. *Journal of Social Behaviour and Personality*, 9: 249–68.

Willis, T. (1684) *Essays on the Pathology of the Brain*, cited in E. Showalter (1997) *Hystories: Hysterical Epidemics and Modern Culture*. London: Picador (p. 16).

Wilson, S.C., and Barber, T.X. (1978) The creative imagination scale as a measure of hypnotic responsiveness: applications to experimental and clinical hypnosis. *The American Journal of Clinical Hypnosis*, 20: 235–49.

Winnicott, D.W. (1971) Transitional objects and transitional phenomena, in D.W. Winnicott (ed.) *Playing and Reality*. London: Tavistock.

Wolf, N. (2001) *Misconceptions: Truth, lies and the unexpected on the journey to motherhood*. London: Chatto and Windus.

Woods, R. (2003) Does my digitally reduced bum look small in this? *The Sunday Times*, 12th January, p. 1.

World Health Organization (1980) *International Classification of Impairments, Disabilities and Handicaps: A manual for classification relating to the consequences of diseases*. Geneva: WHO.

World Health Organization (1997) *International Classification of Impairments, Activities and Participation: A manual of dimension of disablement and health*. Geneva: WHO.

Wright, A. (1996) See: <http://www.medphys.ucl.ac.uk/mgi/alexa/alexawright.html>.

Young, L. (1992) Sexual abuse and the problem of embodiment. *Child Abuse and Neglect*, 16: 89–100.

Zola, I.K. (1993) Self, identity and the naming question: reflections on the language of dis. ability *Social Science and Medicine*, 36: 167–73.

Index

Page numbers in *italics* refer to figures.